DC GREATEST EVENTS

STORIES THAT SHOOK THE MULTIVERSE

Dedicated to
Neal Adams and George Pérez

Senior Editor Cefn Ridout
Senior Designer Nathan Martin
Senior Production Editor Jennifer Murray
Senior Production Controller Mary Slater
Managing Editor Emma Grange
Managing Art Editor Vicky Short
Publishing Director Mark Searle

Packaged for DK by Bullpen Productions
Editor Alan Cowsill
Editorial Assistant Melanie Scott
Designer Gary Gilbert

First published in Great Britain in 2022 by Dorling Kindersley Limited
One Embassy Gardens, 8 Viaduct Gardens, London SW11 7BW
A Penguin Random House Company

The authorised representative in the EEA is
Dorling Kindersley Verlag GmbH. Arnulfstr. 124, 80636 Munich, Germany

Page design copyright © 2022 Dorling Kindersley Limited
DK, a Division of Penguin Random House LLC
10 9 8 7 6 5 4 3 2
002–332248–Nov/2022

ACKNOWLEDGEMENTS
DK would like to thank Win Wiacek for his text and expertise; Benjamin Harper and Josh Anderson at Warner Bros., and Benjamin Le Clear, Mike Pallotta, Leah Tuttle, Hank Manfra, and Steve Sonn at DC for vital help and advice; Gail Simone for her gracious foreword; Bullpen Productions for packaging; Jennette ElNaggar for proofreading; and Vanessa Bird for creating the index.

For the curious
www.dk.com

Contents

Foreword

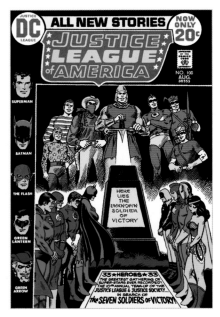

Time consumes memory, even of the things we love most. I can't honestly recall the first book that made me fall in love with reading, or the first movie that made me love going to the cinema, not with any certainty. But I can recall with astonishing clarity the comic that made me a fan forever, which I will likely remain until the end of my days.

It was this comic, *Justice League* #100 (above). Look at that cover. I first read it when I was just a kid, and even now, I get chills seeing this image. Who were all these people? Whose grave is that? But looking at that cover, I knew with absolute certainty that I had to have it. Great comics have that effect.

I grew up on a remote farm. Like a lot of farm kids, I read everything I could get my hands on, so my mother used to take me to garage sales and just buy whatever they had, which would at least shut me up for a few precious hours, I'm sure. At one such sale, I found a stack of old comics, and *this* one promised a whopping *33 heroes* right on the cover. I took it home and read it to tatters.

You see, it wasn't just any comic. It was an *Event* comic. And what an event! The Justice League. The Justice Society. The Seven Soldiers of Victory. Multiple worlds. Cosmic Enemies. Time Travel. All in one comic. My little kid brain was blown.

But the bad news? This was only part one of the story! I had to know everything about these characters. I didn't know it was an old comic, so I rode my bike miles every day to check the racks for part two. I bought note cards and made cards for each of the characters. I was hooked. It felt like a party, and we were all invited.

Since then, I have loved these big event books, both reading them and eventually writing them. It felt like something movies and novels didn't do. Pippi Longstocking never crossed over with Dorothy Gale. You never got a novel that promised 33 literary heroes, right?

That's why I love *DC Greatest Events*. That feeling of excitement, that thrill that anything can happen, is all through the spectacular stories covered in this book. And no one, I mean no one, does event stories like DC.

This book races through the history of the biggest stories ever told in comics, from the creation of Superman to the first meeting of Batman and Superman to Jack Kirby's epic *Fourth World* saga to *Crisis on Infinite Earths*, which took DC's amazing Multiverse and smashed all those worlds together—and changed comics forever.

This book is an epic story as well. The story of one of the largest and most remarkable shared fictional universes in history, and the creative teams that built it.

This sense of scale, it's something comics can do better than any other medium, I believe. Telling tales where a world exploding is only the beginning. Where all your favorites intertwine in battle against enemies too big for a single universe. It's every fan's book of dream stories, where every conversation of "Who's stronger?" or "What if Superman met Swamp Thing?" finds a glorious reality.

In here are all the milestones that make up a story that spans dimensions, galaxies, and histories from the Big Bang until the End of Time. Tales of adventure, imagination, and sacrifice, and from the best creators in the history of comics. Flipping through these entries makes me want to go back and read the ones I missed. Like right now.

Dang. Looks like I'm going to need more note cards!

Gail Simone

> **Gail Simone** has written more than 600 comics and can't resist event and crossover books, as evidenced by her resume: *Villains United*, *Swords of Sorrow*, *Seven Days*, *Tarzan/Red Sonja*, *Wonder Woman/Conan*, and *Catwoman/Sylvester & Tweety.** She currently lives on the Oregon coast and still reads pretty much every event comic from every company—she's hopeless that way.
>
> *A real comic, by the way!

Crisis on Infinite Earths #1 cover (right)

Introduction

Since their invention in the 1930s, comic books have always offered a vibrant portal to adventure and escape for young and old alike. Some of the most potent moments of modern mass-entertainment fiction sprung from those flimsy but colorful pamphlets, molding the tastes and often lives of generations of readers. The eventful stories contained within these comics also formed a resonant, modern mythology, affecting mainstream media: music, drama, apparel, games, the arts, television, and movies.

And what readers recall most are the "big stories."

Debuts and reinventions, colossal team-ups, the death of heroes and villains, and the ending of worlds are all memorable events that profoundly impacted readers caught up in the thrill of the moment. These stories also constructed a vital conceptual landscape: a complex, collaborative, cohesive, and constantly evolving meta-reality enticing and open to all.

Whether you're a seasoned collector or a newcomer contemplating buying your very first comic—on paper or digital download—these stories carry meaning and importance. Moreover, they are interconnected and build upon each other.

All Star lineup
DC's stunning stable of stars combined imagination with longevity by introducing and embracing the concept of iconic Super Heroes inspiring and mentoring successive generations.

When talking of "events," we're actually describing two different things. One is a landmark moment, either immediate or gradual, that alters the status quo. The debut of Superman immediately reshaped the comics industry. Batman, Justice Society of America, and Wonder Woman were equally significant but took longer to change comics and, ultimately, global culture.

The other is a managed project that enhances reader appreciation, company profile, and sales, such as the groundbreaking *Crisis on Infinite Earths*. The roots of this transformative 1980s event lay in an equally crucial 1963 story arc that teamed the Golden Age Justice Society of America with their reimagined Silver Age successors, the Justice League of America. The hero-packed tale's stunning commercial and critical success sparked an annual tradition (and guaranteed sales), while also coining a generic term—Crisis.

"In-world" stories have real-world impact. *Crisis on Infinite Earths* was the breakthrough example—a yearlong epic uniting DC's numerous characters (current and defunct), conceived to reinvigorate company output by instituting universal change at a stroke. Describing the end of a multiversal existence, it remade the comics industry but was at its heart simply another captivating tale.

Shelf life

As we're talking firsts, let's consider timing. Comics occupy a time warp and, as a result, historians endure many headaches seeking to determine provenance. Before the advent of comic book stores, DC's titles vied for

> ## "We fought the good fight. We succeeded."
>
> **Superman (Kal-L of Earth Two)** | *Crisis on Infinite Earths #12*

space and attention not just with rivals and imitators, but also with every other printed publication on a sale or return basis that crowded the newsstands. At the end of a preset time limit, newsstand distributors accepted unsold periodicals in return for cash or credit on future items.

Canny publishers could extend a title's shelf life by designating it as monthly, quarterly, or bimonthly. Thus, covers carried "off-sale" dates, which told retailers when to surrender unsold copies. *Action Comics* #1 is cover dated June 1938, but you were a lucky kid to find one by then. On sale from April 18th, its entire 200,000 print run was snapped up within weeks of its release.

That's why selling out was a big, if double-edged, deal. Soon after *Action Comics* launched, Superman became

the hottest item in America, but the faster issues sold, the longer it took potential readers who hadn't yet seen him to become fans. Eventually, the right balance was struck and some characters—like Captain Marvel (today's Shazam!)—became so popular they were published twice a month!

That's where *DC Greatest Events* comes in. It distills and showcases a

complex mosaic of compelling stories, providing real-world context for pivotal incidents and sagas from across the DC Multiverse and Omniverse, while illuminating the continuities and connections between these events. It also celebrates the visionary, talented writers, artists, editors, and publishers who made these memorable tales possible. Most are available in various formats and diligent exploring will bring welcome delights.

So whether you're looking for game-changing origins, indisputable triumphs, or future milestones like the *Dark Crisis* currently unfolding, *DC Greatest Events* is your guide to Action, Adventure, and Infinite Frontiers of fun. ▪

How to use this book

DC Greatest Events offers a chronologically organized, curated overview of the ever-changing DC universe—a realm made up of not just one Multiverse but a myriad that constitute an elaborate Omniverse. What constitutes an "event" is open to interpretation, but we have combined undeniable landmarks with a selection of lesser known tales deserving a modern reevaluation. Some of these may be found in a **Directory** of notable events. Within the scope of a 200-page book, this has meant that some stories have been reluctantly omitted.

Each entry addresses the achievement and significance of an event, displaying a heading and cover image (not

exclusively a first or last issue) for each event. Cover dates (see above) are specified throughout and do not include preludes, prologues, epilogues, or later additions. Quotes from source comics instill narrative tone and texture.

In focus boxes provide real-world context, a summary of how the event was managed, plus its effects and consequences for DC and/or the comics industry. **Key issues** boxes serve double duty. For early milestones, such as *Zatanna's Search*, they provide the source titles and pertinent subsequent appearances, while mega-events like *Legends* or resets like *DC Rebirth*, are augmented by a compendium of associated titles. In either or both cases, please consider them a shopping list for future enjoyment.

When providing details of the epic stories and sagas that frequently changed the comic book industry itself, a few terms are used that casual readers not steeped in the four-color lore of comic book production may have not encountered before. Below are some of these:

- **Banner:** Subsidiary heading or caption, usually above a cover title (also known as a strap line)
- **Colophon:** A publisher's emblem or brand mark, usually on the cover.
- **Imprint:** A publisher's individual or specifically themed subdivision.
- **Trade dress:** Specially created cover design elements that signify the issue's inclusion and enumeration in an event (also known as "cover furniture" or "livery").

A new world is born
The Man of Tomorrow was groundbreaking from the start. This iconic image—drawn by Joe Shuster—proclaims in no uncertain terms that there has never been a hero like Superman!

Superman and the Birth of the Super Heroes

June 1938

The fledgling comic book industry still followed the traditions of its newspaper strip origins when the eager, imaginative team of writer **Jerry Siegel** and artist **Joe Shuster** created an entirely new kind of hero. Released on April 18, 1938, *Action Comics* #1 introduced *Superman and the Birth of the Super Heroes*—promising action, excitement, and sheer wonderment unlike anything seen before.

Although comic strips had been a mainstay of domestic life since the end of the 19th century, and extraordinary, masked mystery men graced newspapers, pulp magazines, and the (radio) airwaves for almost a decade, the coming of Superman in 1938 reset the boundaries of popular fiction.

The Man of Steel's debut sparked a flurry of new Super Heroes at his publishers National/DC and a wave of imitators as other companies saw the potential of costumed comic book characters. Superman, however, reigned supreme, reinventing the comic industry and modern entertainment in general. He expanded into radio (and eventually film and television), games, toys, apparel, general merchandise, and even

Love for the ages
The interactions between Lois Lane and Superman set the bar for every Super Hero relationship that followed throughout the comic book industry.

newspaper strips. This was especially gratifying for creators Jerry Siegel and Joe Shuster, who had, since 1933, been trying to sell earlier incarnations of their big idea to strip syndicates.

Ready for *Action*

Superman certainly reshaped, and arguably even saved, the entire comic book industry. Comic books had been a commercial proposition since 1933, but had concentrated on reprinting newspaper strips until Major Malcolm Wheeler-Nicholson conceived new stars and material for his 1935 release *New Fun Comics*. Overnight the world became a more open, exciting place with opportunities for young creators to compete and craft their own stories for like-minded audiences.

Action Comics #1 (Jun. 1938) exuberantly launched a physical phenomenon who shrugged off bullets, juggled automobiles, and vaulted over buildings. Behind its now historic and much-imitated cover, a single page described a foundling's escape from an ancient, self-destructing planet and explained his incredible gifts, all in nine brief panels. A year later, when the unstoppable, incredibly popular hero won his own solo title, his origin was revised and Superman's birthworld named as Krypton.

Entitled "Superman, Champion of the Oppressed," the story introduced

> "Listen chief, if I can't find out anything about this Superman no one can!"
>
> **Clark Kent** | *Action Comics* #1

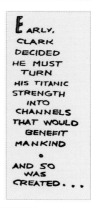

Original thinking

Another key comics innovation was a swift visual biography and convenient contextual rationale that underpinned all the astounding adventure that followed.

From issue #9 (Feb 1939) a cover banner proclaimed Superman's presence within, becoming a cover inset with #12. He permanently secured *Action Comics'* cover spot with #19 (Dec. 1939). The five covers Superman commanded between #1 and #19 outsold all other issues, and editors eventually sacrificed variety for guaranteed sales.

Within three years of his first appearance, the intoxicating blend of action and wish-fulfillment that grew out of the Great Depression and was a hallmark of the Action Ace's early adventures grew to encompass broader themes. Cops-and-robbers crime-busting, science fiction, and fantasy now dovetailed with socially reforming dramas, sports, whimsical comedy, and, once America entered World War II, patriotic fervor for Superman.

Beyond comic books, Superman's syndicated newspaper strip continued into the mid-1960s, spreading the concept of Super Heroes to a wider, international audience. So too did Fleischer/Famous Studios who, between 1941 and 1943, produced some of the most expensive—and best—animated cartoons ever conceived: all starring the mighty Man of Tomorrow! ▨

a brightly caped and costumed crusader who would go on to treat crooks and the forces of authority with equal disdain. He was a vigilante who was hunted by cops for much of the early years and who masqueraded by day as reporter Clark Kent. Superman averted numerous tragedies in a personal crusade against injustice. These included saving an innocent woman from the electric chair and roughing up a serially abusive husband before working over the racketeer Butch to save his journalist colleague Lois Lane from abduction and worse.

The Man of Steel made a big impression on Lois by later exposing an arms industry lobbyist, who was bribing senators on behalf of munitions manufacturers hoping to stoke the profitable fires of war in Europe.

Bestseller

As months went by, the extraterrestrial hero proved far more popular than his stablemates Zatara: Master Magician, Chuck Dawson, Marco Polo, Pep Morgan, Scoop Scanlon, and Tex Thompson (who in 1941 became masked hero Mr. America, the Americommando).

Key issues

Famous Funnies—A Carnival of Comics #1 **(October 1933)**
Maxwell Gaines and Harry I. Wildenberg market the first true comic book.

New Fun #1 **(February 1935)**
First comic book published by National/DC.

New Fun #6 **(October 1935)**
Siegel & Shuster's first comic heroes—Henri Duval and Doctor Occult—debut.

Detective Comics #1 **(March 1937)**
National/DC publish the first specifically themed comic book, a crime anthology

Action Comics #1 **(June 1938)**
A general adventure-themed title inadvertently creates superhero genre.

Batman: Dark Knight Detective

May 1939

As Superman electrified the public, his publishers were already looking for the next sensation. They found it in aspiring writer **Bill Finger** and humor cartoonist **Bob Kane**'s fresh spin on contemporary fictional themes. In *Detective Comics #27*, they mixed movie horror, crime dramas, and pulp fiction mystery men to introduce *Batman: Dark Knight Detective* to Gotham City's mean streets.

Watching the detectives
Sporting a moody yet splashy cover by Bob Kane, the advent of "The Batman" necessitated only the third-ever cover blurb in the magazine's history.

Debuting a year after Superman, "The Bat-Man" confirmed DC as front-runner and conceptual leader of the rapidly expanding comic book world. The industry grew from the vital, viscerally compelling tales of both iconic creations. Light and dark, god and mortal, they encapsulate the entire heroic ideal. Both remain preeminent comic book characters more than 80 years later.

Whodunit?

After redefining conceptual limits of heroism with the demigod-like Superman, DC's next step explored merely mortal, physical, and mental perfection in the form of an implacable Dark Knight Detective. When he took on a junior apprentice, the tone shifted, and dashing derring-do of a strictly human Dynamic Duo rapidly became the swashbuckling benchmark all comic book crime busters were measured by. Significantly, both adult hero and the first costumed junior partner debuted in the company's longest-lived title.

Detective Comics #1 (March 1937) was the third anthology title devised by Major Malcolm Wheeler-Nicholson. In 1935, he sensed the potential in Max Gaines's new comic book invention.

National Allied Publications produced all-new strip material in *New Fun: The Big Comic Magazine* and follow-up *New Comics/New Adventure Comics* (eventually *Adventure Comics*). Following common publishing practice, the owners founded a new company—Detective Comics, Inc.—for the third title. The success of *Detective Comics* (#1 cover-dated March 1937 and on sale from February 10th) led to the company becoming known as "DC Comics."

The initial lineup included adventurer Speed Saunders, Cosmo the Phantom of Disguise, and Gumshoe Gus. It also featured Spy (Bart Regan) and Slam Bradley, both by newcomers Jerry Siegel and Joe Shuster. Issue #20 (Oct. 1938) saw pulp-style masked vigilante the Crimson Avenger premiere. Sheriffs, cops, private eyes, secret agents, and gentleman daredevils now made room for a new kind of hero—the Mystery Man.

Dark omen
Bruce Wayne's alter ego was inspired by a whim of fate and his interpretation of a strange intrusion.

BAT-MAN" QUICKLY PLUGS THE GAS-JET WITH A HANKERCHIEF THE GAS-CHAMBER DESCENDS ENTIRELY OVER THEM ...

...HE THEN UNTIES ROGERS, AND WITH A POWERFUL SWING... CRASH!

The culmination was *Detective Comics #27*'s cover-featured new addition—The Batman. Bill Finger and Bob Kane's "The Case of the Chemical Syndicate" was a spartan, understated yarn introducing playboy criminologist Bruce Wayne, who casually inserted himself into a string of industrialist murders. The killings ended only after an eerie vigilante "The Bat-Man" took over Police Commissioner Gordon's stalled investigation, pitilessly exposing

and destroying the killer. The strange, brooding, single-minded hero was an instant success with readers.

The bat-winged combination of sleuth, action hero, and haunted avenger defeated criminals, crazed scientists, spies, cultists, Super-Villains like Doctor Death and Hugo Strange, and even a vampire. Issue #33's clash with air-pirates included a two-page prologue revealing how young Bruce Wayne trained for decades to wage war against evildoers after witnessing his parents' murder in a holdup.

Father figure

Detective Comics #38 (Apr. 1940) saw a softening shift of focus for Batman, one that changed the comic book landscape forever. Kane, Finger, and Jerry Robinson's "Robin, The Boy Wonder" was child trapeze artist Dick Grayson, whose parents were killed before his eyes. Bruce Wayne was in the audience the night of their demise and invited the orphan into his home. Soon the teenager joined

Robin takes the stage
Robin's youthful glow of eager enthusiasm leavened the taciturn darkness of Batman and provided greater avenues for character development and plot exposition.

No. 38

Detective COMICS APRIL 10¢

THE *Sensational* CHARACTER-
FIND OF 1940...
Robin THE BOY WONDER

Smashing success
Despite diligent planning and carrying a compact personal arsenal, Batman understood the value of improvisation and utilizing whatever came to hand.

Batman's crusade, by bringing to justice mobster boss Tony Zucco, the man behind his parents' murders.

Weeks later, *Batman #1* (May 1940) offered a remastered origin culled from *Detective Comics #33* and #34, and four adventures. These included a return clash with Hugo Strange and debuts for The Joker and Catwoman, as the grim Gotham Guardian gradually evolved into a mentor, protector, and role model.

The Dark Knight became DC's most popular Super Hero, with Robin battling beside him until 1970 when, acknowledging those turbulent times, Robin flew the nest to become a "Teen Wonder" college student. His creation as a character with which younger readers could identify inspired countless costumed sidekicks and kid crusaders. Dick Grayson has evolved into a symbol for and forerunner of a new style of hero reflecting the ever-changing youth culture. ▨

Key issues

New Fun #1 (February 1935)
DC's title launches with many junior protagonists such as "Jack Andrews—All American Boy," "Buckskin Jim," and "Bobby and Binks and the Magic Crystal of History."

Detective Comics #1 (March 1937)
A crime anthology becomes the comic industry's first themed title.

Action Comics #1 (June 1938)
DC introduces the Super Hero genre.

Detective Comics #20 (October 1938)
Crimson Avenger, DC's first masked crime fighter, debuts.

Detective Comics #27 (May 1939)
Batman makes his first appearance.

Superman #1 (Summer/June 1939)
DC premieres the inaugural solo feature comic book.

Detective Comics #38 (April 1940)
Robin debuts as the comic book industry's first costumed sidekick.

Batman #1 (May 1940)
DC launches the industry's second solo Super Hero feature title.

> "...This fellow they call the 'Bat-Man' puzzles me!"
>
> **Commissioner Gordon** | *Detective Comics #27*

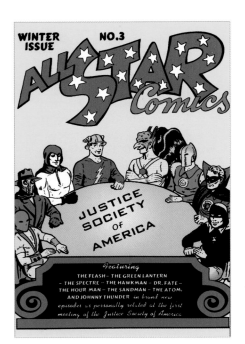

Called to order
Although sedate by modern standards, the image and idea of all Super Heroes working together was radical and thrilling to readers in 1940.

First Meeting of the Justice Society of America

December 1940

It was still early days for comic books when scripter **Gardner Fox** and artists **Everett E. Hibbard, Bernard Baily, Sheldon Mayer, Chad Grothkopf, Howard Sherman, Ben Flinton**, and **Martin Nodell** crafted a commercial collaboration between sister companies to promote their heroes. The result was the invention of Super Hero teams, and the ***first meeting of the Justice Society of America*** in *All Star Comics #3*.

Following the runaway successes of Superman and Batman, both DC Comics and its publishing partner All-American Publications (AA) eagerly sought the next hit to spring from their anthology titles. *All Star Comics* was produced by AA, but was a joint venture designed to give already established characters from both companies an extra push toward winning a solo title.

The Justice Society of America debuted in the third issue of *All Star Comics* (December 1940), which featured characters from National-DC's *Adventure Comics* and *More Fun Comics* and AA Publishing's *Flash Comics* and *All-American Comics*. New stories in the anthology quarterly were accompanied by "A Message from the Editors" asking readers to vote on their favorite feature.

Your country calls!
The greatest heroes of the age first convened for a meal and to compare case notes, but by the end of the initial meeting had started their first case—investigating spies for the FBI!

All together now

The merits of the marketing project were never proved. Instead of a new A-lister emerging and graduating to his own starring vehicle as a result of the poll, something unexpected evolved. For the third issue, prolific writer Gardner Fox and Max Gaines's brilliant, multitalented assistant Sheldon Mayer conceived the notion of linking the previously solo adventures through a lighthearted framing sequence, with the heroes gathering to chat about their latest exploits.

Mayer was a comics polymath who, as legend has it, rescued a rejected strip proposal called "Superman" from the trash and convinced editor Vin Sullivan to run it in new title *Action Comics*. Working with Gaines, Mayer revolutionized the still nascent comics industry. When not editing, designing, or illustrating text stories for All-American, he wrote and drew strips such as "Scribbly, Boy Cartoonist."

A minor character in the strip—washerwoman and landlady Ma Hunkel—was actually an early JSA recruit in her other heroic identity as urban vigilante the Red Tornado. Mayer is best remembered today for his highly addictive humor strip

Team supreme
Over decades, heroes like Robin inherited their mentors' positions as the JSA grew from a team into a family—as seen in this group shot by Murphy Anderson (*Justice League of America* #76 Dec. 1969).

and came back with urgent news from Washington, DC. The FBI needed the heroes to rout a group of fifth columnists trying to destroy America for the Axis powers. This spurred the JSA to work together against a common foe for the first time.

From this low-key collaboration and the natural notion that Mystery Men would probably hang out together, history was made. It wasn't long before the guys—and they were all white men (except Red Tornado who masqueraded as one)—regularly joined forces to defeat the greatest Super-Villains and challenge the social ills of their generation.

front row: ATOM · ROBIN

second row: WONDER WOMAN · GREEN LANTERN · SANDMAN · DR. MID-NITE · DR. FATE · RED TORNADO (#1) · RED TORNADO (#2) · BLACK CANARY

third row: SPECTRE · HAWKMAN · HOURMAN · FLASH · WILDCAT · MR. TERRIFIC · JOHNNY THUNDER · STARMAN

back row: BATMAN · SUPERMAN

"Sugar and Spike," the inventive, antic adventures of preverbal but supremely communicative toddlers.

All Star heroes

In 1940, following two issues of individual adventures, *All Star Comics* #3 saw young, valiant Johnny Thunder idly wish that he could pal around with famous Super Heroes. Accidentally activating the magical Thunderbolt genie bonded to him, Johnny compelled his heroic idols to let him gate crash their first meeting after the he expressed his wish to be one of them.

The wonder of super-teams began with the simple expedient of having assorted heroes gather around a table to regale each other with tales of recent adventures. The Flash told of battling modern pirates, Hawkman had crushed a fire cult, and the Spectre battled moon monster Oom. Hourman tackled criminal impersonators and Red Tornado left early due to a costume malfunction. The Sandman told of a giant-making scientist he'd recently defeated and Doctor Fate described fighting a necromancer, before Johnny shared a recent bad date. The Atom foiled a holdup and Green Lantern shone his light to expose a framing attempt. During the stories, The Flash abruptly left in response to a telegram

Key issues

Famous Funnies—A Carnival of Comics #1 (1933)
Maxwell Gaines and Harry I. Wildenberg market the first true comic book.

New Fun #1 (February 1935)
First comic book published by National/Allied Publications (later DC Comics).

New Comics #1 (December 1935)
The second title, a humor anthology, is released.

Action Comics #1 (June 1938)
Super Heroes are born as Superman debuts.

Adventure Comics #32 (November 1938)
Retitled *New Comics* rebrands as a drama anthology.

All American Comics #1 (April 1939)
Maxwell Gaines launches DC's autonomous sister company—All American Publications—with a general anthology.

Adventure Comics #40 (July 1939)
The DC anthology launches its first Super Hero—the Sandman.

Flash Comics #1 (January 1940)
All American Publications releases new Super Hero heavy anthology.

More Fun Comics #52 (February 1940)
The DC anthology begins transition to Super Heroes with first appearance of the Spectre.

All Star Comics #1 (June 1940)
AA and DC collaborate on Super Hero anthology to promote its midranking stars.

All Star Comics #3 (December 1940)
The Justice Society debuts.

> "I know! I'll contribute an **idea!**— Suppose you each tell the most exciting experience you've ever had... That'll entertain **everybody!**"
>
> **Johnny Thunder** | *All Star Comics* #3

For America and Democracy

March 1941

The superhero phenomenon was less than three years old when comics all-rounder **Sheldon Mayer** and writer **Gardner Fox** devised the next great innovation. *All Star Comics #4* saw each chapter and its solo star individually illustrated by DC's and All-American's top artists, but a true team effort was needed to safeguard the nation. The JSA was ready to respond and fight *for America and Democracy*!

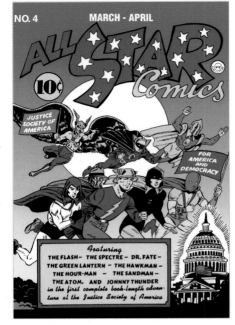

Capitol idea
The JSA's first official mission was a request from the US government to make the nation safe from hidden forces poisoning it from within.

The creation of the Justice Society of America changed the comic book industry. Seeing a favored hero alongside unknown but equally appealing new characters not only thrilled readers but also made sound commercial sense. Now, as the nation braced itself for inevitable involvement in the war ravaging Europe, creators embraced the tone of the times, recasting their heroes as champions of liberty and freedom.

Patriot gains
In the early days, heroes "knew of" each other but respected jurisdictions. However, in *All Star Comics #3* (Dec. 1940, several renowned Mystery Men met to enjoy a dinner and trade tales of recent cases. During the event, The Flash was called to Washington, DC to meet the "Chief of the FBI" (recognizably drawn, but never named, as J. Edgar Hoover). The Flash swiftly returned to tell his friends of a mission only they could accomplish.

Full details came in "For America and Democracy" (*All Star Comics #4*), as the assorted champions made their own way to FBI headquarters to hear the Chief's request. They were told to seek and destroy spies, saboteurs, subversives, and traitors undermining America and corrupting the young and impressionable. The entire espionage operation had a guiding genius controlling the covert campaign, and he, too, had to be stopped at all costs!

Splitting up to cover more territory, the case resolved into separate but connected tales as Gardner F. Fox and illustrators E.E. Hibbard, Martin Nodell, Bernard Baily, Howard Sherman, Chad Grothkopf, Sheldon Moldoff, and Ben Flinton dispatched the heroes where they were most needed. The Flash crushed fascist Greyshirts fomenting unrest in Detroit; Green Lantern destroyed a zeppelin sabotaging US radio transmissions; and the Spectre doomed saboteurs wrecking munitions factories in Pittsburgh. For their part, Hourman saved Oklahoma oil wells and Doctor Fate New England's naval yards from Greyshirt sabotage, while Sandman preserved free press in El Paso, and Hawkman halted the destruction of Californian aviation plants.

In each instance, defeated insurgents gave up the name of their leader, and as the heroes converged on Toledo, Ohio, and Nazi spymaster Fritz Klaver, The Atom quashed propaganda and dissent on college campuses before being

Force for freedom
From the first, America's heroes proved to tyrants and bullies who the real Übermensch were.

"FOR AMERICA AND DEMOCRACY!"

AT THEIR LAST MEETING THE MEMBERS OF THE JUSTICE SOCIETY OF AMERICA ··· THE FLASH — SANDMAN — HAWKMAN — DOCTOR FATE — SPECTRE — GREEN LANTERN — HOURMAN — AND THE ATOM ···· RECEIVED A TELEGRAM FROM THE F.B.I. CHIEF IN WASHINGTON TELLING THEM THEY WERE NEEDED AS PATRIOTIC AMERICANS TO MEET AND CONFER UPON A MATTER OF VITAL IMPORTANCE TO THE UNITED STATES! ····

FROM EVERY PART OF THE NATION THEY COME; FROM THEIR HAUNTS AND BYPATHS, SPEEDING TO THE CAPITOL IN ANSWER TO THEIR COUNTRY'S CALL! · · · ·

THIS IS THE STORY OF HOW THEY MET, AND WHY! OF WHAT THEY DID, AND HOW THEY DID IT! THE JUSTICE SOCIETY OF AMERICA AGAINST THE ENEMIES OF AMERICA ·····

The JSA inspired imitations both within the company and further afield. As 1941 closed, DC created a squad comprising many non-JSA stars. The Seven Soldiers of Victory starred in 14 issues of *Leading Comics* before vanishing as the war ended. Their time would come again, decades later.

Dark days

Once America entered World War II, the Justice Society renamed itself the Justice Battalion. The premise saw the heroes immediately enlist in various military services after the attack on Pearl Harbor, yet continue meeting to maintain the JSA branding during those dark days. Postwar, a smaller team continued into the 1950s, battling aliens, petty criminals, social injustice, mobsters, and magical invaders, as much as the changing tastes of its readership.

The war also had a lasting effect on superheroes themselves, demanding that bad guys were primarily enemy operatives, and thus stifling the development of Super-Villains. As a result, their conspicuous absence may have precipitated the rapid decline of so many costumed characters after hostilities ceased. ■

magically drawn to Johnny Thunder, whose Thunderbolt genie had accidentally whisked them both into the heart of Klaver's citadel. Thankfully, that's when the JSA converged on the HQ to confront and take out the arrogant, unrepentant, fifth column mastermind.

The mission set a pattern for many years to come. The team would identify a problem, initially divide their response into solo missions, and then meet at the end to finish the case together. The format lasted for decades, tweaked in later years to allow for individual pairings of two or three members. The winning formula also became the template for the Justice League of America 20 years later.

> **"I'm going to enjoy this job!"**
>
> **Hawkman** | *All Star Comics #4*

For America and democracy!
Following her sensational 1941 debut in *All Star Comics*, the war against tyranny greatly advanced when Wonder Woman joined the fight.

Wonder Woman Arrives in Man's World

January 1942

National Allied Publications/Detective Comics Inc. set the standard for Super Heroes before sister company All American Publications responded with its own string of stars. AA's most enduring success was *Wonder Woman*. Debuting in *Sensation Comics* #1—the new Super Hero was a complete reversal of established trends, courtesy of psychologist **William Moulton Marston** and illustrator **Harry G. Peter**.

Wonder Woman is the ultimate female exemplar. Since her debut, she has entered global consciousness, a paradigm of comics' values, and an inspirational symbol to women everywhere. The amazing Amazon epitomizes the eternal balance between brains and strength and has joined a select group of literary creations, such as Sherlock Holmes, Dracula, or Tarzan, to achieve meta-reality.

Conceived by psychologist and polygraph pioneer William Moulton Marston—a forward thinker embracing comics' educational potential—Wonder Woman's adventures were a communal effort, credited to "Charles Moulton." Marston's stories were influenced by his wife, Elizabeth, and their life partner, Olive Byrne. He died in May 1947, and former secretary Joye Hummel ghost-wrote around 70 scripts between 1944 and 1947 before writer Robert Kanigher assumed control. Aside from early fill-ins by artist Frank Godwin, the adventures they collectively penned were mostly drawn by illustrator Harry G. Peter, with Irwin Hasen and Bernard Sachs helping out before Peter's death in 1958.

> ## "A man! A man on Paradise Island!"
> ## Quick! Let's get him to the hospital."
>
> **Princess Diana** | *All Star Comics #8*

Wonder Woman was an earnest attempt to offer girls positive, powerful role models, and—for editor M.C. Gaines and his brilliant assistant Sheldon Mayer—a sound move to sell more comics to girls. *All Star Comics* #8 (cover-dated Jan. 1942, but actually on sale from October 21, 1941) introduced Wonder Woman, and she formally debuted one month later as the cover feature of a new anthology. Her debut in *All Star Comics* was an unprecedented move—with pages added to the title—giving the new hero a canny sales boost from the start.

Ready maid alias
The Amazon solved two problems and helped true love's course by acquiring the identity of Army nurse Diana Prince.

Secret origin
In combination, "Introducing Wonder Woman" and "Wonder Woman Comes to America" reveal how a secluded society of immortal super-women changes forever after US Army

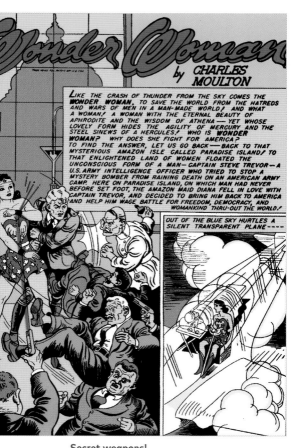

Secret weapons!
Diana arrived in the wider world, bearing unique armaments—indestructible Amazonium bracelets, a throwing tiara, and an invisible plane. Her magical Lasso of Truth would not be created until *Sensation Comics* #6.

Intelligence Captain Steve Trevor crashes on their island. His recovery is supervised by young, impressionable, headstrong Princess Diana.

Dreading her child's growing obsession with the interloper from an intractably violent world, Diana's mother, Queen Hippolyte, recounts the

Role reversal
Gallant and go-getting, action man Steve Trevor found difficulty adapting to the role of hostage and victim in need of constant rescuing.

Amazons' history. They were seduced and betrayed by men but rescued by goddess Aphrodite on condition that they isolate themselves and devote their energies to becoming ideal beings.

After Trevor explains the sinister plot that accidentally brought him to the island, and how the planet is imperiled, Athena and Aphrodite instruct Hippolyte to send an Amazon back with him to America to fight for freedom and liberty. An open contest seeking the best candidate is held and, despite being forbidden to compete, Diana triumphs to become their emissary. Accepting the outcome, Hippolyte dispatches Diana to "Man's World" with an arsenal of super-scientific and magical weapons.

Secret identity
Leading from the front in *Sensation Comics*, the story resumed with "Wonder Woman comes to America" as the culture-shocked hero leaves Trevor in a hospital before foiling dangerous bank robbers and briefly falling in with a smooth-talking con artist. Perhaps the most telling innovation was buying her secret identity from lovelorn Army nurse Diana Prince. This elegantly allowed

The gentle touch
Dedicated to peace, Wonder Woman knew when to apply force and exactly how much was needed to end conflict.

the princess covert access to Steve while enabling the heartsick medic to join her fiancé in South America. Wonder Woman and Captain Trevor then crush a spy ring that had targeted a Draft Induction Center with poison gas. Typically, Steve breaks his leg and ends up in the hospital again, where "Nurse Prince" once more takes care of him.

An instant, game-changing hit, Wonder Woman won her solo title months later (Summer 1942), and her success saw her, along with Superman and Batman, survive beyond the Golden Age of costumed heroes. For decades, Wonder Woman was the most popular female Super Hero on the newsstands and an inspiration to generations of young girls. ▨

When He was a Boy

January 1945

Superman changed the world from the moment of his first appearance, and within a decade, he did so for a second time as **Superboy**. Based on a proposal by **Jerry Siegel** and illustrated by **Joe Shuster** and **Jon Sikela**, the untold tale of a young boy with a magnificent destiny captured the imagination of every kid who ever made a wish.

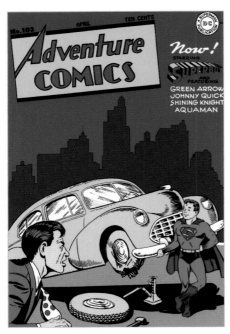

Wonder boy
Despite his astounding powers and alien origins, Superboy was essentially just a kid like any other.

Superman is the primal spark that created the superhero genre. Without him, fiction in all media would be very different. However, his creators—Jerry Siegel and Joe Shuster—felt he was still incomplete. As early as November 1938, Siegel petitioned Detective Comics, Inc. (as DC was known then) to consider a series that looked at the hero's formative years. If Super Heroes were the expression of wish-fulfillment, then Superboy should be the ultimate example of that dream, and once the Man of Tomorrow made his mark as Earth's premier champion, Siegel and Shuster devised a concept nearly as powerful and persistent. Reasoning that a different tone and setting offered fresh vistas for fun, thrills, and amazement, they wondered what life might be like for a fun-loving lad who could do literally anything. The sheer delight of a youth who no adult could dominate or control—surely that would resonate with young readers?

After a few rejections, Siegel's idea finally saw print, while he was still a serving soldier in Hawaii. DC launched the adventures of Superman's childhood, beginning with an untitled five-page short in *More Fun Comics* #101 (January 1945).

Farewell to Krypton
Readers first glimpsed the many wonders of Superman's homeworld in the memories and rediscoveries of the Boy of Steel.

Distant planet

Designated "The Origin of Superboy!" in later reprints, the story actually provides more details of Krypton's civilization and destruction and how scientist Jor-El and wife Lara's unnamed baby was rocketed to Earth. The mighty orphan's adoption and childhood revolves around on his extraordinary abilities and how the serious child decides to hide his gifts behind a meek facade and costumed alter ego—Superboy!

Drawn by Shuster, the script was based on a 1940 Siegel proposal that was adapted by Batman scribe Don Cameron. The charming piece of imaginative whimsy paid off and grew rapidly in the postwar world, where

Destiny's child
The interplanetary foundling learned decency and generosity from his loving foster parents, and realized early that he would dedicate his life to repaying all humanity.

tense action had lost its appeal, and traditional heroes, comfortable drama, and human-interest themes were on the rise.

The experiment was a huge hit. The young hero gained the lead slot of *Adventure Comics* where DC had grouped many of its surviving Super Heroes. The Boy of Steel held or shared

A dog's life
The Boy of Steel's feelings of solitariness were greatly reduced once his mischievous childhood pet Krypto found his way to Earth.

the cover spot until June 1969 when Supergirl took over the title with issue #381. In 1949, he gained his own comic book. In a market still mainly anthological and genre-driven, *Superboy* was DC's first successful Super Hero postwar launch and only its sixth solo title since the company was founded in 1935.

Krypto and friends

Superboy became the biggest hit of the 1950s, with the Boy of Steel living a life two decades behind his adult counterpart. This was a childhood full of escapades, thrills and drama, good deeds, a loving family, and, eventually, a sense of isolation and lack of companionship. The latter would gradually change as repeated narrative return journeys to lost Krypton revealed superpowered animal survivors like Super-Monkey Beppo (*Superboy* #76, October 1959) and, especially, his long-lost pet dog, Krypto, who debuted in *Adventure Comics* #210 (March 1955). Mischievous and dangerously playful, Krypto the Super-Dog heralded a wave of survivors from the destroyed world who made Superboy feel less lonely and unique. Every boy needs a dog.

The Boy of Steel's adventures added many landmarks to Superman's mythology, introducing the Phantom Zone, Bizarro, the Legion of Super-Heroes, Kryptonian villains, many facets of Krypton's culture, and the origin of Lex Luthor, but his greatest

impact came from the idea of juvenile heroes. When continuity changes excised Superboy after *Crisis on Infinite Earths*, he was constantly reinvented. Modern versions have seen Superboy as a survivor of Earth Prime, a clone of Kon-El, and the latest—Jonathan Kent—son of Superman and Lois Lane. ▨

Key issues

***Action Comics* #1 (June 1938)**
Superman debuts.

***Superman* #1 (May 1939)**
The Man of Steel wins his first solo comic book.

***More Fun Comics* #101 (January 1945)**
Superboy quietly debuts.

***Adventure Comics* #103 (April 1946)**
Superboy takes over cover spot in Super Hero anthology.

***Superboy* #1 (March–April 1949)**
The Boy of Steel wins own title.

***Adventure Comics* #300 (September 1962)**
The Legion of Super-Heroes takes cover spot.

***Superboy* #197 (September 1973)**
The Legion takes the cover again.

***The New Adventures of Superboy* #1 (January 1980)**
Modernized Boy of Steel debuts.

***Adventures of Superman* #501 (June 1993)**
New cloned Superboy Kon -El debuts.

***Convergence: Superman* #52 (July 2015)**
Jon Kent debuts.

> # "The lives of all Kryptonians may depend on the success of my experiments!"
>
> **Jor-El** | *More Fun Comics* #101

The Injustice Society of the World

October–November 1947

With the world rebuilding after a devastating global war, spies and criminals were civilization's latest enemies but were no match for costumed champions. Everything changed in *All Star Comics #37*, when editor **Sheldon Mayer** and writer **Robert Kanigher** evened the odds by introducing the *Injustice Society of the World* in a shocking tale of domestic terrorism illustrated by **Irwin Hasen**, **Joe Kubert**, **Carmine Infantino**, **Alex Toth**, and **Jon Belfi**.

Winners take all
The imminent triumph of evil over good, the helplessness of valiant heroes, and the dissolution of America was perfectly captured in Irwin Hasen's iconic cover.

O ne of the guiding propositions of all fiction is that heroes are defined by their enemies. However, for early comic book creators, it was a premise that took time to reach its logical conclusion. Despite fantastic abilities, super-science trappings, and common acceptance of ghosts and magic, the majority of mystery men and superheroes faced very few opponents with powers, capabilities, or gimmicks equal to their own. The majority of comic book tales featured thugs, conmen, and gangsters, with the war years providing spies and venal traitors for the masked wonders to combat. Very few even wore costumes.

Coalition of the wicked

The Justice Society of America (JSA)—a large, ever-shifting alliance of multipowered champions—generally addressed pressing social issues, explored uncanny worlds, or crushed evil masterminds employing standard-issue goons, rather than take on returning nemeses who possessed uncanny abilities. Other than outsider villains like the Psycho-Pirate and Brain Wave, few of the JSA's more eccentric enemies ever sought return engagements, but in the politically charged postwar era, recurring foes became commonplace. Eventually, the bad guys swiped the founding concept of the JSA and formed a super-team of their own.

A coalition of the wicked was not completely unknown. The Seven Soldiers of Victory—DC's second Super Hero team—had fought enemies working for dying genius the Hand in *Leading Comics #1* (Dec. 1941), but not all of those super-foes were established prior to their appearance in that issue, and they never worked together afterward.

The Wizard, Gambler, Thinker, Vandal Savage, Per Degaton, and Brain Wave formed "The Injustice Society of the World" to specifically counter Super Heroes and achieve their aim of conquering America in a criminal blitzkrieg. It began with the schemers dividing the country between them before picking an enemy to eliminate and a sector of government to neutralize. Already in play were robotic duplicates of world leaders and opinion-shapers, and each Super-Villain not only had his particular techniques and tools but also a personal battalion of convicted criminals, who had been

Eyes on the Prize!
After failing individually, the malign malcontents were ready to pool resources and act together... but for how long?

Judgment Day
The show trial and imminent end of the heroes collapses into chaos and defeat, as the supposedly dead Green Lantern turns the tables on the Injustice Society and leads the inevitable fightback.

Justice for all!
The Junior Justice Society of America knew how to handle bad guys like The Wizard as well as social issues such as juvenile delinquency.

sprung from jails across the country in anticipation of the final assault.

Then JSA members Hawkman, The Flash, Green Lantern, The Atom, Doctor Mid-Nite, Johnny Thunder, and Wonder Woman battled bravely but ultimately fell to overwhelming opposition. However, when the triumphant totalitarians tried to humiliate them with a show trial, the tables were spectacularly turned, the heroes snatching victory from certain defeat.

The ending cleverly tapped into current affairs and the tenor of the times, with the Super-Villains holding their own version of the Nuremberg Trials of defeated Nazis. The Allied Powers' tribunals ran from November 20, 1945, to October 1, 1946, but after the judgments, America carried on alone, holding 12 further war crimes tribunals between December 1946 and April 1949. Administered by the US military courts, their findings filled newspapers, newsreels, radio, and television just as *All-Star #37* (Oct./Nov. 1947) hit newsstands.

Organized crimes

The notion of a villainous team heralded a new kind of threat, and the tactic was repeated months later as eight archfoes—all wicked women condemned to Amazon behavior modification and redeeming socialization—escaped Transformation Island to form Villainy Incorporated in *Wonder Woman #28* (Mar./Apr. 1948). Mere months later, The Wizard formed a second Injustice Society—Sportsmaster, Huntress, Icicle, the Fiddler, and Harlequin—to attack the JSA again in *All-Star Comics #41* (Jun./Jul. 1948). Although it came at the end of the Golden Age of Heroes, the device was swiftly revived during the Silver Age, with temporary evil alliances plaguing almost every hero from Aquaman to Zatanna. The innovation led to the creation of formal organizations such as the Injustice Gang, Secret Society of Super-Villains, Secret Six, and The Rogues of Central City. ▪

Key issues

All Flash #12 (Fall 1943)
The Thinker first battles Jay Garrick.

Green Lantern #10 (December 1943)
Vandal Savage premieres.

Green Lantern #12 (Summer 1944)
The Gambler debuts.

All-Star Comics #15 (February/March 1943)
Brain Wave first attacks the JSA.

All-Star Comics #17 (June 1943)
Brain Wave strikes again.

All-Star Comics #34 (April/May 1947)
The Wizard first attacks the JSA.

All-Star Comics #35 (June/July 1947)
Per Degaton debuts.

All-Star Comics #37 (October/November 1947)
Injustice Society debuts.

All-Star Comics #41 (June/July 1948)
Injustice Society returns with new members.

> "...now... on to **Capitol City, Degaton!** When that falls, our war is won!"
>
> **The Wizard** | *All Star Comics #37*

The Mightiest Team in the World

May 1952

The turn of the decade saw superheroes in decline and traditional genres filling comic books. However, the biggest names weathered the storm and even prospered, especially after a seemingly inevitable connection made allies of two distant colleagues. Scripted by science-fiction author **Edmond Hamilton** and illustrated by **Curt Swan**, **Stan Kaye**, and **John Fischetti**, the meeting in *Superman #76* made the two heroes the *Mightiest Team in the World.*

Double trouble
In their initial adventure together, Superman and Batman had more difficulty deflecting Lois Lane's suspicions than catching the fugitive jewel thief who sparked their alliance.

Superman and Batman propelled DC/National Comics to the forefront of the nascent comic book industry, and from the outset, they were marketed vigorously. In 1939, DC won the license to produce a 96-page comic book commemorating the New York World's Fair—a mammoth premium stuffed with DC characters in exploits celebrating the event. Produced before Batman's debut in *Detective Comics #27* (May 1939), the cover featured the exposition's key attractions and head shots of Superman, Zatara, the Sandman, and humor-strip stars Butch the Pup and Gingersnap (both by a pre-Batman Bob Kane).The following year's sequel edition (*New York World's Fair Comics 1940*, Jul. 1940) boasted a stunning cover by top artist Jack Burnley, with just the Dynamic Duo and the Man of Tomorrow. This changed the course of each hero's career when the premium's bumper format was adopted for a quarterly anthology that launched as *World's Best Comics #1* in Spring 1941.

World's Finest

Changing its name to *World's Finest Comics* from the second issue, the title enjoyed a 45-year run that only ended during the *Crisis on Infinite Earths*. Variations of the venerable title soon returned, and remain part of DC mythology today, with the heroes and their cities—Gotham and Metropolis—seen as dark and light echoes of each other. Latterly, fellow Golden Age survivor Wonder Woman has replaced Robin in a new, critically important "Trinity" of heroes.

Despite never meeting and having separate adventures inside *World's Finest* issues, the most memorable aspect of the title was its striking and generally comedic covers of the Batman, Robin, and Superman acting together. As the decade progressed, the title's hefty page count gradually

Partners in time
Although the heroes were first pictured together in 1940 and interacted for over a decade on *World's Finest Comics'* covers, their first official collaboration was a long time coming.

> ## "Your wonderful skill in disguising as Clark Kent saved my secret, **Batman!**"
>
> **Superman** | *Superman #76*

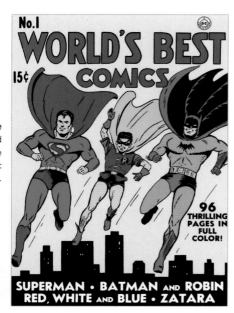

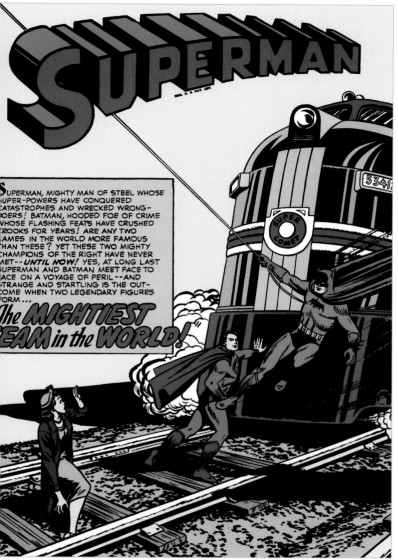

Meet and greet
Heroes overlapping and interacting was rare in comic books, but from the start, Superman and Batman were cordial, respectful, professional, and instantly at ease with each other.

diminished, and in 1954, it joined the rest of DC's line as a 36-page periodical publication.

When spiraling print costs downsized *World's Finest*, the inspired solution to losing all those pages was to create an official three-way partnership and group adventures. For decades thereafter, Superman, Batman, and Robin worked together as the "World's Finest Team." They were friends as well as colleagues, who now encountered each other's very different circumstances and case loads, such as malign magicians, aliens on the loose in Gotham City, and numerous instances of gaining and losing superpowers.

The union made sound financial sense since DC's top heroes—in effect the company's only mainstream costumed superstars—could cross-pollinate and, more importantly, cross-sell their combined readerships. The result was a huge hit, which enhanced sales of the heroes' own core titles, allaying DC editors' concerns about overexposing their stars. But it only happened thanks to a tentative one-off tale in *Superman* #76 (May 1952) that fired readers' imaginations.

Tactical advantage

During the 1950s, and perhaps influenced by the rise of television and the massively popular Superman newspaper strip, "juvenile" action adventure and spectacle generally played second fiddle to human drama, mysteries, and domestic situation comedy.

"The Mightiest Team in the World!" finds Clark Kent and Bruce Wayne booking passage on the same vacation cruise ship, and, after being forced to share a cabin, accidentally discover each other's secret alter egos while attempting to catch a jewel thief. Immediately bonding, their biggest dilemma from then on is keeping

Radio stars

The most inevitable of team-ups finally took place in March, 1945 on the hit *Adventures of Superman* radio show and was later confirmed through an actual comic book collaboration where DC's heavy hitters acted as substitutes for missing members of the Justice Society of America (*All-Star Comics* #36 Aug./Sep. 1947). However, even in that issue, the popular heroes worked apart. Fans had to wait another five years before their favorite Super Heroes appeared in a comic together.

secret-identity-obsessed Lois Lane in the dark. The simple yarn triggered a phenomenon and presaged even greater costumed alliances to come throughout the comic industry. ▪

Key issues

Action Comics #1 (June 1938)
Superman ushers in Super-Heroic age.

Detective Comics #27 (May 1939)
Urban crime-fighter Batman debuts.

New York World's Fair Comics 1940 (July 1940)
First published cover appearance of Batman, Robin and Superman together.

World's Best Comics #1 (Spring/March 1941)
Quarterly anthology begins with Batman and Superman as separate features among many.

World's Finest Comics #2 (Summer/June 1941)
Title renamed with Batman, Robin, and Superman sharing all future covers.

All-Star Comics #36 (September 1962)
Honorary teammates working in Justice Society of America.

Superman #76 (May 1952)
Retroactively adjusted first meeting of the Man of Steel and the Dark Knight.

World's Finest Comics #71 (July 1954)
First official collaboration and start of "World's Finest Team."

The Legion of Super-Heroes

April 1958

Scripted by science-fiction author **Otto Binder** and illustrated by artist **Al Plastino**, a one-off tale in which Superboy is pranked by new friends fired readers' imaginations, creating a new world exploration for the young Super Hero. The story, in *Adventure Comics* #247, grew to encompass DC's entire continuity and would make the future another vital venue for stories as it introduced **The Legion of Super-Heroes**.

Don't judge me!
The iconic cover image by Curt Swan and Stan Kaye caught the eye of readers, artists, and editors and has been constantly revisited and "homaged" by generations of comics creators ever since.

In the future, superpowered teenagers from many alien civilizations, inspired by Superman, will found a club of heroes. One day, they travelled back in time and invited the hero to join them.

Superboy was created in 1945 and quickly became a popular mainstay of the ever-expanding "Superman Family." The original Superboy was the young Superman, still living in Smallville. These comics combined action and fantasy on levels with which young readers could easily empathize. A recurring theme in several stories from both *Adventure Comics* and Superboy's own title was loneliness, the isolation of a youngster with a big secret he is unable to share with anyone his own age.

This inescapable situation yielded many tales of brief but ultimately doomed friendships with young heroes such as Marsboy and Power-Boy, but nothing substantial ever developed. That all changed after an encounter with three captivating teens who seemed to know all his secrets.

Friend zone
The plot was a familiar favorite. Tales of heroes from foreign locales—albeit usually other places, not different times—were frequent during this period. "The Batmen of All Nations" in *Detective Comics* #215 (Jan. 1955) spawned the sequel "The Club of Heroes" in *World's Finest Comics* #89 (Aug. 1957), and just three months after the Legion launched, Jack Kirby would premier "The Green Arrows of the World" in the Emerald Archer's backup slot in *Adventure Comics* #250 (July 1958). Such stories were devised as ways of adding drama, scope, and perspective, showing that heroes were everywhere but America's were always best. There was never any intention of a spin-off series, but somehow, the Legion was different. Readers demanded more, and despite the wave

Work in progress
The Legionnaires were redesigned for their second outing. Lightning "Boy" became "Lad," hurling bolts rather than summoning electricity by clapping; Saturn Girl's "thought-casting" became telepathy, and Cosmic Boy's "magnetic vision" became control of magnetism.

> "How will I ever tell them back in Smallville that their 'super-hero' flunked out of the **Super-Heroes Club**?"
>
> **Superboy** | *Adventure Comics* #247

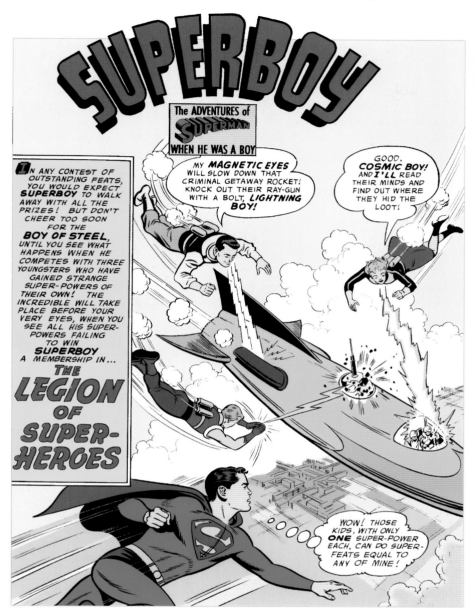

From its humble beginnings, the Legion of Super-Heroes grew and matured into a fundamental aspect of DC continuity. Its mission, settings, membership, and even core characters continually adapted as the team was periodically reinvented to fit the shifting fashions of the readership. Throughout all the decades, it held and still holds the undying devotion of a zealous fan base who forever declare "Long Live the Legion!" ▦

The future is now!
By the time the Legion took over the anthology title *Adventure Comics*, guest appearances had introduced a small army of new members, with issue #300 placing Saturn Girl in command. She was the first female to head a super-team in Silver Age comics history.

of guest appearances in numerous Superman titles that followed, no amount of simple sequels seemed sufficient. Eventually the Legionnaires won their own series, relegating Superboy to the back of *Adventure Comics* with #300 (Sep. 1962), before he left the title completely, except as one of the gang when he visited the 30th century every month.

Teens from tomorrow!
The lead story in *Adventure Comics* #247, which also included Green Arrow ("The 13 Superstition Arrows") and Aquaman ("Aquaman's Super Sea-Squad"), the landmark Legion debut saw three new kids in Smallville who all know the Boy of Steel's secret identity. On confronting them, he learns they are from the 30th century, where his historical exploits have inspired young champions to form a Legion of Super-Heroes.

Touched by the attention and their offer of honorary membership, he joins them in the world of tomorrow but fails every simple initiation test they set for him. He is heartbroken and shocked when they reject him but relieved when the Legionnaires reveal it's all a prank to gauge his temperament. In reply, the Boy of Steel plays a joke on his new allies when a real crisis emerges.

Key issues

More Fun Comics #101 (January 1945)
Superboy's first appearance.

Adventure Comics #247 (December 1959)
Legion of Super-Heroes debuts.

Adventure Comics #300 (September 1962)
Legion begins its own series.

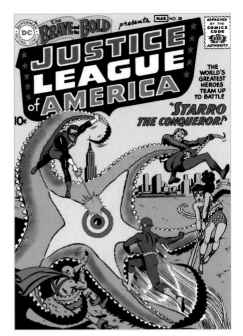

Star power
The first sight of the JLA said it all. Giant monsters! Valiant heroes! Earth defended by colorful super champions! How could any comics reader resist?

The Justice League of America

March 1960

After years when costumed champions were seen as a spent fad, new superpowered characters and careful modernization of Golden Age survivors prompted the creation of a team of the World's Mightiest Heroes. Their initial, all-action exploit in *The Brave and the Bold* #28, courtesy of editor **Julius Schwartz**, scripter **Gardner Fox**, and penciller **Mike Sekowsky**, electrified fans, who clamored for more stories featuring the *Justice League of America.*

The Justice Society of America (JSA) was rightly revered as a landmark in the development of comic books. However, unlike the company's twin blockbusters Superman and Batman, imitators—often seen as the only true indication of success—were few and far between. Despite the long-term benefits of their creation, scant years after the JSA first met, the popularity of superheroes waned as WWII ended. By 1950, almost all were gone, replaced by more traditional heroes in comfortably traditional genres.

Notwithstanding the occasional appearance of science-fiction inspired heroes such as mutant Captain Comet in 1951 and detective John Jones, Manhunter from Mars in 1955, superheroes were generally considered by publishers to be a spent force and minority interest. That began to change after National/DC launched *Showcase* as a vehicle to try out new concepts and characters. *Showcase* #4 (Oct. 1956) and the introduction of a new version of The Flash was the game changer, introducing a streamlined, Atomic Age Scarlet Speedster. His success proved the appetite for outlandishly attired adventurers was strong in the latest generation of readers.

Calling all the heroes
With novel Super Heroes cropping up everywhere, astute editors began subtly revamping the costumed crime fighters in their stables who had survived since the 1940s. The demand for more super adventures increased and editor Julius Schwartz took the next logical step in mid-1959, by introducing something special for companion try-out title *The Brave and the Bold*. Just in time for Christmas 1959, unforgettable adverts started running.

The modern, reinvented versions of The Flash and Green Lantern were selected to be part of new team Justice League of America alongside John

Mountain tension
The League debuted fully formed, democratically run, and hinting that it was large and well-organized, rather than just five heroes sharing similar goals. They even had a cool, secret underground base for debate and planning missions.

> "One among you is not under my influence... He must be destroyed!"
>
> **Starro the Conqueror** | *The Brave and the Bold* #28

Unlike their JSA predecessors, the Justice League battled as a team from the start against monsters, evil scientists, Super-Villains, and invaders from space.

with inking from Bernard Sachs, Joe Giella, and Murphy Anderson. It saw The Flash, Wonder Woman, Aquaman, J'onn J'onzz, Manhunter from Mars, and newcomer Green Lantern—already members in good standing—convene to combat a mind-controlling, marauding alien starfish manipulating stolen atomic forces and imperiling all humanity. Superman and Batman stood by in reserve, but the team instead adopted average American teenager Snapper Carr as a mascot after he gave them the crucial clue to defeating the threat.

Although somewhat conventional by modern standards, the team was groundbreaking at the time. When the Justice League of America premiered in *The Brave and the Bold* #28 (Mar. 1960), their triumph cemented the growth and validity of the genre, triggering an explosion of new superpowered characters at every company producing comics in America. The innovation even spread to the rest of the world as the 1960s progressed. A keystone of the DC Universe ever since, the Justice League of America is arguably the reason we have a comics industry today. ■

Jones, Manhunter from Mars, Wonder Woman, and Aquaman. Batman and Superman were officially on the roster but sidelined to let the others shine, and because editors were concerned that overuse would diminish their popularity. When allied, ever peripherally, with the relatively unchanged big guns who had weathered the first decline of Super Heroes, the result was a fresh, glamorous, Space-Age continuance of the JSA, and the birth of a thrilling new mythology. As if to confirm the fact, the team debuted in situ, already in established existence. Their origins and first case would not be revealed until *Justice League of America* #9 in 1962.

Invader from the stars

"Starro the Conqueror!" was written by former Justice Society scripter Gardner Fox and illustrated by Mike Sekowsky,

Monster mayhem
Reimagined under Comics Code restrictions, Silver Age heroes were primarily defined by science-based themes. Magic was used with restraint, but marauding or benevolent aliens popped up almost daily.

The Flash of Two Worlds

September 1961

After reviving the superhero genre—heralding the start of the Silver Age—The Flash infinitely extended DC's storytelling horizon by linking past and present in *The Flash* #123. When science-fiction author **Gardner F. Fox** and illustrators **Carmine Infantino** and **Joe Giella** orchestrated a meeting of generational superstars in *The Flash of Two Worlds*, it led to even greater innovations and astounding adventures.

Rapid response
The Fastest Men Alive looked very different but were identical in their drive to save lives and battle injustice.

Created by Gardner F. Fox and originally realized by Harry Lampert, Jay Garrick became the first Scarlet Speedster in *Flash Comics* #1 (Jan. 1940). A huge sensation, The Flash was the first All American Comics character to win a solo title, mere months after *All Star Comics* #3 (Dec. 1940) launched the Justice Society of America. Garrick's invention as a single-power mystery man began a new trend in comic books. He headlined in four titles: *Flash Comics*, *Comics Cavalcade*, *All-Flash Quarterly*, and *All Star Comics*, and was one of the last Super Heroes to be canceled. His final appearance was in *All Star Comics* #57 (Mar. 1957).

Five years later, a new generation encountered the concept of Super Heroes when legendary editor Julius ("Julie") Schwartz, scripter (and Schwartz's officemate) Robert Kanigher, and artists Carmine Infantino and Joe Kubert launched a new version of The Flash in *Showcase* #4 (Oct. 1956) as police scientist Barry Allen became the next hero to run with the concept.

Race to revolution

Schwartz ushered in a fresh epoch with his Golden Age revivals. The Flash, Green Lantern, The Atom, Hawkman, and the Justice League of America revitalized the entire comic industry. Thanks to close collaboration with his writers and artists, his titles always sparkled with challenging ideas and novel situations. From the start, The Flash was his core innovation engine.

Fast friends
After initially suffering individual crushing defeats, the speedsters discover the secret of success is teamwork.

Whereas 1940s tales were frequently about mobsters, magic, and monsters, the Silver Age burnished adventures with fashionable scientific notions and rationalistic concepts. The revived Scarlet Speedster was the bedrock of the Silver Age Revolution. Chief writers John Broome and Fox set an extraordinarily high bar for Super Hero dramas with sharp, witty tales of technology and imagination, illustrated with captivating style and clean simplicity by Infantino.

The most significant contribution was "Flash of Two Worlds" in *The Flash* #123 (Sep. 1961), formally introducing parallel worlds to the continuity.

> "I've just had a brainstorm! **Keystone City**? Could it be that... what I'm thinking... is true? 'He' used to live there!"
>
> **Barry Allen** | *The Flash* #123

THE FLASH

HOW CAN *YOU* POSSIBLY CLAIM TO BE *THE FLASH*, BARRY ALLEN-- WHEN *I* -- JAY GARRICK--AM *THE FLASH*--AND HAVE BEEN SO FOR MORE THAN *20* YEARS?!

HOW MANY FLASHES ARE THERE? ONE? TWO?

IS BARRY ALLEN THE REAL FLASH? OR IS JAY GARRICK?

DOES THE FLASH LIVE IN CENTRAL CITY? OR IN KEYSTONE CITY?

ONLY ONE THING SEEMS CERTAIN! BOTH LIVE ON THE PLANET EARTH! AND ONLY BY TRAVELING TO THAT "OTHER" EARTH CAN THE FLASH DISCOVER HIS ALTER EGO AND BECOME THE...

FLASH OF TWO WORLDS!

Who's who?
The tantalizing first encounter of the Flashes promised thrilling wonders and spectacularly delivered on that promise for the next six decades.

either in their individual series or via annual summer collaborations in *Justice League of America*. At the same time, Schwartz attempted relaunching other old favorites in *Showcase* and *The Brave and the Bold*. Set on Earth-Two, Starman/Black Canary and Dr. Fate/Hourman/Wildcat foundered, with only the Spectre graduating to his own short-lived title just as Super Heroes went into a short decline and were supplanted by supernatural themes.

The most important result came from the conceit that author Gardner Fox was a "real" character in continuity terms and able to tune in to alternate Earths. This led to the creation of Prime-Earth (*The Flash* #179, May 1968), the world of DC comics readers, who believed Super Heroes were fictions—until Barry Allen crashed there and needed Julie Schwartz's help to return home. From this first interaction would stem later menaces such as Ultra and the ultimate adversary Superboy Prime. ■

Through follow-up tales and by careful extension, DC's expanded reality embraced a multiversal structure comprising variant Earths without limit. Established as a cornerstone of the DCU through numerous alternate Earth team-ups, the notion underpinned an escalating succession of cosmos-shaking crossover sagas. It also established a pattern that would, after tumultuous decades, culminate in a spectacular *Crisis on Infinite Earths*.

During a benefit performance for orphans, The Flash accidentally slips into another dimension—one vibrating at another frequency—and meets the fictional comic book hero on which he based his own Super Hero identity. Every thrilling tale young Barry Allen had avidly absorbed was reality for Jay Garrick and his comrades on the swiftly designated "Earth-Two." Barry convinces the older speedster to come out of retirement just as three villains make their own criminal comeback, resulting in a spectacular showdown with the Fiddler, the Thinker, and the Shade.

Earths shock

The floodgates had opened. The following months saw several Earth-One stalwarts meet their counterparts,

Key issues

Flash Comics #1 (January 1940)
The first Flash, Jay Garrick, premieres.

All Star Comics #57 (March 1951)
Last appearance of The Flash, Atom, Black Canary, Dr. Mid-Nite, Green Lantern, and Hawkman.

Showcase #4 (October 1956)
The second Flash, Barry Allen, debuts.

The Flash #123 (September 1961)
Barry Allen and Jay Garrick meet for the first time.

The Flash #129 (June 1962)
The Flashes reunite to save both Earths from meteoric dooms.

The Flash #137 (June 1963)
The Flashes save the Justice Society from Vandal Savage.

Justice League of America #21–22 (August–September 1963)
First JLA/JSA team-up.

The Flash #179 (May 1968)
Barry Allen accidentally discovers Prime-Earth.

Crisis on Earth-One and Crisis on Earth-Two

August–September 1963

As the 1960s progressed, for DC Super Hero fans, every month brought fresh wonder. A huge leap forward came in *Justice League of America* #21–22 when twin worlds intersected in **Crisis on Earth-One and Crisis on Earth-Two**. In these pages, history was made by writer **Gardner F. Fox** and artists **Mike Sekowsky** and **Bernard Sachs**, who depicted the moment when old and new heroes joined forces for the first time.

Calling all heroes
Overpowered by sorcery and deprived of The Flash's alternate Earth experience, the JLA resort to magical trophies to establish contact with their Earth-Two counterparts, the JSA.

As the 1940s ended, tastes changed and superheroes all but vanished. Soon the mighty JSA had only seven heroes—Wonder Woman, Doctor Mid-Nite, Black Canary, The Atom, Hawkman, The Flash, and Green Lantern—appearing in their final issue of *All Star Comics* (#57, Mar. 1951). The incredible fantasy and furious, cartoony action of costumed champions gave way to more realistic heroes in western, war, science fiction, horror, and crime adventures, with romance, teen comedy, funny animal, and celebrity comics offering more traditional fare.

Suit up

DC sustained a small core of their Super Hero stable for half a decade, until a new Flash debuted in *Showcase* #4 (Oct. 1956). His compelling exploits sparked a slow but inexorable return for masked crime busters and world savers. When the Scarlet Speedsters of two eras met in *The Flash* #123 (Sep. 1961), the epochal event changed the scope of American comics forever. In a gradually cohering shared continuity, "Flash of Two Worlds" had introduced the concept of alternate Earths—and by extension a Multiversal structure for all future DC books. Now, thanks to a plot conceit that declared Earth-One and -Two were closest in vibratory alignment during summer, it also offered the opportunity for annual team-ups during the months when schools were closed and kids enjoyed well-earned vacations.

The groundwork for the initial group contact had been laid months earlier. *The Flash* #129 (Jun. 1962) saw a sequel tale costarring Golden Age Speedster Jay Garrick and teasingly reintroduced, via flashback, JSA members Wonder Woman, The Atom, Hawkman, Green Lantern, Doctor Mid-Nite, and Black Canary. They appeared in person in *The Flash* #137 (Jun. 1963), kidnapped by immortal villain Vandal Savage and saved by the occasional but effective partnership of the twin Flashes. Clearly editor Julius Schwartz had something bigger and more substantial in mind.

Conference of crime
Arrogant and confident of success, some of the worst villains of two Earths calmly debate ways of neutralizing Super Heroes.

> "Everything went as we planned it! How did you make out on your **Earth?**"
>
> **Doctor Alchemy** | *Justice League of America* #21

Justice is served
The peak cathartic thrill of Super Hero storytelling—evildoers receiving the thrashing they have rightly earned—across an economical, action-packed spread!

These innovative adventures generated an avalanche of popular and critical approval, and commensurate sales. Inevitably the transdimensional tryouts led to the ultimate team-up a few months later in the summer of 1963. The profound pairing began in *Justice League of America* #21 (Aug. 1963) as the League responded to an impending "Crisis on Earth-One!"

The danger came from experienced Earth-Two Super-Villains the Fiddler, the Thinker, and the Shade, allying themselves with indigenous Earth-One criminals Doctor Alchemy, Felix Faust, and Chronos. After trouncing all opposition, the wicked plunderers traded worlds to facilitate easier scores against lawmen unfamiliar with their powers and tactics. As part of the grand

scheme, these "Crime Champions" imprisoned the mighty Justice League of America inside their own secret mountain headquarters. Unable to escape, the Justice League used captured trophies from past cases to broach interdimensional walls and combine forces with the champions of another Earth to save both worlds.

Reshaping the Multiverse
To ensure success, the villains had removed both Flashes beforehand but did not anticipate the JLA and JSA establishing interdimensional contact and trading enemies in "Crisis on Earth-Two" (*Justice League of America* #22, Sep. 1963), a spectacular showdown that would dictate the course of all future group team-ups.

Taken as a whole, these issues form one of the most important stories in DC history. The Golden Age defenders of Earth-Two increasingly cropped up throughout the DCU, and the

subsequent annual summer Crises became a regular fixture. From these came all the successive cosmos-shaking, time-rending Crisis sagas that have repeatedly shaken and reshaped the DC Multiverse. ◼

Key issues

***All Star Comics* #3 (December 1940)**
First Super Hero team—the Justice Society of America—debuts.

***All Star Comics* #57 (March 1951)**
Last JSA story signals the end of the Golden Age of comics.

***The Brave and the Bold* #28 (March 1960)**
Justice League of America premieres.

***The Flash* #123 (October 1961)**
Barry Allen's The Flash discovers Earth-Two.

***The Flash* #137 (June 1963)**
The JSA come out of retirement.

***Justice League of America* #21–22 (August–September 1963)**
JLA and JSA meet for the first time and join forces to combat a multiversal threat.

Crisis on Earth-Three and the Most Dangerous Earth of All

August–September 1964

After reinventing Super Heroes and reuniting two generations of DC stars, editor **Julius Schwartz** and creators **Gardner F. Fox**, **Mike Sekowsky**, and **Bernard Sachs** expanded the cosmic playground even further one year later. If infinite parallel Earths held similar beings, would they also be good and wise? What if they were evil? *Justice League of America* #29-30 had the answers in **Crisis on Earth-Three!**

Friends in need!
The elders of the JSA quickly took on the mantle of mentors as well as brothers and sisters-in-arms.

It's an aspect of human nature and a maxim of popular entertainment to always crave more and bigger and better. That was certainly the case with readers of Super Hero comic books as the Silver Age unfolded, and definitely the result of the second annual team-up of the Justice League and Justice Society of America.

Same as it ever was

With "Crisis on Earth-Three" and "The Most Dangerous Earth of All!" in *Justice League of America* #29 and #30 (Aug. and Sep. 1964), the creative team fully embraced the science-fiction concept of alternate realities and began to explore vastly varied potentialities. While Earth-Two was home to DC's original heroes— all now aged in real time—and Earth-One home to modern-day counterparts such as Barry Allen's The Flash, other Earths were soon introduced and the floodgates opened for truly mind-boggling possibilities.

The event began appropriately with a glimpse of The Flashes from Earth-One and -Two in action before introducing a third Scarlet Speedster, this one plundering his home city. Johnny Quick, reviving the name of another Golden Age DC Super Hero, was one of five superpowered beings who dominated their Earth, a world where history was wildly different and no Super Heroes had ever existed. Later stories would reveal it as a world where the dominant ethos was strength and force, which had suppressed compassion and caring.

In that lawless state, Owlman, Superwoman, Power Ring, Johnny Quick, and Ultraman had formed

a tenuous and fractious alliance as the Crime Syndicate of America but were experiencing unexpected setbacks. A lack of competition and combat complacency resulted in near-defeats for all of them, before Ultraman offered a tantalizing solution.

In his universe, Kryptonians gained additional powers from Kryptonite exposure and his newest talent was transdimensional ultra-vision. Using this new power, Ultraman had seen beings like themselves but who used their abilities to stop crimes and defend the weak. Before long, the wicked warriors of Earth-Three had conceived a scheme to invade Earth-One, plunder its treasures and, most importantly, regain their competitive edge by battling its valiant heroes.

Robbing rampage
The Crime Syndicate ravaged the unfamiliar Earth, not from greed or need but just to prove who was in charge now.

Evil triumphant
The experienced elder heroes of Earth-Two eventually outfought their freakishly familiar foes but were no match for Owlman's fail-safe strategies.

However, the plan to use Earth-One's costumed crusaders as living practice dummies and unwitting sparring partners failed at the first hurdle. The Justice Leaguers proved unbeatable on their home world. That contingency had been anticipated by super-intelligent Batman analogue Owlman, who engineered a fail-safe tactic that transported the heroes to Earth-Three at the moment of victory. Once there, a swift rematch proved the Syndicate was unbeatable on home turf and led to the JLA being imprisoned, while the villains secured a neutral venue for the final decider.

That was to be Earth-Two, but thanks to their years of experience, and prior association with the JLA, the Justice Society veterans were forewarned and ready for the Crime Syndicate.

Planets in peril
The concluding chapter saw the JSA exclusively in action for the first half of the story, but again treachery and forward planning turned Syndicate defeat into victory. Exultant, the villains then transported the JLA to Earth-Two for the showdown, only

Undue process
Although scripter Gardner F. Fox was a lawyer, he frequently had his heroes ignore legal conventions. Here they illegally imprison their defeated enemies between dimensions in the cause of a "greater good."

to be beaten. This time, their fallback plan—to blow up Earths-One and -Two if captured—was spotted in time, and the united hero teams incarcerated their criminal counterparts in the inaccessible wilderness between dimensions.

A rousing and inspirational tale, this thriller cemented the annual tradition of summer team-ups for years to come. More significantly, it provided conceptual and metaphysical underpinnings for later events and Crises. These would determine the structure of the DC Multiverse and inform the ethical and psychological makeup of its heroes and villains, monsters and gods. ▇

Key issues

The Flash #123 (September 1961)
Barry Allen discovers Earth-Two.

The Flash #137 (June 1963)
The Flashes of Earth-One and Earth-Two save the Justice Society from Vandal Savage.

Justice League of America #21 (August 1963)
The JLA and JSA meet for first time.

Justice League of America #22 (September 1963)
JLA and JSA defeat the Crime Champions.

Justice League of America #29-30 (August–September 1964)
The JLA and JSA are attacked by Earth-Three's Crime Syndicate and eventually snatch victory from the jaws of defeat.

> "Great Hera! The Crime Syndicate must have defeated the Justice Society!"
>
> **Wonder Woman** | *Justice League of America #30*

The Teen Titans: Birth of Teen Teams

July 1964

The notion of stories starring kids was tricky in the first decades of the comic book industry. Opportunities for readers to empathize with young champions never really matched the heady thrill of self-determination promised by adult heroes. That changed in *The Brave and the Bold #54*, when author **Bob Haney** and artist **Bruno Premiani** repositioned junior crime fighters as the stars of their own show—heralding the ***Birth of Teen Teams.***

No sidekicks allowed!
The initially fractious team-up of junior partners quickly became an impressive alliance of equals working in harmony and efficiency.

Once DC had invented the concept of juvenile partners with Robin in *Detective Comics #38* (Apr. 1940), the innovation quickly spread across the entire comics industry, not only for Super Heroes but in countless other types of adventure feature. The company's own Congo Bill mentored "jungle boy" Janu for decades, and historical privateer the Black Pirate gave his son on-the-job training throughout the Golden Age. The concept even had strong literary antecedents, harking back to Jim Hawkins in *Treasure Island* and Tom Sawyer in *Huckleberry Finn*.

During World War II, "kid-gang" teams were commonplace, with DC's Newsboy Legion and Boy Commandos meeting each other, and the Golden Age Sandman taking on a young partner, Sandy. Later comics included Superboy's encounters with Robin and young Green Arrow, so the concept of kid heroes working together was not a new one when DC tested the commercial waters with a one-off union of their current star heroes' assorted apprentices.

Group think

At that time, *The Brave and the Bold* employed a model of pairing established Super Heroes in unique exploits—presumably in hopes of finding a new "World's Finest" team. The policy ultimately led to the title becoming a legendary vehicle for Batman team-ups, but many of the early alternative pairings have also become true classics.

The story in *The Brave and the Bold #54* (Jul. 1964) was timely and truly important, striking a chord and growing beyond the simple experiment of putting juvenile heroes together. Blessed with perfect timing, it emerged just as the Sixties started to swing, and as teenagers everywhere began developing notions of autonomy and self-determination as the decade changes society.

Kid heroes with their own regular comic featuring an ever-shifting, fab, hip, and groovy ensemble dedicated

Ganging up
The unnamed, unruly alliance of young champions would eventually grow into one of DC's most popular and well-populated teams, with a membership in excess of 80 heroes, antiheroes, and even villains.

> **"Flash...** like all adults, you forget that you were once a teen-ager, too!"
>
> **Kid Flash** | *The Brave and the Bold #54*

Generation gap
A widening gulf between "responsible" parents and "misunderstood" kids was subtly addressed from the start—a fact experienced and understood by most readers.

Wet and wild
The peculiar powerset of the first Titans frequently demanded peculiar plot situations and bizarre solutions, highlighting the heroes' specific talents.

to helping their peers and fighting evil may have felt patronizing to some, but for the target preteen audience, it was revelatory. Even though they didn't merit a distinctive group moniker yet, the creation of the Teen Titans was clearly part of the burgeoning 1960s phenomena of "the teenager" as a social and commercial force. Here were kids who could—and should—

be allowed to do things themselves without overbearing adult supervision.

Magical menace

Bob Haney's gripping mystery was illustrated by Bruno Premiani as "The Thousand-and-One Dooms of Mr. Twister." It united Kid Flash, Aqualad, and Robin the Boy Wonder against a modern wizard seeking to abduct all the teens of small town Hatton Corners. The young heroes collide there by chance after individual students separately invite them to mediate a long-running dispute with

the town's adults. After a spectacular battle, the youngsters triumph, but Twister would return in later years to bedevil the young heroes and their many successors.

The element of a teen "court of appeal" was a motivating principle in many subsequent cases. One year later, they reformed, this time under a team banner and with Wonder Girl added to the roster. This took some doing as she was not actually a sidekick, or even a person at that juncture, but rather a simulation of Wonder Woman as a child—a fact the writer and editor of the series simply ignored.

From these quirky beginnings, an irresistible force of young heroes have since sprung. Iterations of the Teen Titans have entertained generations, addressed social issues, and saved the universe, proving they are not just a junior Justice League but truly "Titans Together!"

Key issues

Detective Comics #38 (April 1940)
Robin makes his first appearance.

Detective Comics #64 (June 1942)
Boy Commandos premiere.

Wonder Woman #98 (May 1958)
Wonder Girl debuts.

The Flash #110 (January 1960)
Kid Flash's first appearance.

Adventure Comics #269 (February 1960)
Aqualad debuts.

The Brave and the Bold #54 (July 1964)
Teen Titans premieres.

Teen Titans #1 (February 1966)
The team wins its own title.

Zatanna's Search

October–November 1964

Scripted by **Gardner F. Fox** and illustrated by the cream of DC's stable of artists, a new female—and first "legacy"—Super Hero of the Silver age debuted in a bold experiment in storytelling. *Zatanna's Search* was an epic quest across numerous titles edited by Silver Age architect **Julius Schwartz** that culminated in a classic confrontation and changed the ever-expanding DC Universe forever.

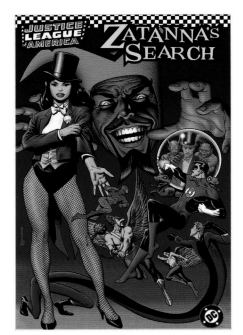

Nothing up her sleeve
The breakout star of the series, Zatanna, had to wait for the 2004 collected edition to truly take center stage in her own origin saga.

Gardner F. Fox, fellow scribe John Broome, and editorial mastermind Julius Schwartz laid the foundations of the modern DCU. A Golden Age veteran and canny innovator, Fox created or reinvented many characters while devising extended storylines that met the contemporary demands of being self-contained in one episode. These foreshadowed today's "braided crossovers" and company-wide "events."

A polymath and qualified lawyer, Fox began his comics career on major and minor features, in every genre, and for numerous publishers. As well as co-creating The Flash, the Sandman, Hawkman, and Justice Society of America, one of the many B-list strips he scripted was Zatara: a magician-hero who battled evil in *Action Comics* and *World's Best/World's Finest Comics* from their first issues until tastes changed at the end of the 1940s.

For my next trick...

In 1956, Schwartz revitalized the superhero genre by introducing modern iterations of DC's past pantheon of characters. The Flash, Atom, Green Lantern, and Hawkman were retooled for the sleek, scientific Atomic Age. Eventually, their legendary—mainly magical—predecessors returned as denizens of an alternate Earth. Innovation became a trend and then policy, as enduring characters Superman, Batman, Green Arrow, Aquaman, and Wonder Woman were updated to match. Before long, original heroes also arrived, like ductile detective the Elongated Man. The superhero had become ascendant and public appetite seemed inexhaustible.

Bells, books, and candles
Zatanna's multipart quest gave Gardner F. Fox plenty of scope to display his encyclopedic knowledge of mystic literature and mythic lore.

Fox and Schwartz then revisited the 1940s and DC's oldest magician, Zatara—first seen in *Action Comics* #1. Rather than consign him to Earth-Two, they made Zatara DC's first "legacy hero," whose stories took place in Earth-One's past. To explain his long absence, they introduced a daughter who embarked on a far-reaching quest to find him. Zatanna debuted in *Hawkman* #4 (Oct./Nov. 1964) in "The Girl Who Split in Two," Illustrated by Murphy Anderson. Following separate mystical trails, she divided her body, traveling simultaneously

> "If necessary, I must sacrifice myself to safeguard **Green Lantern** and keep the **Warlock** confined to his own world!"
>
> **Zatanna** | *Green Lantern* #42

HAWKMAN

STORY GARDNER FOX

ART MURPHY ANDERSON

FROM THE MUSEUM IN MIDWAY CITY THE TRAIL OF THE MYSTERY-TREASURES LED TO THE LOST CITY OF YIN AND TO THE HILL OF TARA IN IRELAND!

CONFRONTING HAWKMAN WERE ORIENTAL BANDITS! FACING HAWKGIRL WERE CRIMINALS FROM LONDON! AND AT TRAIL'S END FOR BOTH WAS THE ADDED MYSTERY OF...

The GIRL WHO SPLIT IN TWO!

Women warriors
Zatanna joined the small but growing ranks of Silver Age female Super Heroes, including Wonder Woman, Supergirl, Batwoman, Mera, Elasti-Girl, and Hawkgirl.

to Ireland and China, but lapsed into paralysis until Hawkman and Hawkgirl answered her distress call.

Zatanna's search took a strange turn in *Detective Comics* #336 (Feb. 1965). Drawn by Sheldon Moldoff and Joe Giella, "Batman's Bewitched Nightmare" pitted a broom-riding witch against the Dynamic Duo. It later transpired (in *JLA* #51) that the witch was in fact Zatanna in disguise and under the thrall of mutant menace the Outsider.

Witch hunt
Artist Gil Kane and inker Sid Greene illustrated the next two chapters. "World of the Magic Atom" (*The Atom* #19, Jun./Jul. 1965) found Zatanna and The Atom battling Zatara's old nemesis the Druid in the microcosmic world of Catamoore. This was followed by Green Lantern joining forces with Zatanna in an extradimensional realm on "The Other Side of the World!" (*Green Lantern* #42, Jan. 1966), to defeat the malevolent Warlock of Ys. Their victory also secured another clue in the trail that would lead to Zatara.

Depicted by Carmine Infantino, the Elongated Man's backup feature in *Detective Comics* #355 (Sep. 1966) revealed "The Tantalizing Trouble of the Tripod Thieves!" as a stolen eldritch artifact brought the sorceress closer to her goal, before the hunt concluded in *Justice League of America* #51 (Feb. 1967). Illustrated by Mike Sekowsky and Sid Greene, "Z—as in Zatanna—and Zero Hour!" finds the heroes Zatanna previously met transported to a mystical plane to fight for her before she saves the day in a classic good versus evil battle and reunites with her father.

This experiment in continuity is one of the Silver Age's best epics. It is a tale that subtly addressed changing tastes as science-oriented Earth-One welcomed Zatanna as its first Super Hero magic wielder. ■

Key issues

***Action Comics* #1 (June 1938)**
Debut of Zatara the Magician.

***Detective Comics* #27 (May 1939)**
Batman begins.

***The Flash* #112 (May 1960)**
Elongated Man makes his first appearance.

***Showcase* #22 (October 1959)**
The Silver Age Green Lantern debuts.

***The Brave and the Bold* #28 (March 1960)**
The Justice League of America begins.

***The Brave and the Bold* #34 (March 1961)**
First appearance of Silver Age Hawkman.

***Showcase* #34 (October 1961)**
Birth of the Silver Age Atom.

***Hawkman* #4 (October/November 1964)**
Zatanna debuts.

***Detective Comics* #336 (February 1965)**
A bewitched Zatanna battles Batman and Robin.

***The Atom* #19 (June/July 1965)**
Zatanna and the Atom search the Microverse.

***Green Lantern* #42 (January 1966)**
Zatanna and Green Lantern save reality from an extradimensional invasion.

***Detective Comics* #355 (September 1966)**
Zatanna and Elongated Man team up.

***Justice League of America* #51 (February 1967)**
Zatanna rescues Zatara.

***Justice League of America* #161 (December 1978)**
Zatanna officially joins the JLA.

Secret Origin of the Guardians

October 1965

By 1965, the superhero revival was approaching its peak, with almost a decade of stories forming a shared universe of alternate Earths. The inevitable next step was forming a cohesive history. Editor **Julius Schwartz**, writer **John Broome**, and artists **Gil Kane** and **Sid Greene** delivered a stunning starting point, as the old and new guard clashed in *Green Lantern* #40's *Secret Origin of the Guardians*.

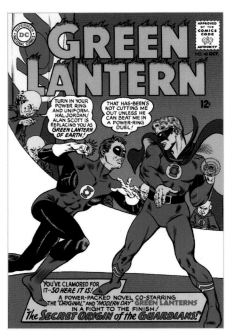

History in the making
Despite a complex backstory and revelatory clues to the nature of reality, this epic clash of heroes never stints on blockbusting action and nerve-jangling suspense.

The Silver Age of comic books saw the evolution of an increasingly complex and shared continuity. This new continuity was a network of cities, each with its own Super Hero, and worlds, all connected to alternate realities. Virtually every story was an act of universe-building, as heroes and villains crossed over, shared opponents, and developed a cohesive, communal history. This happened in the middle and peripheries of superbly engaging action, adventure, and mystery tales in which entertainment was paramount.

When mystical adventurer Alan Scott, the original Green Lantern, was reimagined as all-too-human space cop Hal Jordan, the newcomer met and befriended his 1940s predecessor in the first JLA/JSA team-up in *Justice League of America* #1 (Aug. 1963).

Scott's crime-fighting heyday was revealed to have been decades earlier in the parallel reality of Earth-Two. However, although a generation apart, the Emerald Gladiators became firm friends, with their amazing power rings able to sunder the vibrational barrier between existences at will.

To protect and serve

Hal Jordan had rapidly established himself as a major star of the DC firmament. His *Green Lantern* title spotlighted his benefactors, the benign Guardians of the Universe, who had policed creation since the dawn of time. The series also increasingly provided conceptual milestones and "big picture" foundations that affected other series as successive creators expanded a tight-knit history and the continuity of

the DC universe. In the 1960s, there was also a preference for a down-to-Earth action hero who could solve problems with his mighty fists rather than a wondrous ring that could do anything.

In "The Secret Origin of the Guardians!" (*Green Lantern* #40, Oct. 1965) Scott encounters a bizarre meteor on Earth-Two, which removes his ring's weakness to wooden objects. He selflessly travels to Earth-One, hoping to share his fortune by removing Jordan's powerlessness against the color yellow but instead discovers his own vulnerability has been returned. Using his mystic ring, he and Hal probe the mystery and learn that the "meteor" was in fact an energy prison for an immortal scientist named Krona. The ring relates how the renegade researcher came from an early civilization of super-beings and how his obsessive search for the origins of existence unleashed evil and suffering into reality billions of years ago.

Most shockingly, Krona was from Oa. His actions compelled his immortal brethren to reduce him to energy and condemn him to an endless circuit of

Emerald oversight
Foreshadowing later events when they sought to control, not simply safe guard the universe, the immortal Oans reveal that they monitor their agents extremely closely.

creation before they themselves eternally atoned for his deeds by becoming protectors of life and civilization. As part of their contrition, the Oans, the self-appointed Guardians of the Universe, founded a multispecies force of cosmic peacekeepers—the Green Lantern Corps.

> "We shall become the **Guardian**s of our universe! Wherever wickedness arises, we will combat it... and protect justice!"
>
> **Oan Leader** | *Green Lantern #40*

Infinite obsession

Krona was two steps ahead of the heroes and the Guardians. Liberated and restored by Scott's well-meaning efforts, he resumes his catastrophic inquiries, triggering chaos on Earth-One before possessing Scott's body and telepathically overcoming the Oans. However, his attempts to sideline Jordan lead to a cataclysmic clash between the two Green Lanterns and, ultimately, Krona's own defeat and reincarceration.

Simultaneously high-concept and action-packed, this team-up tale became the keystone of DC cosmology and a springboard for many intertwined publishing events such as *Crisis on Infinite Earths* and *Millennium*. "The Secret Origin of the Guardians" is a landmark that doubled down on the incredible revelations of "Flash of Two Worlds" and the early Justice League/Justice Society team-ups that sprang from it. It also displayed Gil Kane's peerless ability to stage a Super Hero fight like no other. ▨

Emerald action
The tradition of Super Heroes misguidedly battling each other has rarely been better illustrated than by masters of dynamic action, penciller Gil Kane and inker Sid Greene.

Key issues

All-American Comics #16 (May 1940)
Green Lantern Alan Scott debuts.

Showcase #22 (October 1959)
Hal Jordan becomes a Green Lantern.

Green Lantern #1 (August 1960)
The Guardians of the Universe first contact Hal Jordan.

Justice League of America #1 (August 1963)
Two eras converge when the JSA and JLA meet.

Green Lantern #40 (October 1965)
Two Lanterns first adventure together.

Green Lantern #76 (April 1970)
Guardian Appa Ali Apsa experiences humanity, alongside Green Lantern and Green Arrow.

Crisis on Infinite Earths #1–12 (April 1985–March 1986)
Multiple universes are destroyed and a new singular reality is born.

Millennium #1—8 (January–February 1988)
Guardians and Zamarons depart the universe after creating the New Guardians.

Green Lantern: Ganthet's Tale #1 (November 1992)
Reframes Krona's crime, casting doubt on the Guardians' true motives.

Fourth World

October 1970–March 1974

As a product traditionally intended for youthful consumers, comic books sought to be topical, and as America underwent social and cultural revolution in the 1960s and 1970s, many creators seized the zeitgeist to underpin their stories. Returning to DC after more than a decade, supreme imagineer **Jack Kirby** combined passion with audacity and a lifetime of entertainment experience to create a new mythology of Biblical scope that revolutionized comics forever and became known as *Fourth World*.

Escapist literature
Gods, monsters, and heroes were perennial comic book fare, but they had rarely been used so forcefully to probe the human condition and grand themes of existence.

Famed for larger-than-life characters and colossal cosmic imaginings, Jack Kirby was an astute, spiritual, family man who lived through the most dramatic years of the 20th century. He survived the Great Depression, global conflict, Cold War paranoia, and political cynicism yet always saw the best in people. A gifted artist and writer, he devoutly believed comics were worthy of greater respect and that sequential narratives should be published as "real books" like other literary art forms. And he dedicated his life and abilities to proving it.

Genesis
With partner Joe Simon, Kirby first worked for DC in the 1940s, reviving moribund strips "Manhunter" and "Sandman" and creating landmark hits "Boy Commandos" and the "Newsboy Legion" before leaving to serve in World War II. He was a free agent after the war and started a company with Simon. Kirby returned to DC in the mid-1950s, working his magic on Green Arrow and conceiving pioneering feature The Challengers of the Unknown, before making his next career move to DC's rivals.

When he returned to DC in 1970, it was to fashion his most powerful concept. The *Fourth World* inserted an entire novel mythology into existing DC continuity and changed the direction of the industry forever. Co-opting ailing title *Superman's Pal Jimmy Olsen*, he transformed it into a showroom for cutting-edge concepts. Via top-secret government venture "The Project," readers encountered the notion of cloning and how humans might be mass-produced and tailored to specific functions. At the height of America's counterculture movement, Kirby explored how technology might forge

> ## "Are we truly **beyond** time? Are we beyond **Death**?"
>
> **Esak** | *New Gods #4*

Fire in the sky
Afflicted by their forebears' demons, the New Gods' fate changed once Izaya of New Genesis abandoned warfare to pursue the Source's benign mysteries.

Forge of evil
Despotic Darkseid set Apokolips ablaze for fuel, repurposing his subjects as machines, cannon fodder, or weapons of mass destruction.

new kinds of societies, such as the techno-pacifist "Hairies" and dropout biker clan "the Outsiders."

Wedded to drama, intrigue, and stunning action, while also using the youthful reporter as a participant but also "honest witness" to unfolding events, Kirby introduced Morgan Edge, the new owner of the *Daily Planet*, alien-backed mobsters Intergang, an "Evil Factory" unleashing clones and monsters, and Darkseid—the ultimate enemy of universal free will.

Revived through cloning, a new Newsboy Legion and their Super Hero mentor the Guardian provided action and laughs as Olsen followed Edge's curious agenda, blithely unaware that the media mogul was actually the agent of an alien power. Whether working beside Superman or his new allies, Olsen's astounding exploits were simply

the appetizer for something truly innovative—comics' first meta series.

Revelations

Over two years, Kirby, with inkers Vince Colletta and Mike Royer, wove a tapestry of love, honor, death, and ideology, drawing Earth into an ancient war between rival factions of gods— dark and light—risen out of the ashes of a previous Armageddon to fight forever. The saga was intended to unfold as an interlinked triptych of finite series forming one epic mosaic. But fate had other ideas.

When the old gods died in ultimate battle, their final struggle sundered their home into two planets—dark, evil Apokolips and light, joyous New Genesis. However, even after eons, old philosophies still dominated and conflict reignited, due to the hubristic Darkseid. He sought the "Anti-Life Equation,"

a cosmic force that could negate free will and choice in all beings. Darkseid believed it lay hidden and dormant in some unsuspecting Earthling's mind, needing only agony or terror to awaken it for him to seize.

Bloodshed between the New Gods had paused for years, thanks to a trade of child hostages—noble Highfather's infant Scott Free for Darkseid's ferocious spawn Orion. Reared in their hereditary enemy's camp, both grew up proud and independent, but when Scott escaped Apokolips to seek a different path on Earth, the war began anew. Reflecting differing public concerns over the ongoing Vietnam conflict, the *Fourth World* saga even had its own conscientious objector. As super escape

THE FOREVER PEOPLE!

THEY'RE FROM A PLACE THAT MEN HAVE SOUGHT, BUT NEVER FOUND-- WE'VE SEEN THEIR LIKE BEFORE-- IN DIFFERENT AGES-- IN DIFFERENT GUISE-- BUT NEVER LIKE THIS-- YET, ALWAYS LIKE THIS-- WHEN MAN'S CIVILIZATION FACES DESTRUCTION...

IN SEARCH OF A DREAM!

EDITED, DRAWN AND WRITTEN by JACK KIRBY (OUR MAN IN THE BOOM TUBE) INKED by: VINCE COLLETTA

GUEST-STARRING THE IMMORTAL SUPERMAN

Together forever
Exploding out of a transdimensional "Boom Tube," Supertown's young gods sought to solve Earth's woes with boldness and staggering overconfidence.

artist Mister Miracle, Scott Free and his beloved Apokolips defector Big Barda found their own way to resist the call of war, even as the scheming Darkseid began his campaign in earnest.

Although renowned for cosmic scope, cataclysmic consequence, and infinite grandeur, the *Fourth World* saga was most powerful in moments of intimate human interaction. Whether it was the sheer hilarity of murderously frustrated Morgan Edge trying to get rid of annoying snoop Clark Kent and aggravating employee Goody Rickles with Apokoliptian Pyro granulate, or Orion's shame at revealing his hidden monstrous face to friend and comrade Lightray, or Darkseid's misguided pride

in his hated son Orion and loathing of his actual heir Kalibak, all evinced a level of sophistication never seen in Superhero comics before.

Proverbs

A consistent theme was isolation and alienation. Kirby portrayed Superman as someone who could be homesick and hungry for the company of his own kind. In *Forever People* #1, potential contact with New Gods is what draws the Man of Steel into the cosmic conflict, but it is only at the end of Kirby's run that Superman finally realizes his dream of making it to Supertown. However, once there, he finds the experience unsettling and,

Chariot of the gods
New Genesis technology like the sentient Super-Cycle was wondrous and friendly, working with its users and fully one of the family.

Fires of creation
The original god-world's final annihilation polarized matter into opposing planets where the ancient ideologies continued, two tribes forever at war.

Close calls
Mister Miracle's alternative to his proposed destiny was no guarantee that danger, death, or Darkseid could be avoided or escaped.

after some sage advice, chooses to return to the fight while his friends are still at risk.

Despite the many overarching interconnections and the shared scenario of an intergalactic war for hearts, minds, and souls played out in secret on Earth, each title of the saga was largely self-contained and pursued a different agenda. The Forever People were well-intentioned, idealistic kids, seeing a bad scene and rashly overeager to fix it, while the stories of the New Gods explored the view of experienced soldiers called back to onerous duty in defense of home and a hopeful future.

Scott Free sought a third path, seeking peace but instead attracting a throng of wildly unforgettable monsters, such as Granny Goodness, Virman Vundabar, and Doctor Bedlam, who would never permit a third way as they tried to appease the insatiable, diabolical Darkseid. Mister Miracle's high-octane escapades with human assistant Oberon, future wife Big Barda, Shilo Norman, and the militia-like Female Furies against Darkseid, Granny Goodness, Apokoliptian hordes, and grifter extraordinaire Funky Flashman—

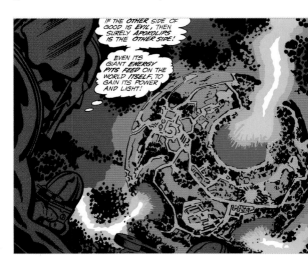

Proxy war
Guided by the nurturing Source, Apokoliptian outcast Orion led New Genesis's forces in a battle for life and choice imperiously imposed on Earth and humanity.

> **"We serve only Darkseid... and Darkseid serves conflict!"**
>
> **Big Barda** | *Mister Miracle #4*

Big-sky thinker
Building a new reality, Kirby grounded his epic in solid human interactions, reintroduced historical DC heroes, and even inserted himself into the mix.

Face of evil
The eternal struggle spawned many iconic stars, but none with the terrifying charisma and chilling philosophical assurance of deadly Darkseid.

Shadows and echoes
The Fourth World's repercussions resonated across the traditional DC universe, involving the most unlikely of the company's stars.

not to mention incipient bankruptcy—was bright and breezy in contrast to the weighty content of the epic's other titles.

Kings

Kirby's world and characters arrived fully formed for the interlocking epic he had devised, and other editors—especially those in the Superman family of titles—incorporated many aspects seemingly overnight in related titles. The *Daily Planet* newspaper was absorbed by Galaxy Communications, and evil corporate overlord Morgan Edge became Clark Kent's boss in all other Superman titles.

Edge's schemes and crimes were most closely detailed in core title *Superman's Pal Jimmy Olsen*, but he

also prowled through *Action Comics, Superman, World's Finest Comics,* and *Justice League of America* before his incredible secret was finally exposed in an extended story arc in *Superman's Girlfriend Lois Lane.*

Evolving organically with crucial scraps of information appearing everywhere, the climax began as a sub-strand with Lois Lane discovering that the communications magnate had been replaced by a clone. "Edge of Darkness" (*Superman's Girlfriend Lois Lane* #118, Jan. 1972, by Robert Kanigher, Werner Roth, and Vince Colletta) detailed how Darkseid's Evil Factory minions had installed a replacement to act as a human intermediary between Apokolips and Intergang agents. Simyan and Mokari botched the removal of the original who escaped death by hiding with Lois.

When the New Gods saga wound down, the original Morgan Edge reclaimed his role at Galaxy Communications, which allowed all Superman-related continuity changes and renovations generated by Kirby to remain in place.

Numbers

Like other creative landmarks—such as DC's own "Hard-Traveling Heroes" Green Lantern and Green Arrow, who reshaped comics but still couldn't avoid cancellation due to perceived poor sales—the *Fourth World* saga succumbed to economic pressures at the time of release. The marketplace was changing and the economy depressed, and both *New Gods* and *Forever People* were canceled just before their proposed conclusions. A far better fit with readers, *Mister Miracle* escaped the fate of its sister titles with

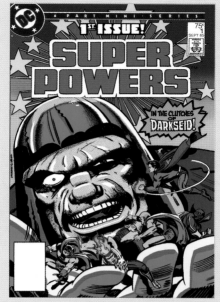

Toying with you
Super Powers launched in July 1984 as a five-issue miniseries with Kirby covers and his signature Fourth World characters prominently represented.

Apocrypha

During the 1980s, costumed heroes became big toy business, and DC licensed many of its stars as action figures. The Super Powers line came with mini-comic inclusions of individual characters and ultimately led to a line of tie-in comic books. DC's most recognizable Super Heroes and Villains now included Darkseid, Parademons, Orion, Mister Miracle, and other Fourth World icons, and Kirby was asked to contribute to a line of limited series.

Plotting the sagas, co-writing with Joey Cavalieri, and illustrating with Adrian Gonzales and Pablo Marcos, Kirby's tales of cosmic quests across time and space and bombastic battles between agents of Good and Evil were fully integrated romps. They starred the assembled DC Pantheon, confirming how the New Gods had become an inextricable part of mainstream continuity while setting the scene for the long-awaited conclusion of the original saga in *The Hunger Dogs* graphic novel.

Wicked game
Kirby constantly introduced astounding concepts and symbols, like miraculous Mother Boxes, to serve his true message—good must always confront evil.

a run of divergent non-Apokoliptian tales that only returned to course for its final issue, *Mister Miracle* #18 (Mar. 1974)—the hasty wedding of Scott Free and Big Barda, with the rest of the New Gods in contentious attendance.

The *Fourth World* saga was only controversially completed years later, after a high-quality reprinting of *New Gods* #1-11 in 1984 included an all-new episode by Kirby. It was not the intended finale—too much time had passed and society had moved on— but rather an intermediary tale. It led in 1985—via a toy company license—to a true, fitting conclusion in the format Kirby had long predicted, a graphic novel entitled *The Hunger Dogs*. The lasting effects of the *Fourth World*'s starburst of creative energy spread far and wide, however.

While the saga was all-but-finished by 1974, the characters began resurfacing in work by other creators as early as 1976 and have remained as constants ever since. Moreover, the original epic also contributed possibly the most charismatic villain in comics—the mighty, conflicted, ever-arrogant, and tragically flawed Darkseid. ▪

Key issues

October 1970–March 1985

Superman's Pal Jimmy Olsen #133–149
The Forever People #1–11
The New Gods #1–11
Mister Miracle #1–18
The New Gods Vol. 2 #6
Super Powers #1-5; Vol. 2 #1–6
DC Graphic Novel #4: *The Hunger Dogs*

Non-Kirby tie-ins (July 1971–September 1972)

Superman's Girlfriend Lois Lane #111, 115, 116, 118
Superman's Pal Jimmy Olsen #152

The Great Disaster

October 1972–October 1978

Postapocalyptic scenarios are a staple of fantastic fiction, and many had previously graced the pages of DC's comics. However, it took master imagineer **Jack Kirby**, collaborators **Mike Royer** and **D. Bruce Berry**—with later contributions from scripter **Gerry Conway**—to weave those subgenres into an overarching, shared continuity. Dubbed *The Great Disaster*, it featured characters and concepts that would inspire epic new adventures in the decades that followed.

Future tense
Armed with courage, ingenuity, and the outdated teachings of his dead grandfather, Kamandi set out to repair a ravaged world where nature had run amok.

As America experienced social and political unrest in the early 1970s, comic book tastes shifted away from Super Hero fantasy. The Cold War was gripping humanity and cinema of the era brimmed with tales of atomic destruction and postapocalyptic struggles for survival.

Wild world
Following the boldly innovative *Fourth World* saga, Jack Kirby created *Kamandi: The Last Boy on Earth* #1 (Nov. 1972). A speculative, all-action peek at a probable tomorrow, it was the biggest commercial success of his third tenure at DC.

Set a generation after atomic devastation had ravaged Earth and the evolution enhancing chemical Cortexin had seeped into the environment, it saw a boy emerge from underground bunker "Command D" into a deadly wonderland of mystery and mutation. Earth AD (After Disaster), housed species of talking, reasoning animals, who scavenged the technological achievements of a lost civilization while hunting human brutes.

Fast-paced and high-concept, *Kamandi* was Kirby's perfect vehicle, offering endless opportunity for satirical speculation. He lampooned the Watergate crisis, human arrogance,

and wastefulness, as well as ecological issues and environmental abuse as Kamandi roamed the strange new world in search of humans like himself to help restore mankind to its true destiny.

Reared by his grandfather and schooled by history tapes glorifying human existence, Kamandi was proudly steadfast, wandering a shattered continent, winning allies, and earning enemies among fiercely contending species. Seeking to drag debased humanity up from its devolved status, Kamandi learned that animals were prone to their predecessors' failings. Thankfully, though, many also shared human virtues too.

While gorillas, rats, tigers, bats, gophers, snakes, killer whales, and more battled for dominance,

Continental drift
Like his distant forebears, the Last Boy on Earth charted an astounding course across atomically altered America, finding danger and wonder at every turn.

Scavenger hunt
Devastated outposts provided Kamandi with glimpses of mankind's achievements and seemingly human mutant companions but no vestige of people like himself.

as science and wealth trumped compassion and reason, and humanity teetered on the brink of self-inflicted extinction. In this world, super-rich rogues beyond the law, WMDs, made-to-measure biological horrors, artificial companions, water wars, satellite surveillance, and ecological collapse were forestalled by the Global Peace Agency. This agency policed a species with hair-trigger fingers on nuclear stockpiles and worse. Their only asset was artificially induced super-soldier Buddy Blank, and when he inevitably failed to stop the apocalypse, he retreated to Command D bunker with his infant grandson, determined to survive until After the Disaster. ◼

picking over the carcass of the past, dogs and dolphins (with humans as service animals) shepherded mankind, and Lion Rangers thwarted poachers in a Human Preserve. There were also monsters aplenty—giant mutated insects, crabs, worms, and worse. Kamandi's journeys revealed many miracles, including not just hyper-evolved beasts but also aliens, gods, time travelers, and other dimensions. Kamandi even confronted the ultimate apex predator—intelligent, homicidal germ Morticoccus, who was intent on eradicating all life, eventually succeeding in a later crossover crisis.

Kamandi #29 (May 1975) saw the hero defeat a religious zealot gorilla to secure a holy relic—the remnant of a promised messiah known as the Mighty One. The remnant turned out to be Superman's costume and confirmed Earth AD was once protected—and failed—by Super Heroes.

In *The Brave and the Bold* #120 (July 1975), Kamandi met Batman and, latterly, other past and future champions like Legion of Super-Heroes' stalwart Karate Kid. Ultimately, the "Last Boy" traversed dimensions, allying with the Justice League against multiversal menace Perpetua.

Kamandi and his world were eased into DC's shared history as the Great Disaster was incorporated into other postatomic war series such as John Broome and Murphy Anderson's "Atomic Knights" in *Strange Adventures*, the extensive short-story feature "The Day after Doomsday" and *Hercules Unbound*, but the most crucial addition was another "Kirby Kreation."

Grandaddy dearest

OMAC: One Man Army Corps #1, (Oct. 1974) expressed Kirby's darkest prognostications. His "World that's Coming" seems remarkably prescient,

> ## "I'm betting Man can be smart **again** someday!"
>
> **Kamandi** | *Kamandi: The Last Boy on Earth* #39

Primed and ready
Maniacal villain Per Degaton mastered time and terror in his overwhelming blitzkrieg against humanity across the infinite Multiverse.

Crisis on Earth-Prime

October–December 1982

The JLA and JSA teamed up every year between 1963 and 1985 in summer blockbusters, expanding horizons and consistently upping cosmic stakes. Scripted by **Roy Thomas** and **Gerry Conway**, and illustrated by **Adrian Gonzalez**, **Don Heck**, **Jerry Ordway**, **Romeo Tanghal**, and **Sal Trapani**, *Crisis on Earth-Prime* spanned time and parallel dimensions to deliver doom and salvation for multiple Earths.

The Justice Society of America inspired many Super Heroic imitators, successors, and devoted fans. Possibly their most passionate follower is comics writer, editor, and historian Roy Thomas, who crafted many of the team's latter campaigns against tyranny and injustice. For DC in the early 1980s, Thomas created *Arak, Son of Thunder*, *Infinity Inc.*, and *Captain Carrot*, wrote *Batman* and *Wonder Woman,* and, most significantly, revived the world's original Super Hero team. Crucially, he convinced DC to set them back where they truly belonged, battling for freedom and democracy in World War II.

All-Star quandary

Thomas's All-Star Squadron comprised 1940s characters created or acquired by DC and formerly published by other comic companies such as All American, Quality, and Fawcett

Meet and greet
Generations of pandimensional costumed champions converged in 1942 to ensure Per Degaton's dream did not become a Multiversal extinction event.

Comics. These heroes supplemented a rotating number of JSA stalwarts, and was devised as an adjunct to the original team, telling "untold tales" from wartime.

When the time came for 1982's annual JLA/JSA team-up, Thomas and then Justice League scripter Gerry Conway brought the 1940s iteration into the epic and, for good measure, included Earth-Three's nefarious Crime Syndicate. Spanning alternate universes and divergent histories, the time-warping drama impacted multiple Earths, beginning in *Justice League of America* #207 (Oct. 1982), when members of the JSA were accidentally shunted across dimensions

Man of the moment
Per Degaton's only advantages were cunning, narcissism, and a manic determination to rule. However, the chronal pirate's many attempts to rule the world usually ended with his triumphs erased from history and his name forgotten.

Zatanna, Firestorm, Hawkman, and Aquaman rushed to Earth-Two and found a fascistic state that had been ruled by Degaton for 40 years. Voyaging down the corrupted timeline to January 1942 to solve the mystery, they stumbled into the JSA's wartime branch, the All-Star Squadron. Inevitably, confusion led to conflict between the heroes.

The newcomers' arrival in *All-Star Squadron* #14 (Oct. 1982) coincided with Degaton recovering his erased memories—a recurring hazard of time manipulation and restoration—and stealing a prototype time machine from his bosses at the Time Trust. In the time stream he encountered Ultraman, Owlman, Superwoman, Johnny Quick, and Power Ring and opportunistically released them from the energy-prison where the JLA and JSA had left them.

Axis of evils

Joining forces, the murderous Crime Syndicate crossed realities and traversed histories. On Earth Prime in 1962, they savagely stole nuclear missiles Russia had stockpiled in Cuba, precipitating a clash of wills between President John F. Kennedy, Fidel Castro, and Soviet premier Nikita Khrushchev that ultimately resulted in nuclear catastrophe.

The transdimensional triple threat concluded in *Justice League of America* #208 (Nov. 1982) after Degaton issued his ultimatum to humanity on Earth-Two—accede to total surrender or face the successive detonation of dozens of atomic super bombs in many nations.

The heroes of twin worlds and two eras were ready to counter the scheme. In *All-Star Squadron* #15's (Nov. 1982) all-action clash, they deployed into smaller units to destroy the stolen nukes, bolstered by their JSA comrades from 1982. These heroes had escaped a prison dimension before heading back 40 years for the beginning of the end. *Justice League of America* #209 (Dec. 1982) delivered the stunning conclusion, course-correcting chronal status quos and restoring the various Earths to normality. And once again, ambitious lab assistant Per Degaton awoke from his dreams of conquest and resumed his dreary toil at the Time Trust. ▨

while traveling to Earth-One during a scheduled rendezvous with the JLA.

They arrived in a postapocalyptic dystopia, born when the Cuban Missile Crisis of 1962 sparked global atomic war. The heroes' investigations revealed that it was Earth-Prime—a world with no Super Heroes—that had been devastated decades previously due to the machinations of malign time-tyrant Per Degaton. He had employed Earth-Three's Crime Syndicate to steal nuclear missiles and callously triggered an atomic Armageddon.

In 1982, on the Justice League satellite, the waiting heroes were brutally overwhelmed by the sudden appearance of their evil counterparts from Earth-Three. Barely surviving the surprise attack, Superman,

> ## "Figures... all **fading**! Then it was all just a **dream**... a **nightmare**..."
>
> **Per Degaton** | *All-Star Squadron* #14

Key issues

All Star Comics #3 (December 1940)
The JSA premieres.

The Flash #123 (September 1961)
Multiple Earths confirmed by meeting of Earth-One and Earth-Two.

Justice League of America #21 (August 1963)
JLA and JSA team up for first time.

Justice League of America #29 (August 1964)
Evil Earth-Three and Crime Syndicate of America discovered.

The Flash #179 (May 1968)
Introduction of Prime-Earth.

Justice League of America #153 (April 1978)
Ultraa becomes Earth-Prime's first—and covert—Super Hero.

Justice League of America #193 (August 1981)
New 1940s-set JSA exploits begin as All-Star Squadron debuts.

Justice League of America #207–209 (October–December 1982)
Crisis on Earth-Prime.

All-Star Squadron #14–15 (October–November 1982)
Per Degaton is defeated.

The Great Darkness Saga

August–December 1982

The period between DC's contemporarily set stories and the seemingly set-in-stone, millennia-distant era of the Legion of Super-Heroes was varied, packed with potential probabilities, and fluid by nature. Readers assumed this 30th century was the one true future and **Paul Levitz**, **Keith Giffen**, and **Larry Mahlstadt** apparently confirmed that belief when every hero of that age faced the greatest terror of the past reborn to bring about *The Great Darkness*.

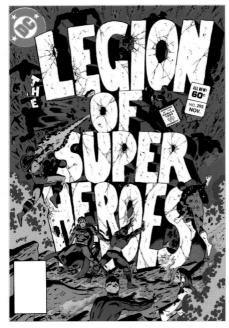

Total war
Old hands at universe-saving, the Legion were still utterly unprepared for the unrelenting evil of history's most feared foe revived in their time.

The fortunes of the Legion of Super-Heroes had waxed and waned for decades since their debut in 1958, but in all their incarnations, the bold future force had inspired a truly devoted fan base. In anticipation of the 25th anniversary, that loyalty was repaid in 1982 as an epic storyline capped a string of increasingly thrilling and memorable tales.

It began slowly with an ominous prologue in *Legion of Super-Heroes* #287, with tantalizing teasers in succeeding issues, including the first *Legion of Super-Heroes Annual*, gradually building to a magnificent main event.

Sleep no more

With the Legion suffering growing internal dissent, political attack from government, and possible dissolution, a dead world wandered into United Planets space, destroying all probes sent to investigate it. Thousand-year-old teen Daxamite Mon-El and Shadow Lass of Talok VIII were dispatched to deal with the intergalactic interloper but barely escaped with their lives after ancient weapons were engaged. The heroes fled, unaware that a force of evil long forgotten had awoken.

Marshaling malign forces and scouting a proposed new empire, the revenant attacked the universe, using debased clones of heroes and villains from history and legend as his agents. This advance guard ruthlessly gathered arcane artifacts to fuel their Master's recovery—shattering cities and brushing aside the best efforts of the Science Police and the Legion to stop them.

Told as a mystery, readers were given many clues to the revived villain's identity as he ravaged and stole power from the Legion's greatest adversaries with ease. The heroes scored a few precious victories, and the tide only began to turn after precognitive Dream

Blast from the past
Infused with the energies of Izaya of New Genesis and the Source, Superboy, and Supergirl deftly delivered immortal Darkseid's most humiliating experience.

Girl and her sister, the White Witch of Naltor, secured a rapidly aging infant from an unknown but benevolent realm.

Eventually, the Master was revealed as the ancient horror Darkseid, and his wandering world as the former bastion Apokolips. Reborn, the tyrant was in the

Legacy issues

The *Great Darkness Saga* was a gift to fans by former fans made good. At that time, Paul Levitz and Keith Giffen were on fire, consistently delivering groundbreaking stories and constructing a comprehensive, completely credible future. Their world-building feat still informs the Legion's adventures today. Famously, the saga involved every heroic character ever to appear in the series.

The storyline has become a landmark of DC continuity. One final episode was added decades later, when time-traveling hero Booster Gold visited Daxam (*Booster Gold #32*, Jul. 2010) just before Darkseid struck. As often happened, the hero failed in his intended mission but saved one child—Rani—who would become his adopted daughter.

The lasting effects of the *Great Darkness* were vast and widespread. In its wake, Darkseid's earlier stories were reprinted in a vibrant new collector's format (*New Gods* Jun.–Nov. 1984), which culminated in an

all-new chapter by Jack Kirby, who delivered the long-anticipated conclusion in the pioneering graphic novel *The Hunger Dogs*.

The New Gods became popular toys and featured in all-ages title *Super Powers* and mainstream series like the *Justice League of America*. In 1989, the New Gods were relaunched with contemporary exploits as the Fourth World became an active component in DC continuity.

Doom deferred

Exposed, defeated, and with an entire universe hunting him, Darkseid realized his cause was lost but left a dark curse to blight the Legion forever.

ascendant and would rule in this time if not in his era of origin. Victory seemed assured after he enslaved the planet Daxam. The isolated world was filled with potential supermen when removed from its red sun, and by corrupting the population, Darkseid unleashed a wave of terror across creation. In response, the Legion and Substitute Legion, aided by Kryptonian survivor Dev-Em, the Wanderers, and the Heroes of Lallor counterattacked, but all hope was lost until the child discovered by Dream Girl and the White Witch was finally revealed as Darkseid's archnemesis, Highfather of New Genesis.

Machina ex deus

The New God was not meant to linger and transformed Darkseid's last clone-servant back into his true identity. As Darkseid's prophesied executioner Orion, the forgotten warrior attacked and a long-deferred final battle

resumed. Ultimately, a hard-fought victory for life and free will was snatched from certain doom, but the aftermath changed the future forever.

The *Great Darkness Saga* has survived as part of history in every reboot and relaunch, from *Crisis on Infinite Earths* to *DC Comics: The New 52* and *Rebirth*, a testament to the Legion's valor and competence. However, its greatest significance is that reader response convinced DC of the power of its fan base.

In 1984, this led to DC turning both the *Legion* and *New Teen Titans* into experimental deluxe-format titles. The new *Legion of Super-Heroes* (#1, Jul. 1984) was available only from comic book stores and set a year ahead of then-current continuity. The newsstand edition, renamed *Tales of the Legion of Super-Heroes* from #314, carried a year's worth of untold adventures until it caught up, after which it reprinted those deluxe adventures for readers unable to reach comic book stores. ◼

> ## "**Worship** the darkness, fools... until the day it comes for **you**!"
>
> **Master of Darkness/Darkseid** | *Legion of Super-Heroes #287*

Key issues

August 1982–March 1985

Legion of Super-Heroes #287, 290–294
Legion of Super-Heroes #313
Legion of Super-Heroes #1 (direct sales edition)
Tales of the Legion of Super-Heroes #314
DC Graphic Novel #4: The Hunger Dogs

End of everything
Readers and fans had no conception of how much would change in the DC universe by the time this Super Hero spectacular concluded.

Crisis on Infinite Earths

April 1985–March 1986

In 1985, worlds lived, worlds died, and comics changed forever. The DC universe made comics history in a defining event—the first company-wide crossover to deliver lasting change. Writer **Marv Wolfman** and illustrators **George Pérez**, **Jerry Ordway**, **Dick Giordano**, and **Mike DeCarlo** set the event template for decades to come as New Earth rose from the rubble of the *Crisis on Infinite Earths*.

Nothing happens suddenly in print publishing. There are inescapable time factors and processes baked in to the production and distribution of a physical comic book. From a rough story plot and final script; to penciling; inking, and coloring; to editing, correcting, lettering, and assembling the final artwork; to printing and shipping, weeks can turn into months before the printed comics land on bookstore shelves. In short, there was always time to plan the next big thing.

Adventure comics
In 1985, DC Comics editorial staff were finalizing details for celebrating 50 years of publishing, enjoying a creative upswing that had been some time coming. As part of the festivities, and at the suggestion of star writer Marv

Wolfman, it was decided to rationalize character duplications and confusing anomalies that had cropped up since 1961, when "Flash of Two Worlds" *(The Flash #123, Sept. 1961)* and its popular sequels reintroduced the Golden Age inspirations for Silver Age Super Heroes such as Green Lantern, The Atom, Hawkman, and The Flash.

Intent on streamlining and clarifying five decades of often conflicting and contradictory stories, the decision to craft a truly epic, yearlong saga that would impact every DC title and reconstruct history, revitalized the entire DC Universe. Also envisioned was an appearance—however brief— by every character the company had ever published. The resulting saga was a monumental success, both critically and commercially, enabling DC to reboot many of its most cherished, but dated properties.

First seen in *New Teen Titans #21* (Jul. 1982), following an instruction to all group editors, a mysterious being

spent years insinuating himself into every corner of DC continuity. A satellite-based arms and information-broker, the Monitor catered to villains but now disclosed his true alien nature and critical mission. His previous enterprise let him assess extraordinary beings— surveillance that included every era of history on many Earths.

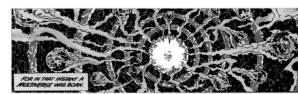

In the beginning
Creation's mystery and magnificence was forever marred after Krona's arrogant and callous intervention divided reality into weak fractions of the real thing.

> ## "Worlds lived, worlds died. Nothing will ever be the same."
>
> **Psycho-Pirate (Roger Hayden)** | *Crisis on Infinite Earths #12*

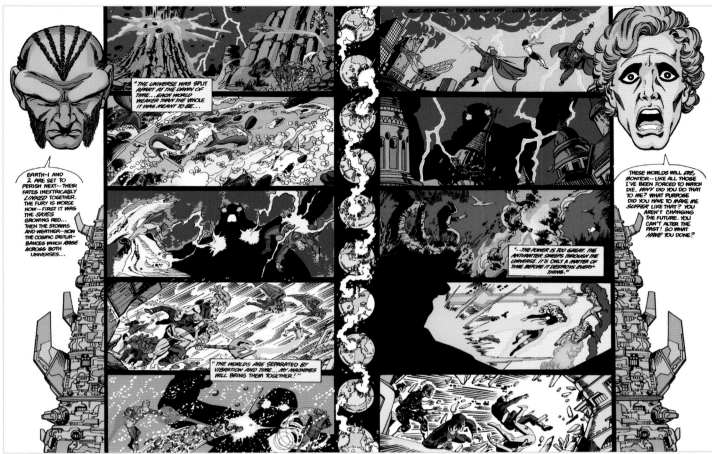

Threads and portents appeared across DC titles, as the Monitor and his enigmatic, immensely powerful assistant Harbinger gauged potential allies on Earths and associated planets with a view to saving reality from impending annihilation. At last, it began. Cover-dated April 1985 to March 1986, the series was in stores from January to December 1985, officially supported by crossovers in dozens of regular titles.

Multiplicity

At this juncture, countless parallel Earths coexisted, largely oblivious of each other, with differences that varied from slight to staggering. This was because, at the dawn of time, a curious scientific meddler from the future caused a unified universe to fracture. His name was Krona, and in eternal penance for his actions, his people forever after policed creation as Guardians of the Universe.

Now an unstoppable wave of antimatter began Multiversal eradication by voraciously consuming individual universes. Before each Armageddon, a tormented immortal named Pariah appeared, somehow summoned to witness its end. On Earth-3, he saw the Crime Syndicate fail to save the planet, unaware that Alexander Luthor and his wife, Lois Lane, preserved their infant son—casting him into the void between realities. Above Earth-1, the Monitor claimed the child while Harbinger gathered heroes and villains

Visions of doom
Pariah had been forced to witness the end of countless worlds and was convinced the Monitor had devised the phenomenon to punish his curiosity.

Missionary zeal
As old as existence itself, the Monitor was prepared to sacrifice himself and everyone else to preserve some vestige of life.

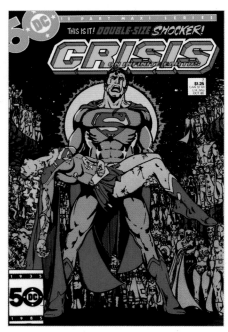

Fallen hero
Dying in battle to save her friends, Supergirl's only regret was leaving her cousin even more alone.

from across realities and throughout time. However, while the Monitor explained his purpose, the already anxious assemblage was attacked by shadow-beings.

The Monitor was as old as creation, and opposed by an evil antimatter counterpart who destroyed realities and strengthened itself on their energies. With almost all life expunged, the prospective savior built colossal technological towers in different time periods to smoothly remerge remaining universes into a single, stronger, more sustainable one. The Monitor needed defenders to preserve the towers from shadow-demons but was only fighting a holding action. The Monitor's greatest ally, Harbinger, had been compromised and the primordial protector's own murder was imminent.

The Crisis intensified as the Monitor's sinister antithesis, the Anti-Monitor, commanded Harbinger, now his enslaved pawn, to kill her mentor, while scattered champions defended the preserving towers from shadow-fiends. The caveman Anthro, western heroes like Gunhawk, and regular soldiers

joined masked wonders in their desperate endeavors but were vastly outmatched.

Soon only five Earths remained beyond Anti-Monitor's reach—Earths 1, 2, 4 (home to the Charlton Comics Action Heroes), Earth-S (the world of Shazam!), and Earth-X (where the Freedom Fighters battled a global Nazi Reich).

Five and counting
The Anti-Monitor had been cunning and subtle, using Harbinger, kidnapping key threat Barry Allen, and deploying emotion-twisting Psycho-Pirate Roger Hayden to control his enemies. The Monitor had factored in his own murder, however, and apportioned his life energies to create a pocket dimension to shelter the remaining Earths.

Alexander Luthor Jr. aged at hyper-accelerated rates, gaining superior intelligence and trans-dimensional powers that the Monitor had counted on. After Psycho-Pirate failed to foment war between the five Earths, Harbinger and Luthor transported a task force into the Antimatter Universe to sabotage a weapon built to bombard Earths. The sortie succeeded, but Anti-Monitor killed Earth-1's Supergirl as she

Relentless
The enemy of all life seemed impossible to kill and constantly rebuilt his body to resume his pitiless attacks.

stalled the cosmic menace, allowing time for the task force to retreat.

Brainiac led a Super-Villain army to conquer the last Earths, but in the end they united with the heroes against the Anti-Monitor. The world destroyer had constructed an antimatter cannon to pick off planets in the limbo pocket but had miscalculated. He believed Barry Allen was broken, but The Flash

> "You've seen the destruction... you know the end was near... but you do not know why... or who was behind it. We do."
>
> **Alexander Luthor of Earth-3** | *Crisis on Infinite Earths #5*

Ends of an era

Although a bonanza for superhero, supernatural, and science-fiction storytelling, and after scrupulously deploying most characters from DC's traditional comic book divisions, *Crisis on Infinite Earths* signaled the end of a genre-inclusive continuity. A major strand of the saga incorporated the final mission of joint-services task force the Losers

(*The Losers Special #1*, Sep. 1985) by Robert Kanigher, Judith Hunt, Sam Glanzman, and Mike Esposito.

A number of gunslingers and G.I.s played significant roles in the Crisis, but within a year, their once obligatory and ubiquitous fare vanished. *G.I. Combat* ended with issue #288 (March 1987), and DC's 33-year dominance of the war comics market was reduced to sole star *Sgt. Rock*. The valiant WWII hero held on until

1988 (#422, Jun.), after which new combat titles were sporadic, on the fringes of mainstream continuity, and often released under separate imprints.

The same was true for westerns, once a bountiful setting for magical and masked heroes dispensing frontier justice. DC's last western title of the period, *Jonah Hex*, ended with #92 (Aug. 1985, during the *Crisis*) and was replaced by a future-set, road-warrior iteration, as science-fictional themes started to come to the fore in comics and wider entertainment markets.

---

raced back through time, destroying himself to wreck the weapon.

Frustrated and furious, the Anti-Monitor attempted one final ploy, journeying to the beginning of time to prevent existence from being born. In response, the Spectre assembled an army of superpowered beings, bringing Super Heroes and an army of villains to the creation point to stop Krona from fracturing the primal Universe into a Multiverse. Their last ditch plan failed and a catastrophic explosion merged the five worlds into one, with all its various peoples unaware of what had transpired. Only those outside the event remembered what had happened and many were baffled and terrified to find themselves on an Earth that was not quite right and with no place for them.

Anti-Monitor attacked again, dragging the unified Earth into the antimatter universe and prompting a united front from heroes and villains—even Darkseid of Apokolips joined the war for existence. The death toll was devastating, but eventually the heroes were able to restore New Earth to its proper place.

Even after his physical body was shattered, the Anti-Monitor continued his frenzied assault in the expanse between existence and the Void. Facing him were Superboy of Earth-Prime,

Alexander Luthor Jr., and Earth-2's Kal-L (the first Superman), who ultimately ended the war, smashing the last remnants of the Anti-Monitor.

Resolved to perish outside reality with only satisfaction at having eliminated the Anti-Monitor to sustain him, the first Superman was astounded to learn that Luthor Jr. had preserved his wife, Lois, against erasure from existence and had found the four survivors a pocket paradise to happily live out the rest of their lives. It was a beautiful dream doomed to disappoint.

Standard bearer

Crisis on Infinite Earths was a groundbreaking cosmic spectacle. It set the benchmark for all future crossover publishing events and remains a high point seldom reached and yet to be surpassed. As well as being a gripping blockbuster, accessible to even the most neophyte reader, it is the foundation

Gone, for good
After experiencing the loss of so many loved ones, Earth's first Super Hero Kal-L of Krypton made sure that the Anti-Monitor was finally finished.

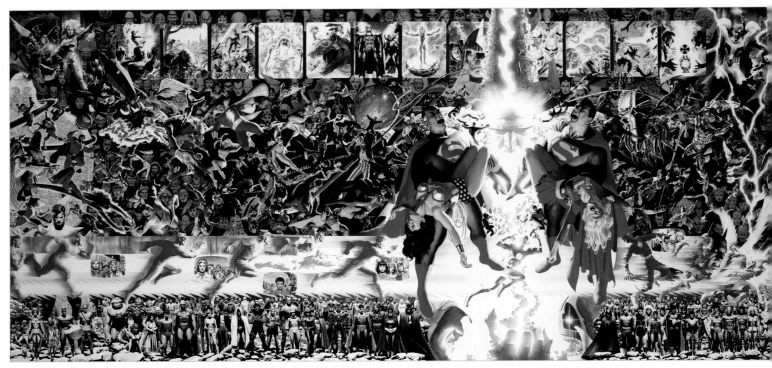

Epic in the making
The inspirational story is a highpoint of comics storytelling, as seen in this stunning tableau painted by Alex Ross for the collected edition.

of all DC stories since 1985, and laid the groundwork for many of the events that would follow.

No comics publisher had ever attempted anything like *Crisis on Infinite Earths*. There had been stories started in one title and concluded in another, like the origin of Captain Marvel Jr. in *Master Comics* #21 and *Whiz Comics* #25 in 1941, or a 1966 team-up tale begun in *Challengers of the Unknown* #48 and finished in *Doom Patrol* #102, and continued stories such as Justice League of America's *Crisis on Earth-One* and *Crisis on Earth-Two* (*JLA* #21-22, Aug.–Sep. 1963). There had even been tales told across multiple titles like *Zatanna's Search* (Oct. 1964–Feb. 1967) or Kirby's *Fourth World* (Oct. 1970–Mar. 1974), but never an epic that invited readers to follow events in every title currently published.

All ancillary stories were identified by additional trade dress announcing not just participation but also the 50th anniversary. The event's complex

Gone but not forgotten

With a significant anniversary to aim for, *Crisis on Infinite Earths* took literally years to plan. The intention was to celebrate the half-centenary of America's oldest comic book publisher by simplifying and rebuilding the framework to reinvent its major stars. Although creatively fruitful and beloved by fans and creators, the concept of multiple Earths was seen as confusing to some younger readers and daunting for potential new consumers—

almost requiring a scorecard to differentiate all the Flashes, Supermen, Green Lanterns, Atoms, and Hawkmen, in tales across dozens of Earths and multiple time periods. As if to underscore that, DC published a series to help readers.

In parallel with the *Crisis* saga, a monthly catalogue and guidebook listing and contextualizing all their characters and locales began at the same time. *Who's Who: The Definitive Directory of the DC Universe* (#1-26, Mar. 1985-Apr. 1987) was an indispensable guidebook. It offered statistics, story history, and art by the best illustrators from every company in the comic book business. It was followed by updates in 1987, 1988, and 1990. In an era before home computers and an online world, it was a crucial aid to old and new readers.

A more conventional and contemporary follow-up was *History of the DC Universe* (#1 and #2, Jan.-Feb. 1987). where Wolfman, Pérez, and inker Karl Kesel detailed the official revised history of the remade New Earth from the dawn of creation through the rise and fall of Atlantis and successive Ages of Heroes to the end of time. The stories were related through the deeds of their heroes and told by the former Harbinger.

> ## "Better to go into the **unknown** than die here alone..."
>
> **Superboy-Prime** | *Crisis on Infinite Earths* #12

momentous, official chapters were added years later, such as *Starman Annual* #1 in 1996 and *Legends of the DC Universe—Crisis on Infinite Earths* #1 in 1999. The latter one-off saw writer Marv Wolfman returning to his epic. Echoes of the event also informed and affected storylines forever after, the Multiversal reconfiguration directly impacting later crossover events such as *Zero Hour* and *Infinite Crisis*. ■

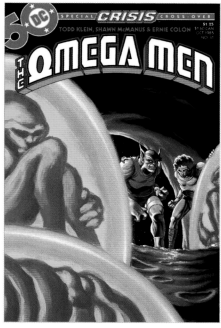

No escape

Even the ever-escalating war between the Omega Men and tyrants dominating the Vega system was paused to respond to the threat menacing existence.

titles were particularly active, as their role was critical. After the dust settled, there would only have ever been one Earth with a modified single history. The 1940s All-Star Squadron would overnight lose pivotal stalwarts Superman, Wonder Woman, Batman and Robin, Green Arrow and Speedy, and Aquaman, whose debuts were moved ahead two generations.

In the aftermath on the singular New Earth, the still extant Justice Society saw their actions replaced and their historically verified feats reaffirmed by debuting team the Young All-Stars and its oddly familiar replacement Super Heroes, Iron Munroe, Fury, Fling Fox, Dyna-Mite, Tigress/Huntress, Tsunami, and Neptune Perkins.

Carefully synchronized, repercussions of the main narrative spread through 40 crossovers, and the event was so

orchestration saw some titles starting on different Earths and time periods, but by the end, all titles were set on one world in one timeline.

Endings and beginnings

While the location and time of All-Star Squadron and Infinity Inc. may have been relatively easy to assign, who could tell whether Jonah Hex or the Haunted Tank were set on Earth-1 or -2? And what about teen caveman Anthro, Travis Morgan, Warlord of Skartaris, or Arak, Son of Thunder?

Before *Crisis on Infinite Earth's* official start, a number of titles (unmarked by trade dress) featured or cameoed the Monitor, but once the core series launched, almost every title over the year announced its place in the saga. Writer Roy Thomas's Earth-2

Untold tales

1999's tale revealed how The Flash (Barry Allen)'s last mission to save Earth-D allowed the Anti-Monitor to capture him before *Crisis on Infinite Earths*.

Key issues

Pre-Crisis Monitor appearances (July 1982–June 1985)

New Teen Titans #21, New Teen Titans Annual #2, Green Lantern #176–178, Action Comics #560, 564, Batman and the Outsiders #14–15, Blue Devil #5, The Flash #338–339, The Fury of Firestorm #28, Tales of the Teen Titans #47, 58, Infinity Inc. #8, Justice League of America #232, Swamp Thing #30–31, Tales of the Legion of Super-Heroes #317, Wonder Woman #321, All-Star Squadron #40, DC Comics Presents #76, 78, Superman #402–403, Justice League of America #234, World's Finest Comics #311, Tales of the Legion of Super-Heroes #319, Amethyst #2, G.I. Combat #274, Tales of the Legion of Super-Heroes #320, Vigilante #14, Wonder Woman #323, G.I. Combat #274, Warlord #91, Jonah Hex #90, Batman #384, Detective Comics #551

April 1985–March 1986

Crisis on Infinite Earths #1–12

Badged participants (September 1985–March 1986)

Wonder Woman #327–329, Infinity Inc. #18–24, Infinity Inc. Annual #1, All-Star Squadron #50–56, The Losers Special #1, The Omega Men #31, New Teen Titans #13–14, Blue Devil #17–18, DC Comics Presents #86–88, The Fury of Firestorm #41–42, Green Lantern #194, 195, 198, Justice League of America #244–245, Justice League of America Annual #3, Superman #414–415, Legion of Super-Heroes #18, Amethyst #13, Swamp Thing #46

Unbadged tie-ins/continuations (October 1985–September 1986)

Detective Comics #555–558, Vigilante #22, Batman #389–391, Legion of Super-Heroes #16, Blue Devil #17, 18, The Omega Men #33, Superman #413, Green Lantern #196–197, Swamp Thing #44, Infinity Inc. #25, All-Star Squadron #57–60, DC Comics Presents #94, 95, 97, Superman #423, Action Comics #583

Later official additions

Starman Annual #1 (1996), Legends of the DC Universe: Crisis on Infinite Earths Annual #1 (February 1999), JLA Incarnations #5 (November 2001)

Watchmen

September 1986–October 1987

In a time of rapid change and restless experimentation, the very concept and traditions of the superhero was being deconstructed, reexamined, and put to the test. Controversial and shocking, one storyline shook the ethical underpinnings of the genre, bursting into public consciousness when writer **Alan Moore**, illustrator **Dave Gibbons**, and colorist **John Higgins** brought British impertinence and irreverence to the American dream and unleashed *Watchmen*.

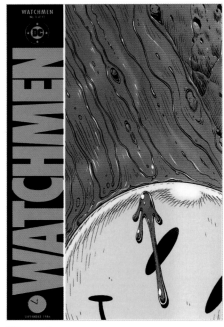

Killer smile
A fantastic, convoluted scheme to save humanity from itself unraveled because one misguided "hero" saw blood on a button and jumped to the wrong conclusion.

Success breeds success. Following the huge triumph of *Crisis on Infinite Earths*, DC exploded with creativity, generating innovative formats, various ways to schedule ongoing and fixed-length series, and new kinds of storytelling. It also saw DC produce a literary masterpiece courtesy of Alan Moore, Dave Gibbons, and John Higgins.

Comics grow up
In 1986, a 12-chapter superhero mystery thriller set on an alternate Earth gripped public attention far beyond the usual comic book audience. Dauntingly sophisticated and politically satirical, this reexamination of the genre, American culture, Cold War ethics, and human nature forever elevated the comics medium.

At a time of heightened cultural and political tensions, "Who watches the watchmen?" was a commonplace street slogan, a rough translation of "Quis custodiet ipsos custodes?" (from the second century Roman poet Juvenal's *Satires*). It was a universal challenge from the oppressed, speaking truth to power, and when deployed in this multilayered saga, underpinned the state of a world on the brink of catastrophe.

Back in 1983, DC acquired Charlton Comics' "Action Heroes" stable of characters. All played significant roles in *Crisis on Infinite Earths* and many won their own series on New Earth at the end. When Alan Moore submitted a proposal to use them in a challenging limited series that would effectively end their viability, DC managing editor Dick Giordano instead suggested he create his own cast of characters. Moore's tale required heroes and villains who resonated with readers, familiar archetypes who would be sympathetic actors in the drama. Working closely with illustrator Dave Gibbons, the end result was a fractured "round table" of isolated former champions floundering in a world with a history of failed heroes.

The story began with excerpts from the distressing journal of obsessive vigilante Rorschach. Dated October 12, 1985, it signaled his initial involvement in the murder of Edward Blake. On this Earth, masked heroes ("masks") had come and gone in the 1940s. A brief 1960s resurgence spawned a small

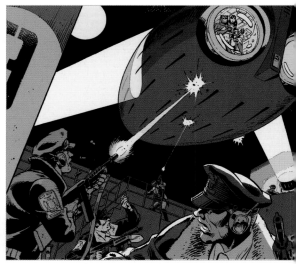

Jailbreak
With time running out, previously law-abiding Nite Owl and Silk Spectre had to spring Rorschach from prison to help stop their hidden opponent.

> "But it's too late, always has been, always will be too late."
>
> **Jon Osterman (Doctor Manhattan)** | *Watchmen #4*

Red planet
On Mars, Silk Spectre convinced former lover Doctor Manhattan to halt humanity's imminent extinction.

flowering of new champions eager to continue the legacy of their forebears before they were outlawed in 1977. Most retired—except Rorschach.

Earth's only true super-being was Jon Osterman, who had miraculously reconstructed himself after being vaporized in a science experiment. A quantum god, his idealistic Super Hero role as Doctor Manhattan ceased as his connection to humanity faded. Joining the government, his scientific discoveries transformed society, and his actions won the Vietnam War for President Nixon.

Save the world

Another freelance mask with a federal commission who served in Southeast Asia was the mercenary Comedian. The administration's chief wet work fixer also ensured the Watergate scandal never became public. His civilian name was Edward Blake and his inexplicable death sent a paranoid Rorschach into overdrive. Suspecting someone was targeting masks, he dutifully warned former associates like Doctor Manhattan, Silk Spectre, Nite Owl and Ozymandias, utterly oblivious to the cunning conspiracy actually in play—one that old enemies and the government knew nothing about.

When the hidden plotter manipulated Osterman to abandon Earth for Mars, the political balance of power shifted and the Soviet Union invaded nearby states, pushing the planet into a nuclear showdown no one could win. This was the mystery schemer's plan and led to a shock ending that challenged every convention of comic book storytelling.

Detailing an immense epic through small personal interactions, layered with levels of meaning, and employing visual motifs and techniques possible only in the comics medium, *Watchmen* changed how comics worked and altered the industry. On completion, it was one of the earliest successes of the nascent graphic novel market and has remained in print since the first collection in 1987. *Watchmen* is the only comic on *Time Magazine*'s Best 100 English Language Novels from 1923 to the present.

Who watched the Watchmen? Everyone did... and does. ◾

Crimson tide

Watchmen was meticulously constructed with inherent symbolic elements, such as clockworks and smiley faces, and worked on multiple levels. A bleak parallel story about comic book pirates echoes the failing efforts of the bewildered heroes trying to stave off nuclear Armageddon. Gibbons's detailed art is rendered on a classic and strict nine panel grid, and the unfolding, highly structured plot also takes in minor incidents—such as Rorschach stealing sugar cubes—that resonate throughout the story. It was published on higher-grade paper stock than regular newsprint titles and reflected a more mature depiction of sex and violence.

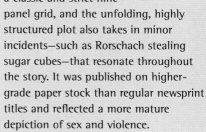

The limited series was published without ads, leaving room for supplementary in-world text material. These included excerpts from autobiographies and dossiers, faux features on pirate comics (with "real" masked adventurers in a world where superhero comics never caught on), and other backstory extras that flesh out a large cast of characters and expound on a story told over two separate time periods. Back covers displayed a countdown clock progressively drenched in red.

Watchmen's high design trade dress marked it as something different, and each cover doubled as the first panel of the story inside. The system was revived for 2012-2013's 37-issue prequel event *Before Watchmen* and 2018-2020's thematic sequel *Doomsday Clock*.

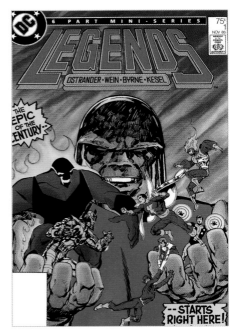

Legends

November 1986–April 1987

In the wake of *Crisis on Infinite Earths*, as ripples of a new universe settled, DC recreated its stars. Some were reinvented and fresh iterations of classic heroes were incorporated into a singular new reality. Conceiving the sequel mega-crossover, *Legends*, plotter **John Ostrander**, scripter **Len Wein**, and illustrators **John Byrne** and **Karl Kesel** challenged the very nature of heroism and its implications for humanity.

Better together
The reconfigured DC continuity was blessed with heroes in abundance, but not if New God Darkseid had his way.

Fan interest was intense when DC launched a sequel event capitalizing on the success of *Crisis on Infinite Earths*. Many of their major properties—and in fact the entire continuity—was wide open for radical change, innovation, and renewal. However, what could possibly follow cosmic catastrophe? Perhaps a smaller-scaled, intimate "great disaster," spotlighting the strangers now wearing familiar costumes—and a wealth of beginnings, rather than multiversal deaths and endings?

Like its predecessor, *Legends'* core narrative spread out into other DC series, but this time each tie-in was consecutively numbered and every cover badged. The saga touched 22 other comic books and spawned three new series—*Justice League*, *The Flash,* and *Suicide Squad*—while publicizing the new Wonder Woman, Blue Beetle, and a fresh beginning for Billy Batson (in a follow-up *Shazam!* limited series). Fans couldn't help but read them in the right order.

In "Once Upon a Time...!" (*Legends* #1, Nov. 1986), tyrannical god Darkseid of Apokolips conspired to shatter humanity's spirit by crushing its concept of heroism and individuality. He ordered psychic influencer Glorious Godfrey to America, fomenting a crusade against extraordinary heroes, and initiated targeted plans to demoralize and destroy humankind's key champions. His first triumph was the naïve, youthful Billy Batson—the juvenile alter ego of Captain Marvel—whom he deceived into believing his formidable powers accidentally killed the monstrous Macro-Man.

Task Force X

As Darkseid's flaming minion Brimstone ravaged the nation—despite the herculean efforts of Firestorm, time-displaced Legionnaire Cosmic Boy, and Justice League Detroit—the US government activated its own covert, illegal solution to the crisis. Devised by civil servant Amanda Waller, Task Force X comprised volunteers like Colonel Rick Flag and masked martial artist Bronze Tiger, who supervised convicted Super-Villains offered a pardon in return for secret services rendered.

Glorious Godfrey's influence on Earth spread, inciting riots that hospitalized second Robin

Gathering of heroes
Darkseid's scheme and Glorious Godfrey's rabble-rousing ultimately affirmed the stalwart dedication of Earth's Super Heroes.

Blockbuster finish
From the start, the coerced criminals of the new Suicide Squad knew that their lives now belonged to ruthless bureaucrat Amanda Waller.

Jason Todd, while driving Batman, Blue Beetle, and Green Lantern Guy Gardner into hiding. A "Breach of Faith!" (*Legends* #2, Dec. 1986) saw President Ronald Reagan respond to rampant civil unrest by outlawing costumed crime fighters. Unsure whether to comply or rebel, Super Heroes were forced to search their consciences as global chaos ensued. Super-heated plasma monolith Brimstone tried to reduce Mount Rushmore to slag but was stopped by America's latest secret weapon in "Send for… the Suicide Squad!" (*Legends* #3, Jan. 1987) And after heartbroken Billy Batson met the hero-worshiping Lisa, whose family took him in, Billy gained a fresh perspective on the ongoing calamity.

Brave new world
Events quickly escalated in "Cry Havoc…!" (*Legends* #4, Feb. 1987) as the emboldened Super-Villains ran amok, prompting several heroes to ignore the Presidential Edict. On Apokolips, the Phantom Stranger challenged Darkseid, while on Earth, the immortal mystic Doctor Fate gathered allies for the imminent final battle he foresaw. At that moment, Godfrey made a desperate power grab using brutal human-fueled Apokoliptian Warhounds in "Let Slip the Dogs of War!" (*Legends* #5, Mar. 1987) The separate story strands eventually converged in the tense "Finale!" (*Legends* #6, Apr. 1987) as Doctor Fate's substitute Justice League, aided by an enigmatic

Sensational stranger
An utterly unknown quantity, Diana of Themyscira's public debut confirmed the Wonder Woman as an irresistible force for good.

stranger calling herself Wonder Woman, drove back the forces of anarchy. The heroes came together to prevent the conquest of humankind and preserve its most vital belief.

The enthralling tale was carefully designed to stand alone, easily accessible without its connected

> **"Somebody** has to protect the **innocent** from monsters like **you!"**
>
> **Batman** | *Legends* #4

Company of strangers
Familiar stars in a strange new world, Earth's heroic legends seamlessly and triumphantly united to save humanity and its heroic beliefs.

crossovers and tie-ins. It remains a compelling mission statement for that new DC universe—gritty, witty, cohesive, and modern. Playwright and indie comics author John Ostrander was new to DC. He was paired with veteran writer Len Wein, whose long experience with DC's characters ensured the scripts delivered the right tone and texture. Together, they crafted a boldly controversial tale for newly arrived superstar artist John Byrne to draw and Karl Kesel and Dennis Janke to ink.

New world order
This multipart story was the first mass Super Hero event since *Crisis on Infinite Earths* reshaped a Multiverse into one singular reality. It gave DC an opportunity to showcase its revamped stars Superman, Batman, and Wonder Woman. The saga also breathed new life into revered, long-established properties such as Captain Marvel and the Blue Beetle—

Heritage hero
Created by Bill Parker and Charles Clarence Beck, orphan Billy Batson was empowered by ancient gods and heroes. He battled injustice with the might of Solomon, Hercules, Atlas, Zeus, Achilles, and Mercury by speaking aloud the name of the wizard Shazam!

Call of fate
Generations of DC Super Heroes joined the greatest champions of previous realities to save their new shared universe from Darkseid's diabolical schemes.

who had been acquired from Fawcett Comics (in 1972) and Charlton Comics (in the early 1980s) respectively, and bring them firmly into DC's expanding Super Hero pantheon.

The clean slate was fully exploited in *Legends*, with major roles for relative newcomers such as Green Lantern Guy Gardner, Blue Beetle Ted Kord, and established heroes such as Black Canary, Cosmic Boy, Doctor Fate, and Wally West, who graduated from sidekick Kid Flash to inherit Barry Allen's mantle, The Flash. The most significant changes were the revival of the Suicide Squad, a new backstory for Wonder Woman, and a redefined Captain Marvel (now called Shazam!), heralding a new—International—Justice League. ■

Secret origins

Unlike most crossover events, *Legends* was editorially curated—the trade dress of every tie-in issue carried a banner indicating not only that it was part of

the event but also where in the unfolding saga it took place. This reading order advisory/alternate numbering system was a prime example of the close coordination between the many writers, artists, and editorial staff involved in the process.

This carefully orchestrated approach was especially important in *Legends*. The event not only intersected with ongoing storylines, but also introduced new characters and concepts while reintroducing reconfigured older ones—such as the Suicide Squad—in both crossover chapters and spin-off titles only tangentially impacting the larger story.

Although a fresh team and concept sprang forth in *Legends* #1, the untold histories of numerous pre-*Crisis* Suicide Squads were told in parallel with Amanda Waller's origins in John Ostrander, Luke McDonnell, and Dave Hunt's "The Secret Origin of the Suicide Squad" (*Secret Origins* #14, May 1987).

Never forget
The *Secret Origins* story set up future plot threads for the new *Suicide Squad* title while dissecting the complex history of military hero Rick Flag.

Key issues

Crossovers and spin-offs (November 1986–April 1987)

Batman #401 (November 1986)
Crossover.

Detective Comics #568 (November 1986)
Crossover.

Legends #1–6 (November 1986–April 1987)

Green Lantern Corps #1 (November 1986)
Crossover.

Cosmic Boy #1–4 (December 1986–March 1987)
Spin-off.

Justice League of America #258–261 (January–April 1987)
Crossover.

Secret Origins #10 (January 1987)
Spin-off.

Firestorm #55–56 (January–February 1987)
Crossover.

Blue Beetle #9–10 (February–March 1987)
Crossover.

Warlord #114–115 (February–March 1987)
Crossover.

Superman #3 (March 1987)
Crossover.

Adventures of Superman #426 (March 1987)
Crossover.

Action Comics #586 (March 1987)
Crossover.

Secret Origins #14 (April 1987)
Spin-off.

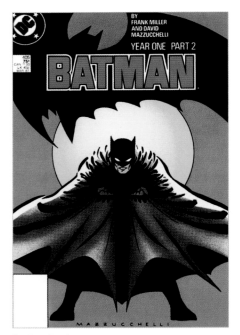

Back to basics
Batman's new noir grittiness reflected a corrupt world that would be hell for the just—even without costumed crazies, who were waiting in the wings.

The Reinvention of Batman

March 1987–October 1989

In a new, unified universe, many of DC's biggest guns were rapidly rebooted, but Batman was in no need of an overhaul—his origins, cast, and Gotham City location remained ideal. Instead, creators like **Frank Miller**, **David Mazzucchelli**, **Max Allen Collins**, **Jim Starlin**, **Jim Aparo**, **Grant Morrison**, and **Dave McKean** explored the inner landscape of DC's most human hero and delivered a *Reinvention of Batman*.

Batman is one of DC's heroic trinity, who has achieved global fame and meta-reality. Like Sherlock Holmes and Tarzan, everybody knows some version of Batman, Wonder Woman, and Superman. However, unlike his DC co-megastars, while the character has been modernized, Batman's mythos and origin have never been formally rebooted or reimagined.

World's Greatest Detective

Batman remained constant as tastes changed around him. A powerful barometer of his contemporary environment, he was a grim avenger in the gangster-ridden era of his debut and a morale-boosting spy catcher in WWII. Postwar, he became everything from caped cop to interplanetary warrior, and briefly an affable adventurer. Throughout these transitions, he battled the most memorable gallery of villains ever imagined.

In 1964, editor Julius Schwartz and his chief artist Carmine Infantino proclaimed a "New Look," for the Caped Crusader, by streamlining, modernizing, and reconcentrating on crime. It gradually restored a driven, relentless, near-infallible hero who crystalized into a more recognizable masked avenger as the next decade began. With minor shifts, this Batman survived beyond *Crisis on Infinite Earths*. Crucially, his growing popularity opened the door for innovation in both story content and publication formats.

As New Earth began, there was no grand relaunch, only a subtle shift in tone. The biggest revision was made

By the book
Batman's inevitable migration from simple comics to grand tomes and mature markets only confirmed what fans and readers already knew— comics weren't just for kids!

to Robin. When original sidekick Dick Grayson went solo, assuming command of the Teen Titans, new junior partner Jason "Jay" Todd debuted in *Batman* #357 (Mar. 1983). Another circus acrobat whose parents were murdered, Todd first donned a costume in *Detective Comics* #526 (May 1983), soldiering on until *Crisis* changed everything.

A groundbreaking retelling of the hero's origins in writer Frank Miller and artist David Mazzucchelli's *Batman: Year One* (*Batman* #404–407, Feb.–May 1987) preceded a new approach, with crime novelist Max Allen Collins scripting and Jason Todd reinvented. Following Dick Grayson's departure, Batman worked alone until he caught a streetwise delinquent in the act of stealing the Batmobile's tires. Realizing the troubled teen had potential,

> "You can never escape me. Bullets don't harm me. Nothing harms me."
>
> **Batman** | *Batman* #407

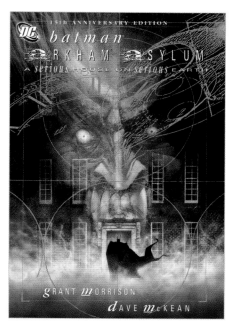

Ark enemy
The complex, multilayered thriller offered chilling insights into the nature of madness, raising a question pondered by Batman himself—did he belong in Arkham alongside the deranged villains he put there?

Batman began training this post-*Crisis* Jason Todd as a second Robin.

During this era, Batman's mythology readily transferred to sophisticated formats like Frank Miller's dystopian *The Dark Knight Returns* (Jun.–Dec.

1986), collected as a hugely popular early triumph of the graphic novel market. Batman became an industry pioneer, helming true novel-length sequential narratives like 1987's *Batman: Son of the Demon* and sequels *Bride of the Demon* (1990) and *Birth of the Demon* (1993).

As the decade closed, mainstream sagas and provisionally noncanonical novels both delivered milestone hits. With Batman drifting apart from and often at odds with standard comics fare, *Death in the Family* (*Batman* #426-429, Dec. 1988–Jan. 1989) showed just how far removed from conventional plots his stories had become. His new apprentice Robin had serious emotional problems, growing cold and brutal in response to the daily horrors he encountered. After causing the death of a vicious drug dealer with diplomatic immunity, Todd guiltily spiraled out of control, which culminated in a landmark event.

Comics grow up
Writer Jim Starlin and penciller Jim Aparo had shifted focus from fantastic super-crime to real-world themes like organized crime and global terrorism. During this period, the increasingly violent and incautious Jason was

suspended by Batman. Todd went looking for his long-missing mother and stumbled into The Joker and nuclear blackmail, leading to his own brutal murder—following a poll of readers!

As a result, Batman plunged into his own self-destructive, guilt-fueled decline until young Tim Drake saved him and began his own Super Hero career as the third Robin.

The Dark Knight's evolution was confirmed as the market for complex, mature storytelling enjoyed a game-changing baptism with the release of Grant Morrison and Dave McKean's graphic novel *Arkham Asylum: A Serious House on Serious Earth*. The seemingly straightforward tale of Batman quelling a riot in the infamous psychiatric facility was elevated by an expressionistic, symbolic narrative and cutting-edge illustration and typography to a new level of creativity. A jarring, intense, and psychologically disturbing experiment, it paid huge dividends commercially and critically, inspiring a revolution in intellectually challenging superhero comics. ▨

Voice of the people
While Superman, Wonder Woman, The Flash, Justice League, and other treasured DC characters were recreated in attention-grabbing new titles, Batman and his stories continued as usual in his eponymous title and *Detective Comics*. However, that did not mean he and his creators were coasting. The primal hero was not only expanding into more mature markets in more expansive stand-alone stories but also pushing boundaries in the mainstream. Increasingly using modern technology and techniques in both publishing and marketing, especially in the rapidly expanding direct-sale comic book sector, when the plot for

A *Death in the Family* was discussed, it was decided that readers should be invited to participate in the conclusion.

With Robin (Jason Todd)'s predicament fully trailed in advance thanks to a press campaign, two endings were drawn up and the then-new marketing tool of a 1-900 telephone number was set up. Readers were offered the chance to vote on whether Robin would live or die in the story.

Against all editorial expectation, a democratic vote determined that Jason should die and he did. It led to darker, tougher nights for Batman until his friends, before a young boy named Tim Drake staged a timely intervention.

Millennium

January–February 1988

On a high following the success of *Crisis on Infinite Earths*, *Legends*, and relaunches of Superman, Wonder Woman, and the Justice League, DC's next shared event, **Millennium**, further pushed comic industry conventions and the creative envelope to deliver a landmark epic in two short months. Crafted by **Steve Englehart**, **Joe Staton**, and **Ian Gibson**, this superstar get-together once more altered the shape of DC's reality.

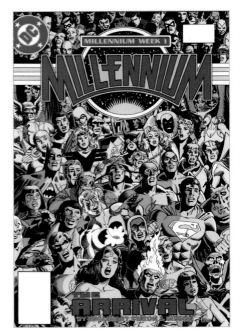

Cosmic congregation
The Guardian/Zamaron decree of a new beginning affected every hero on Earth, but not as much as the discovery that evil robots had been spying on them.

Millennium brilliantly exploited the incomprehensibly ancient history of the Guardians of the Universe by expanding upon a revelatory tale scripted by Steve Englehart a decade earlier in *Justice League of America* #140–141 (Mar.–Apr. 1977). The event also tapped into the writer's later tenure on the Green Lantern Corps in the aftermath of *Crisis on Infinite Earths*.

Coming of age

Billions of years before the Guardians armed and empowered sentient recruits with green power rings, they had deployed autonomous robotic peacekeepers called Manhunters to police and create order in the universe. Eventually, these mechanoids rebelled against their creators and disappeared.

Decades later, readers would learn that their rebellion was, in fact, a major programming aberration that triggered the Manhunters' extermination of all life in Space Sector 666.

Wake-up call
The Manhunters' scheme to disrupt universal advancement by destroying the Guardians and Zamarons was foiled by Superman and Hal Jordan.

The mechanoids who survived the Guardians' retaliation seemingly vanished. They had adapted and gone undercover, infiltrating scattered space-faring civilizations to enact their core drive of hunting those they deemed wrongdoers. Across thousands of worlds, including Earth, a cult dubbed the Shan selected, equipped, and trained well-intentioned beings

> ## "It is not an issue of right or wrong. It is one of duty. Of obeying orders."
>
> **Captain Atom** | *Captain Atom* #11

Rogue red
While readers tried to guess the identity of the potential traitor in each title, it was pretty clear who would betray the recently formed Justice League International.

such as human Mark Shaw to enforce a higher form of justice than mere law.

The true purpose of the hidden robot overlords remained the Guardians' destruction, and to that end they insinuated themselves into every potentially significant situation across existence. When baby Kal-El crashed in Smallville, a local doctor and many citizens were either willing or brainwashed Manhunter drones. World War II hero Manhunter was

Beware our power
Green Lanterns led a team of heroes to the Manhunter homeworld, offering a glimpse of future days when the post-Crisis Man of Steel would join the Justice League.

the Shan's unwitting spy, the reborn Justice League International inadvertently invited one in as Rocket Red 7, while 10 centuries after the *Millennium* crisis ended, Legion of Super-Heroes candidate Laurel Kent remained an extremely deep cover android traitor-in-waiting. One audacious automaton even invaded Olympus, murdering and replacing godling Pan simply to be close to Wonder Woman.

Sleeper cells
Ever since Krona's experiments had disrupted creation, the Oan Guardians of the Universe had worked toward creating a rational, emotionless cosmos. Their belief was not shared by a breakaway faction calling themselves Controllers, nor the

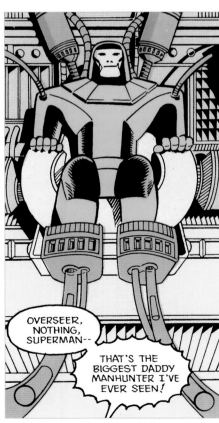

Father figure
The Highmaster responsible for creating new generations of the androids was willing to destroy any threat to his "children."

Cult status
The secret history of the rampaging robots also explored and exposed the exploits and true nature of three Super Heroes who had shared the code name "Manhunter."

majority of Oan women, who abandoned the Guardians at the start of their grand scheme. Seeking to embrace the emotion of love, they migrated to another world and became the enigmatic Zamarons.

Following *Crisis on Infinite Earths*, the two immortal factions reconciled and left the (post-Crisis) reconstructed universe together, entrusting its security to the remaining Green Lantern Corps. In *Millennium*, they returned to spark the evolution of a successor race of immortals drawn from Earth's teeming human masses. As Guardian representative Herupa Hando Hu and Zamaron Nadia Safir asked Earth's Super Heroes to protect "the Chosen," Manhunters activated all their hidden assets to thwart the plan.

Embedded in all aspects of society throughout the universe, they moved to stop the birth of the Chosen by seduction, connivance, and brute force. Gathered and galvanized, Earth's heroes worked to protect the project, all confronting the Manhunters in their own solo titles.

The epic crisis spanned time and space, offering many memorable moments such as a Justice League task force locating and destroying the Manhunter homeworld or Smallville taken over by crimson-clad automatons. And it concluded on an uncharacteristically downbeat note. Not all the Chosen survived, not all were even good or heroic beings, as was

Ordinary people
The forced evolution of the startlingly unconventional New Guardians continued in an eccentric new series far from standard Super Hero fare.

seen when their evolution continued in spin-off series *The New Guardians*.

DC's third mega-series touched all corners of the newly rebuilt universe, highlighting the company's broad

Seeds of destruction
Secret Origins was vital to publishing events. It shared past key moments that allowed revisions to enter the official DC canon. In #23, the triumphs and failures of the Oan Immortals were exposed, and their future plans were now seen to depend on human rebels, outcasts, and even former villains like Floronic Man Jason Woodrue.

Millennium and beyond

Each weekly chapter of *Millennium* was both springboard and catalyst for stories that played out across the DC Universe for months and sometimes years to come. In addition to the eight issues that comprised the core limited series, *Millennium* also unfolded across 21 titles for two months—another 40 issues— and managed to squeeze in two unofficial prequels.

Once again, striking covers presented a badged trade dress design on all titles. Every tie-in issue displayed a cover banner indicating its participation in the saga and which week it pertained to. Before long, this carefully devised reading order and secondary numbering system would become the industry standard for most crossover storylines, large or small. It remains a crucial means of curation that goes a long way toward enhancing understanding and enjoyment of such epic events.

range of rationalistic, science-fictional, and supernatural titles. It introduced new characters, cross-selling the company's now wide variety of heroes in an array of diverse formats. If that wasn't ambitious enough, the entire saga interlaced a weekly limited series into ongoing stories across the company's regular monthly titles.

Hidden agendas

Crucial to *Millennium*'s success was establishing the post-Crisis status quo: confirming for old and especially new readers which aspects of DC's previous continuity and history were still valid in this new singular reality. This offered creators opportunities to flesh out the backstories of their assigned stars such as John Byrne and Jerry Ordway having Clark Kent discover that he and his loved ones had been closely monitored throughout his childhood in *Adventures of Superman* #436 and #437.

The event provided scope for visual experimentation, too, such as a shared background for the covers of Week 4 titles *Captain Atom* #11, *Detective Comics* #582, *Suicide Squad* #9, and *The Spectre* #10 (Jan.–Feb. 1988). Most importantly, *Millennium* allowed a closer integration between mystical heroes such as the Spectre or Doctor Fate and the rational worlds of

Superman, Batman, and Green Lantern. It also revealed the true stories of the Guardians and the Manhunters in bookended editions of *Secret Origins* #22–23 (Jan.–Feb. 1988). This presaged the formation of a very different kind of superteam with *The New Guardians* in October 1988, leaving the DC Universe a much-changed place. ▪

Key issues

Millennium #1–8 (January–February 1988)

Firestorm #67–68 (January–February 1988)

The Flash #8–9 (January–February 1988)

Justice League International #9–10 (January–February 1988)

The Outsiders #27–28 (January–February 1988)

Wonder Woman #12–13 (January–February 1988)

Batman #415 (February 1988)

Blue Beetle #20–21 (January–February 1988)

Legion of Super-Heroes #42–43 (January–February 1988)

Secret Origins #22–23 (January–February 1988)

Superman #13–14 (January–February 1988)

Young All-Stars #8–9 (January–February 1988)

Adventures of Superman #436–437 (January–February 1988)

Booster Gold #24–25 (January–February 1988)

Green Lantern Corps #220–221 (January–February 1988)

Infinity Inc. #46–47 (January–February 1988)

Action Comics #596 (January 1988)

Captain Atom #11 (January 1988)

Detective Comics #582 (January 1988)

Suicide Squad #9 (January 1988)

The Spectre #10–11 (January–February 1988)

Teen Titans #18–19 (January–February 1988)

The New Guardians #1 (September 1988)

Batman: The Killing Joke

March 1988

Law versus injustice and good against evil are fundamental principles of superhero storytelling, but with Batman and The Joker, the principles evolved into perpetual war between logic and chaos, reason and ruthlessness, and—life and death. The celebrated creative team of writer **Alan Moore**, artist **Brian Bolland**, and colorist **John Higgins** delivered definitive proof of this in an unforgettable confirmation that all philosophical disputes can be reduced to a *Killing Joke*.

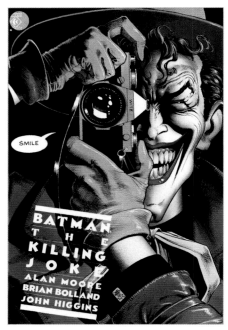

Smile!
In The Joker's hands, even a simple camera could become an instrument of cruelty and torment.

After *Crisis on Infinite Earths*, Batman and his "family" developed a detectably darker tone. During that purposeful evolution, a daring 48-page prestige format one-shot emerged, confirming how much the Dark Knight had grown apart from the rest of DC's Super Hero community.

The Joker is Batman's ultimate nemesis and karmic opposite. And he has always reflected the tone of the times. In his earliest appearances—premiering twice in *Batman* #1 (Mar. 1940) in the first and final stories, with Hugo Strange and Catwoman completing the four-story roster—he was a flamboyant mastermind ruthlessly killing for profit and to prove his superiority over the forces of law and order.

Hard act to follow

As comics were forced to take on a lighter tone following the introduction of the comics code in 1954, The Joker gradually lost that lethal edge, becoming an entertaining yet essentially harmless bandit with a comedy fetish. Eventually rediscovered rehabilitated by a succession of writers eager to reaffirm that bad guys should be really scary, he evolved into DC's primary unpredictable menace. That process began in the 1970s, mirroring Batman's own return to a figure of grim mystery and unrelenting retribution.

Batman: The Killing Joke teamed leading creators of the "British Invasion"—a time starting in the mid-1980s when UK creators stormed the US comic scene—on an editorial passion project. Garnering several awards, it was deemed by many to be the quintessential comic book clash of the implacable foes. Alan Moore's script

Jester minute
Although always trying out new and experimental gag material in his schemes, every Joker gig ended in a traditional all-action finale.

offered a (potentially) definitive origin for the Harlequin of Hate—adopted by most writers ever since—while illustrator Brian Bolland referenced classic visual landmarks like the original Batmobile to set the scene for a chilling, violent tragedy that unfolds in two distinct time frames.

The story draws upon seminal classic "The Man Behind the Red Hood" by Bill Finger, Lew Sayre Schwartz, and Win Mortimer from *Detective Comics* #168 (Feb. 1951), expanding a mystery into a study of human frailty and motivations. It begins with Batman seeking to reason with the Mountebank of Menace, only to discover that The Joker has already escaped Arkham Asylum, leaving an unwilling understudy in his place.

On the outside, while murderously "acquiring" a derelict carnival, The Joker's mind wanders. He pictures a past where an engineer burdened with an adored, pregnant wife risks everything on a drastic career change. However, stand-up comedy falls short and he ends up helping crooks rob a playing-card factory by guiding them through the Ace Chemical Processing plant where he used to work. Despite his wife suddenly dying, he is forced to finish the heist, disguised in a seamless scarlet metal helmet. During the robbery, he runs into Batman, and, while escaping, the "Red Hood" is

No laughing matter
Tragedy and comedy are inextricably linked and never more powerfully at war with one another than in the Clown Prince of Crime.

disfigured by toxic waste, bleaching his skin and turning his hair green. Or at least that's how he remembers it this time.

In the present, driven to affirm his chaotic worldview, The Joker targets Police Commissioner Jim Gordon, shooting, paralyzing, and tormenting

> ## "Because I've heard it **before**... and it wasn't funny the **first** time."
>
> **Batman** | *Batman: The Killing Joke*

his daughter Barbara (aka Batgirl and—due to this assault—future Super Hero tech expert Oracle). The villain then abducts Gordon, attempting to drive him to madness and moral collapse. Ultimately, Gordon proves unshakable and Batman arrives to end this latest episode of trial and terror.

One bad day

By exploring the psychological underpinnings and lowest single moment of the unnamed man who became The Joker, the tale argues that the pitiless villain and his heroic counterpart are, at heart, the same—two extraordinary humans who used a tragic, motivating incident to change and steer their lives into something altogether different—and darker.

For powerless school boy Bruce Wayne, witnessing the murder of his parents created an obsession that drove his lifelong pursuit of physical and mental perfection in the service of justice and humanity. However, the successive poor choices of the man who would be the king of comedy created a convoluted path filled with bad outcomes: pain, cruelty, and death.

Happy Daze

The introduction of the comics code took the edge off Batman's most prolific returning foe. By the 1960s, The Joker was, in all ways, a "Clown Prince of Crime," but in the 1970s, he started reclaiming his macabre mystique. The process culminated in Dennis O'Neil and Neal Adams's "The Joker's Five-Way Revenge" (*Batman* #251, Sep 1973). This major reworking reversed The Joker's zany image and reshaped the arch-antagonist and his relentless protagonist by reclaiming the original 1930s concept of a grim and obsessive dark avenger chasing an appalling avatar of pure evil.

His star again ascendant, The Joker won his own solo title, and, true to form, broke all the rules. His absurdist exploits against non-Bat heroes and criminal rivals ran for nine issues until October 1976, but issue #10 seriously missed its cue and was not published until August 2019, as the entire Batman franchise prepared for the epic story arc "Joker War."

Key issues

Batman #1 (March 1940)

Detective Comics #168 (February 1951)

Batman #251 (September 1973)

The Joker #1–9 (May 1975–October 1976), #10 (August 2019)

Detective Comics #275–276 (February–April 1978)

Batman: The Killing Joke (March 1988)

Batman #429 (January 1989)

Arkham Asylum: A Serious House on Serious Earth (October 1989)

"Joker War" crossover event (September–December 2020)

The Joker #1 (May 2021)

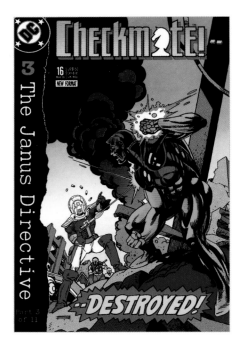

The Janus Directive

May–July 1989

At a time when DC titles increasingly focused on geopolitical issues, writers **John Ostrander**, **Kim Yale**, and **Paul Kupperberg** wove a complex web of disinformation between their overtly spy-based titles and similarly themed superhero comics. With additional scripts by **Cary Bates** and **Greg Weisman**, *The Janus Directive* devastated and reshaped the status quo, setting the scene for darker days to come.

Hostile agents
The sheer number of rival intelligence agencies made them easy pawns for any foe subtle, ruthless, and patient enough to methodically pull their strings.

Espionage has long been a facet of fiction, and valiant covert operatives have graced DC's comic books from day one. With nefarious secret agents threatening freedom, Sandra of the Secret Service debuted in DC's first title *New Fun* #1 (Feb. 1935), while Bart Regan defended America from *Detective Comics* #1 (Mar. 1937) until his retirement in 1944.

Golden Age superheroes often foiled enemy espionage and, when their mystery men days ended, hard-hitting American agents like King Faraday (debuting in *Danger Trail* #1, Aug. 1950) stepped in to protect the nation from insidious foreign threats.

The Cold War era and 1960s superspy fad spawned many clandestine agencies, such as Task Force X/Argent, G.O.O.D. (Global Organization of Organized Defense), and G.E.O.R.G.E. (Group for Extermination of Organizations of Revenge, Greed, and Evil), who worked in parallel with the CIA, NSA, and FBI.

New world order
After the reality of DC's comic books realigned in 1985, a darker, more complex post-*Crisis* Earth saw a cynical and suspicious US government monitoring a proliferation of rogue states hostile to America and the west. Thus, successive presidents took steps to control, if not actively exploit, metahuman assets and resources. In times of war, earlier examples had included military monster manufacturing Project M and a covert penal battalion offering deals and pardons for extraordinary services rendered. The latter was revived during the *Legends* crisis by government agent Amanda Waller, co-opting super-criminals to join her ominously designated Suicide Squad.

Groups like the Agency and Checkmate used intensive training, cutting-edge technology, and innate patriotism to equip elite operatives and run a network of intel gatherers, while the military simply bought, built, or drafted empowered soldiers (like Major Force and Captain Atom) for

> "Gentlemen, **Checkmate** and the **entire** intelligence community is about to enter into a **war!**"
>
> **Amanda Waller impostor** | *Suicide Squad* #30

Order of battle
Despite all having vastly different reasons for obeying orders, the Suicide Squad strictly believed in the mantra "get in, get it done, and get out."

HAVE YOU READ
CHECKMATE! # 17
MANHUNTER # 14
FIRESTORM # 86
FIRST?

Snake in the glass
Death-crazed fanatic Kobra easily redirected the US agencies' mistrust of each other to his advantage, using them to trigger the end of humanity

No love lost
The natural distrust of most intelligence operatives was magnified in the Suicide Squad where everyone had personal agendas and usually hated each other.

their Project Atom. One rival unit psychologically manipulated a manic super-vigilante in Project Peacemaker. Some groups, like corporate-sponsored Captains of Industry and ultra-patriots the Force of July, were privately funded and believed any action was acceptable to counter international intrigue, alien threat, and super-terrorists, as long as the American public remained unaware.

War in the shadows
This atmosphere fostered mistrust and rivalry, especially when most groups officially depended on the same federal funding. Despite employing the best administrators, such as former Super Hero Valentina Vostok and Gotham City cop Harvey Bullock, the tense stand-off between agencies inevitably led to chaos and disaster when a truly brilliant and evil opponent emerged.

The Janus Directive was illustrated by Steve Erwin, John K. Snyder III, Rick Hoberg, Doug Rice, and Tom Mandrake. An epic crossover clash spanning a dozen issues, it saw the groups manipulated into decimating each other to further the ambitions of death-cult messiah Kobra. His scheme hinged on replacing Amanda Waller with a fanatical impostor. As official head of or liaison to these organizations, Waller "uncovered" a Janus Directive indicating each agency was secretly planning to eliminate its competitors.

Successful at first, the plan foundered because many individual operatives refused to follow orders and ultimately because Waller had already killed her intended replacement, playing a double game to gain intel and uncover the hidden mastermind.

The strands converged in orbit above America where mercenary Mark (Manhunter) Shaw, Firestorm, Major Force, Peacemaker and the survivors of the Force of July, Checkmate, and Suicide Squad all invaded Kobra's space ark as he prepared to fire a ray-cannon at despised humanity. Meanwhile, new security chief Sarge Steel attempted to nuke everyone, whatever the cost to the US Midwest beneath the target.

Following Kobra's defeat, the Suicide Squad continued to operate as a more foreboding America emerged. A surveillance society under constant impending threat, which proved to be painfully prescient in the decades that followed. ▨

Key issues

May–July 1989

Suicide Squad #27–30
Checkmate #15–18
Suicide Squad #27–30
Manhunter #14
Firestorm the Nuclear Man #86–87
Captain Atom #30

Invasion!

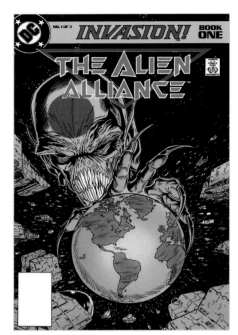

Watch the skies
Earth had repelled alien attacks before, but this time it seemed the entire universe wanted humanity gone!

December–February 1989

By the end of the 1980s, regular readers were familiar with the mechanics of comic book crossovers, and DC explored alternate ways to maintain the freshness and vitality of these now annual events. Writers **Keith Giffen** and **Bill Mantlo**, and artists **Todd McFarlane** and **Bart Sears** combined high concept, artistic superstars, nostalgia, and epic spectacle to create *Invasion!*

Having reaped success with company-wide events *Crisis on Infinite Earths*, *Legends,* and *Millennium*, and smaller, concentrated, character-specific crossovers such as *The Janus Directive*, DC aimed to close the decade with another blockbuster that would reset the status quo. The company was also eager to foster a receptive atmosphere for radical new concepts and characters that were in development. The result was the last word in alien-attack stories, involving all the heroes and villains of an embattled Earth.

Matinee monsters
The core narrative was told in three, triple-length, square-bound editions that referenced DC's beloved Silver Age *80-Page Giants*. The concept and story was drawn from classic matinee science-fiction B-Movies.

It began as star-faring, tyrannical culture the Dominion—and its allies the Khunds—conducted murderous tests on captured humans to confirm that many carry a gene that activated random super-abilities in the face of imminent death.

For eons, humans had inexplicably mutated and the proliferation of super-beings in recent decades was observed by many alien invaders successively repelled by Earth's costumed defenders. Proof came when "Dominators"—biologists of the Dominion's ruling elite—began exterminating human captives under laboratory conditions. Their hypothesis that a dormant "metagene" in the human genome was substantiated when seven out of 50 subjects reacted to the execution methods by developing powers to escape and retaliate. These survivors, later called the Blasters, exacted a heavy price from their captors.

The aggressively expanding Dominators, fearing loss of influence, petitioned a number of other opportunistic stellar civilizations, convening an Alliance to end the future

Survival tactic
The Dominators hoped and believed that no human being could survive their various extermination procedures. They were proved dramatically wrong.

threat of Earthlings. The key members consisted of shape-shifting Durlans, militaristic Thanagarian Hawkmen, aquatic Gil'Dishpan, the rapacious Spider Guild, Okaaran warlords, brutish Citadellians, and cruelly curious Psions. The Dominators and their new allies

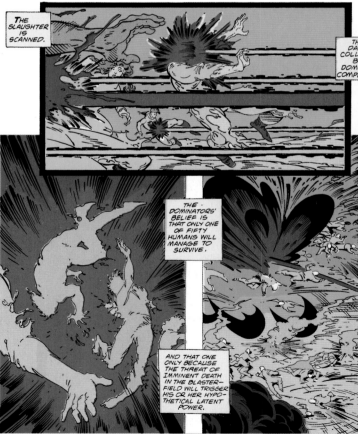

THE SLAUGHTER IS SCANNED.

THE DATA COLL... BY DOMI. COMPL...

THE DOMINATORS' BELIEF IS THAT ONLY ONE OF FIFTY HUMANS WILL MANAGE TO SURVIVE.

AND THAT ONE ONLY BECAUSE THE THREAT OF IMMINENT DEATH IN THE BLASTER-FIELD WILL TRIGGER HIS OR HER HYPO-THETICAL LATENT POWER.

> THEN LET THIS INVASION COMMENCE!

> LIKE DARTS AIMED AT THE BULLSEYE OF A TARGET, THE ALLIANCE ADVANCE FLEET DIVES DOWN AT THE UNDEFENDED PLANET.

Invasion Earth
Sol's third planet looked weak, primitive, and inviting to the assembled astral armada, but its ultimate triumph would reshape the politics of the universe.

were joined by a small group from the red sun world Daxam—genetics researchers intrigued by the potential discoveries of the mission.

As the Alliance converged on Earth, it detained human heroes such as Adam Strange, pro-human sympathizers like the Omega Men— survivors of the recently decimated Green Lantern Corps—and dissident

> "Earth cannot be allowed to breed metahumans that may one day threaten us all."

Dominator Commander | *Invasion!* #2

Defiance!
Humans and Super Heroes constantly battle each other, but will always suspend internal hostilities to unite against a mutual foe.

Thanagarians, interning them aboard a huge mobile jail designated Starlag. The appalling prison camp ultimately proved to be a breeding ground for resistance heroes.

Masters of biological sciences and plant-based technologies, the Dominators' initially removed Earth's elemental guardian the Swamp Thing. They dispatched his consciousness back in time, leaving the planet to rely on more conventional powers. The mighty Spectre was neutralized by otherworldly politics. He was ordered to stand down and to stop mystic heroes joining the conflict in case their actions reignited the ancient war between the Lords of Order and Chaos.

The first strike targeted Australia and was followed by continental assaults from individual Alliance members. The Gil'Dishpan war against Earth's water-breathers was particularly hard-fought, decimating Atlanteans, the Doom Patrol, and Sea Devils. However, casualties were high everywhere, with former Green Lanterns, New Guardian Jet, and Omega Men Primus, Green Man, Felicity, and Ynda among the fallen.

> Chapter ONE
>
> THE INVASION MOUNTED BY THE ALIEN ALLIANCE HAS BEEN DEFEATED, THE SURRENDER NEGOTIATED AND ACCEPTED, AND THE ENEMY SENT PACKING BACK OUT INTO SPACE.
> IT IS A HEADY MOMENT ON AN EARTH FLUSHED WITH THE VICTORY WON FOR HER BY HER SUPER-HEROES.

> IMAGINE, THEN, WHAT IT MUST FEEL LIKE TO WIN THE WAR--AND LOSE THE PEACE.

> GENE BOMB DETONATED!

> WITHIN THE HOUR, ITS EFFECTS SHOULD BE APPARENT TO EVERY HERO ON THE PLANET!

Explosive mistake
Detonation of the Dominator gene bomb seemed to herald Earth's last moments but in fact triggered a last-ditch fight back and victory for humanity.

ordinary, valiant, cunning mankind turned back the tide, at which point a rebel Dominator upset all the invaders' carefully constructed plans.

The Dominion was a vast, single-species empire of many worlds. Fast breeding, ever-expanding, and locked into a hierarchical social caste structure, only individuals of astounding ability rose beyond an assigned rank and position. Seeing his species' imminent defeat, and boldly ignoring status and the orders of superiors, one nameless Dominator devised and detonated a Gene-bomb that warped the powers of all metahumans. It left many close to death but, unfortunately, also triggered powers in those previously undiagnosed with a metagene. This included Maxwell Lord, whose transformation would impact the entire DCU for years to come.

The presumptuous Dominator's reward was a recall to the homeworld and extreme punishment, since his actions rendered human metagene-carriers useless to the Dominion. The goal of the whole campaign

> ...PATIENTS???

Turning point

The Dominators' campaign was further disrupted when a Daxamite died due to an extreme reaction to Earth's environment. Superman desperately tried to save him, and this apparently futile act of kindness caused the other Daxamites to switch sides and call home for reinforcements. A huge battalion

of Superman-analogues then brought the war home to the Alliance.

Inevitably, the Dominators' worst predictions proved correct. Indomitable metahumanity, friendly aliens, and

Fallen heroes
Spontaneous activation of the metagene critically depleted Earth's most vital resource—super-beings—just when they were most needed.

Invasion and beyond

The ultimate space-invader story began quietly and covertly. Cover-dated December 1988, Holiday 1988, and January 1989 respectively, unbadged prequels *Adventures of Superman #449*, *Swamp Thing #80*, *The Flash #20* and *The Spectre #22* all hinted at a conflict about to erupt. *Invasion! #1* of the limited series was supplemented by *The Daily Planet Invasion! Special*— a promotional faux edition of the legendary newspaper.

The war's broad strokes were covered in the miniseries while tie-ins badged either "Invasion First Strike! Extra" or "Invasion Aftermath Extra" detailed individual skirmishes impacting particular heroes and teams. A tight schedule at the busiest time of the publishing year even demanded an extra time slot. Some titles were released between December and January bearing the cover-date "Holiday 1988."

A reading order was featured in each issue of *Invasion!*, but shipping across a continent and globally meant tie-in issues didn't always reach readers in the hoped-for manner. Thankfully, the saga's episodic nature and thrilling storytelling meant it didn't matter much. Further complicating the matter, some titles (such as *Wonder Woman Annual #1*) obliquely mentioned the events in passing without officially

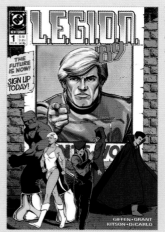

Peacekeeper power
Former Starlag internee Vril Dox channelled his wartime experiences and contacts into a new force to police the lawless galaxies.

participating. Nevertheless, *Invasion!* remains one of the 1980's most important tales. It repositioned Earth in DC's expanding interstellar theater of operations, introduced major series like Alan Grant's *L.E.G.I.O.N. '89*, and Grant Morrison's new direction on *Doom Patrol*, set mature suspense hero *Swamp Thing* down a fresh and controversial path, and brought a second title to the Justice League franchise. It achieved all this while setting the scene for many epic dramas to come.

EXTRA ★ EXTRA ★ EXTRA
DAILY PLANET
MONDAY, DECEMBER 5, 1988   A GREAT METROPOLITAN NEWSPAPER   25 CENTS

REBIRTH!
EARTH'S HEROES CURED!

(STORY BEGINS ON PAGE TWO)

Paper tigers
History is always written by the winners, and *The Daily Planet* proudly broke the news that humanity was safe again... until next time.

had been to secure, monopolize, and unlock the genomic secrets of the wild transformative force, developing it as weapon for Dominators alone.

Counterstrike

With earth reeling from the shocking effects of the Gene bomb, and its greatest defenders removed from the field, a last-ditch attempt to save the day featured a strike team of extraterrestrial Super Heroes, surviving Green Lanterns, and non-powered human champions, linking up with the Omega Men and Blasters to invade Dominion Homeworld. Their goal was information and a possible cure, but the successful sortie—thanks to the Martian Manhunter's telepathy—led to a liberating raid on Starlag and humiliating defeat of the Dominion. Repercussions were slow to end.

In the power vacuum, former Starlag inmates built an intergalactic mercenary security force—L.E.G.I.O.N.—and the Justice League opened branches all over Earth. Many heroes such as Animal Man and Fire endured months of difficulty thanks to radically altered powers, while the shattered Doom Patrol rebuilt and evolved into a formidable force tackling threats at the very fringes of perception. Of most concern were the many rogue states and criminal empires of Earth who greatly benefited from captured alien technology and scientists left behind in the retreat. ∎

Key issues

December–February 1989

Invasion! #1–3
The Daily Planet Invasion! Special
Checkmate #11–12
Firestorm #80–81
The Flash #21–22
Justice League International #22–23
Manhunter #8–9
Wonder Woman #25–26
Superman #26–27
Adventures of Superman #449–450
Animal Man #6–7
Doom Patrol #17–18
Power of the Atom #7–8
Starman #5–6
Swamp Thing #81
Suicide Squad #23
Captain Atom #24–25
Detective Comics #595
The New Guardians #6–7
The Spectre #23

War of the Gods

July–December 1991

An icon since the dawn of comic books, Wonder Woman was recreated in the wake of *Crisis on Infinite Earths* by **George Pérez** and a number of close collaborators. His groundbreaking five-year association with the Amazon ended in her 50th-anniversary year, in an epic event illustrated by **Cynthia Martin** and **Russell Braun**, depicting the universe in flames because of an all-consuming *War of the Gods*.

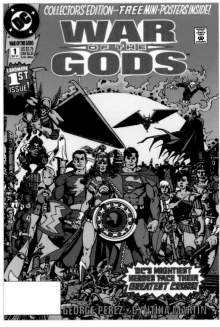

Holy wars
Most humans considered Super Heroes modern demigods, and Circe easily proved they were just as quick to anger and punishment.

In 1987, Wonder Woman was radically reimagined for the new DCU. Her adventures restarted with a new first issue in February 1987, crafted by writers Greg Potter and Len Wein, cowriter/penciller George Pérez, and inker Bruce D. Patterson, which unveiled an entirely new history and mythology. Here and now, Amazons were twice-born—reincarnated souls of women murdered by men in primordial times and blessed with potent new bodies by female gods of ancient Greece.

Gods forsaken
The Amazons thrived, aloof and indomitable, as an example of idealized humanity, peacefully and studiously occupying a miraculous city. Life was idyllic until envious war god

Gods and monsters
Circe's schemes depended on the pride and arrogance of declining and near-forgotten rival pantheons overtaking their common sense.

Ares orchestrated their downfall and enslavement through his bellicose demigod dupe Hercules.

Abused, subjugated, and despondent, the Amazons were rescued by their patrons—the female gods of Greece—in return for eternal penance in strict isolation. On hidden Themyscira, the Amazons became sentinels of Doom's Doorway, overseeing ancient evils and guarding monsters of mythology that their gods had imprisoned.

The price their heavenly benefactors levied for liberating them from slavery split the Amazons. A breakaway sect formed, becoming nomadic mercenaries in the Middle East. These "Bana-Mighdall" replenished their ranks from female fighters of many tribes, who also chose different gods to worship.

After many millennia, future Wonder Woman Diana was born on Themyscira. She was a unique soul—the spirit of the unborn child of the first woman murdered by man. Imbued with life in an infant body made from magical clay, Diana grew up cherished, powerful, and wise, excelling in every endeavor and, after meeting a man from the outer world, she became Wonder Woman. Relocating to modern civilization, she became an inspirational figure, a global hero striving to integrate into contemporary society and understand the madness of the Patriarch's World, while upholding Amazon principles. However, hostility and suspicion followed her everywhere.

> **"Prepare yourself, Amazon princess, for a journey beyond mortal senses!"**
>
> **Hermes** | *War of the Gods #1*

The Amazons had earned many enemies over the millennia, and sinister sorceress Circe had long plotted their downfall. When Themyscira's first ambassadors visited Gotham City, she used a coalition of Wonder Woman's foes—The Cheetah, Dr. Psycho, and Bana- Mighdall mercenaries—to frame the Amazons for a brutal massacre. It was part of Circe's grand scheme to secure mystical artifacts and eliminate Earth's divine pantheons by having them eradicate each other. Hunted in America, the Amazons retrenched, but at the cost of their queen, Hippolyta.

Circe's goal was to murder Earth spirit (and Mother of All Gods) Gaea, installing her own patron goddess Hecate in her place. The resultant conflict spread off-world, affecting gods of Thanagar, New Genesis, Apokolips, and elsewhere.

Everywhere, Super Heroes and Super-Villains empowered by gods—like Captain Marvel/Shazam!, Black Adam,

Divine inspiration
Wonder Woman's destruction was intended to crush the heroes' morale but instead fueled her friends' hunger for vengeance and victory.

Spoils of war

Designed to commemorate Wonder Woman's 50th anniversary, *War of the Gods* suffered scheduling and shipping problems, with some chapters reaching readers out of sequence. Originally, the core limited series' four double-length issues were intended for direct-market comic stores, but a belated decision to include them in general newsstand distribution left DC playing catch-up for a short time.

Additionally, at a time of numerous crossover events, participating *War of the Gods'* characters were double-booked. Some of them simultaneously featured in overlapping story arcs such as *Armageddon 2001* (May—Oct. 1991), Captain Atom's Quantum Quest (Jun.—Sep. 1991), *Justice League America/Justice League Europe* "Breakdowns" (Aug. 1991—Mar.1992), and *New Titans* "Titans Hunt" (Nov. 1990—Mar.1992).

Happily, the 25 official chapters were distinctively cover-badged, with core title and crossovers displaying reading order numbers in the trade dress, indicating where and when incidents occurred.

After the wide-ranging epic reached its thrilling conclusion, writer/artist George Pérez left the series, having guided the reborn Wonder Woman's path for five years (62 regular issues and *Wonder Woman* Annual #1, which spanned 1987-1992).

Hawkman, Firestorm, Quetzalcoatl, Ice, and Doctor Fate—were drawn into clashes of ancient theocracy. As proxy warriors, they unwillingly supported rival pantheons battling each other— Ares facing Mars, Zeus against Jupiter, Hermes opposing Mercury. Inevitably, heroes and deities died as the scheme unfolded. Even the demons of countless Hells and the resurrected dead were called upon to fight.

Godlike power

After killing Wonder Woman by reverting her to clay, Circe's victory seemed assured, but she had not reckoned on the valiant heroism and virtuous self-sacrifice of a minor hero touched by the Heavens.

Johnny Mann was a human journalist who had been loaned the power of Roman divinities by his adoptive father. Calling himself Halciber Filius, he was known to humanity (but not widely or well) as Son of Vulcan. One of the contingent of Charlton Comics' "Action Heroes" incorporated into DC continuity during *Crisis on Infinite Earths*, the Son of Vulcan became the sacrificial lamb who crushed Circe's plot by sacrificing his own twice-blessed life. This triggered an armistice and alliance of the clashing gods, the resurrection of Diana, and Circe's (apparent) doom. ▨

Key issues

The Death of Superman

December 1992–June 1993

For years, the world's most popular Super Hero, Superman, had slowly evolved over half a century into a safe and stalwart hero. Determined to restore his star status and reputation without abandoning his cherished ideals, a canny creative team, including **Louise Simonson**, **Jerry Ordway**, and **Dan Jurgens** crafted a yearlong, interlinked saga to revive his fortunes. It proved that *The Death of Superman* was just the beginning.

No mercy
Superman had no time for strategies or tactics, but could only react and resist the mysterious monster that was seemingly set on destroying Metropolis.

After decades at the forefront of Super Hero adventures, in the 1990s, Superman was seen by many as staid and traditional, with little to offer modern readers. The buzz following John Byrne's 1987 reinvention had settled into solid sales, but the close-knit team of writers and artists who succeeded him felt the world needed reminding of what made The Man of Steel unique in DC's pantheon.

Team effort
Reacting to a wave of violently nihilistic antiheroes, a creative summit attended by editor Mike Carlin, writers Louise Simonson, Roger Stern, Dan Jurgens, Jerry Ordway, and artists Dennis Janke, Jon Bogdanove, Jackson Guice, Denis Rodier, Tom Grummett, Brett Breeding, Doug Hazlewood, Rick

Burchett (with later contributions from Karl Kesel and Walter Simonson) brainstormed ideas and settled on the death and resurrection of Superman. The latter part was kept quiet when the saga began, and the wider world truly believed an era was ending.

Preceded by teaser prologues in the previous month's titles, showing a hooded, manacled figure relentlessly pounding metal walls, the event opened in *Superman: Man of Steel* #18 (Dec. 1992). It revealed a sinister shape bursting from the ground and moving inexorably forward, killing all in its path.

Superman was occupied with aliens, terrorists, and monsters as the horrific escapee carved a devastating swathe across the country. The Man of Steel arrived late, in time to see his Justice League allies Fire, Ice, Booster Gold, Blue Beetle, Guy Gardner, and others brutally crushed by the mystery terror they dubbed Doomsday. It sparked a

Last battle
To permanently put down Doomsday, Superman had to become as relentless and ruthless as his ferocious foe.

huge gas explosion and the Leaguers succumbed to punishing injuries as Superman resolved to stop the rampaging creature at all costs. Approaching Metropolis, Doomsday brushed aside the police, cloned Super Hero/Cadmus security chief Guardian, Lex Luthor's armored private army, and Supergirl.

> ## "We've never faced **anything** quite like this before."
>
> **Superman** | *Action Comics #684*

With hundreds dead and casualties rapidly mounting, a battered, utterly exhausted Man of Steel emerged as the last man standing. The clash of titans concluded in a flurry of full splash pages from writer/penciller Jurgens and inker Brett Breeding as the combatants went toe to toe in the rubble, with the hero ultimately taking the monster down with him.

At Breeding's suggestion, the saga's last chapters visually intensified story pacing by making each issue a countdown. *Adventures of Superman* #497 featured four fight-filled panels per page, reducing to three in *Action Comics* #684, two in *Superman: Man of Steel* #19, until *Superman* #75 detailed the brutal, tragic climax in one big picture after another.

Dead to the world

The shocking conclusion was followed by a somber epilogue across the titles looking at the "World Without a Superman." Proclaiming a *Funeral for a Friend*, Superman's titles related how his super-powered colleagues and human friends paid their respects by finding ways to honor his sacrifice.

Last goodbye
The world had lost its greatest hero, but Lois Lane only saw the end of her future with the man she loved.

The world had changed and crime increased everywhere—especially in the shattered city Superman had loved. Heroes like Gangbuster and citizens like Bibbo Bibowski found ways to counter the chaos, while Luthor and Cadmus Director Paul Westfield secretly warred for possession of Doomsday and Superman's corpses. They sought biological revelations, but far more disturbing was a religious movement that sprang up, declaring the "Last Son of Krypton" to be a messiah who would soon return.

Outside of time, temporal custodians, the Linear Men, reviewed the battle, seeking some legitimate way to turn back the clock, but the greatest heartbreak was felt by Lois Lane and Superman's Earth parents, Jonathan and Martha Kent. Unable to publicly grieve, they did so in silence and Pa Kent suffered a heart attack. Revived by doctors, he claimed to have seen and saved his boy from Krypton's afterlife. He left the hospital's ER mumbling "Clark is back." ■

Media storm

DC's monthly comic book output was released in weekly batches, with a Superman title in each. Under the Superman writing team system, the hero's regular titles—*Action Comics, Superman, Adventures of Superman,* and *Superman: Man of Steel*—were interlinked. The vast weekly serial utilized two numbering systems. A specific title's issue number was augmented by a trade dress shield dictating the reading order and confirming which week of the epic battle readers were currently enjoying.

The system was crucial in amplifying tension during the unbadged *Doomsday* story arc. Although it displayed no specialized trade

dress, follow-up arcs *Funeral for a Friend,* and *Reign of the Supermen!* prominently featured cover banners.

Pounced on by mainstream media, *The Death of Superman* became a global phenomenon. The final chapter, *Superman* #75 (Jan. 1993), was the top-selling comic book of the year, with over six million copies of its assorted printings sold. This included a sealed, black, polybagged collector's edition that also contained a memorial armband, faux *Daily Planet* obituary (written by Roger Stern), a trading card, commemorative postage stamps, and a poster by Dan Jurgens and Brett Breeding.

Key issues

Doomsday (December 1992—January 1993)
Superman: The Man of Steel #18–19, *Justice League America* #69, *Adventures of Superman* #497, *Action Comics* #684, *Superman* #74–75

Funeral for a Friend (January—June 1993)
Adventures of Superman #498–500, *Justice League America* #70, *Action Comics* #685–686, *Superman: The Man of Steel* #20–21, *Superman* #76–77, *Superman: The Legacy of Superman* #1, *Supergirl and Team Luthor* #1

Reign of the Supermen

June–October 1993

It seemed that the entire world was shaken by *The Death of Superman*, and with everyone now watching, the Man of Tomorrow's return had to be spectacular. However, despite the fact that Clark Kent was "back," he was nowhere to be seen as Superman team-writers **Dan Jurgens**, **Louise Simonson**, **Roger Stern**, **Karl Kesel**, and their artistic collaborators instigated a baffling and ultimately cataclysmic *Reign of the Supermen*.

Fight without pity
Resolute and indomitable, the real Superman proved heroism comes from within, not from incredible powers or costumes.

After a horrific rampage across Middle America, mystery monster Doomsday was only stopped through an overwhelming effort by Superman. Dying at the scene, the Man of Steel's body was subject to legal battles and outright bodysnatching before receiving a state funeral and being ostensibly laid to rest in a tomb in Metropolis's Centennial Park.

Four thought

As resurrection cults grew around him in the comic book stories, the real world waited expectantly for a restored Superman to return—but his four comic book series instead premiered four new heroes. Three claimed to be the Man of Steel, while another simply reinvented himself in the hero's honor. Readers already knew Superman was back, rescued from Krypton's afterlife by his human father Jonathan Kent.

The writers fostered a misapprehension that Superman's spirit had transferred to one of the newcomers—the merciless Last Son of Krypton, adolescent Superboy (Conner Kent), a compassionate

blue-collar worker, or the Cyborg Superman, whose DNA tests confirmed he was all that remained of the hero. Each seemed to represent some part of Superman's makeup.

The Last Son came from Superman's Antarctic fortress, powered by energy bestowed on him by a Kryptonian Regeneration Matrix that housed Superman's confiscated corpse. He remembered Doomsday and dying and reasonably concluded that he was Superman restored through technology. Greatly diminished and unable to process solar radiation, he returned to Metropolis, resuming the "never-ending battle" with callous disregard for life.

The immature Superboy was an unprogrammed clone who had escaped from Cadmus with the help of the Newsboy Legion before publicly

Taking charge
Barely returned to life and little more than merely human, Kal-El instantly took command of the mission to stop the destroyers of Coast City.

> ## "I have risen from the dead to continue the never-ending battle!"
> **Last Son of Krypton** | *Adventures of Superman #500*

announcing his existence via numerous sponsored media appearances.

African American inventor and construction worker John Henry Irons—who was once saved by Superman—felt compelled to continue his savior's work in home-built, high-tech armor and later became known as Steel.

Each one attracted the attention of apparently benevolent Lex Luthor II (actually the evil original in a cloned body) who sought to co-opt them as he had naive extradimensional visitor Supergirl. Failing that, Luthor wanted to destroy them before they interfered with his plans.

Back for good

After months clashing for prestige and credibility—and battling heroes like Guy Gardner—a fantastic plot was revealed after cosmic tyrant Mongul landed in California and eradicated Coast City and seven million citizens. The federal authorities had spotted the ship early and sent Cyborg Superman to intercept, unaware that their last hope was Mongul's secret master, who was bent on rebuilding Earth into galaxy-spanning planetary weapons platform Warworld.

In the Antarctic, a fifth, true Superman emerged from the Regeneration Matrix,

Friends and family

Illustrated by Jon Bogdanove, Jackson Guice, Tom Grummett, Dan Jurgens, Brett Breeding, Doug Hazlewood, Dennis Janke, and Denis Rodier, *Reign of the Supermen* unfolded across Superman's linked weekly titles, all carrying a simple banner over the title. The event referenced a prose story, "The Reign of the Superman" (Jan. 1933), by Jerry Siegel and illustrated by Joe Shuster 60 years previously. The comic book pioneers later retooled the story's villainous telepath to create the physical wonder whose 1938 debut altered forever the nature of comic books.

Superman titles went on hiatus after *Funeral for a Friend*, furthering belief

that the original Super Hero had been destroyed. When four new champions emerged, all wearing the S-Shield, speculation was rife over who would replace Kal-El. Their presence added more "Superman Family" stars to the publishing roster and prompted a limited series for Supergirl.

The destruction of Coast City reshaped DC continuity. Bereft, Hal Jordan sank into madness, destroying the Green Lantern Corps and, as Parallax, would trigger company-wide reboot *Zero Hour* and further changes that flowed from it. *The Death of Superman* event officially closed with a *Funeral for a Friend* epilogue (*Superman #83*, Nov. 1993) as Earth's Super Heroes joined Superman in building a memorial in the Coast City crater.

while the Last Son was revealed as an ancient, severely damaged artifact called The Eradicator, which drew power from Kal-El as the hero fought his way back to life. Although barely stronger than an ordinary human, the real Man of Steel quickly adjusted, heading for Metropolis in a Kryptonian warsuit, while Cyborg Superman—aka machine-controlling, disembodied intelligence Hank Henshaw—fatally wounded the Last Son and captured Superboy.

Henshaw and Mongul's plan was to raze Metropolis and install extraterrestrial warriors and a second colossal world-moving

engine in the crater to make Earth a weapon capable of dominating the universe. They had grievously misjudged the new heroes and previously ingenuous Supergirl, who all valiantly aided the depowered Superman in attacking the West Coast Engine City.

Things looked bad for the heroes until Coast City native Hal Jordan unleashed the power of an outraged Green Lantern against the plotters. Eventually, his inability to save home, family, and friends shattered him, but for now victory was assured when the Eradicator transfered his failing energies to Kal-El, fully restoring the Man of Steel's powers to end the threat forever. ▪

One and only

Restored, recharged, and ready for action, the Man of Tomorrow led his new allies from the front.

BUT NOW, IT'S TIME TO GO HOME!

YOU DESERVE A BREAK. WE'LL BE TYING UP AND TAKE CARE OF THE INCARCER-ATOR— INCARCER... MONGUL.

YOU THINK THE WORLD CAN HANDLE TWO SUPERMEN?

CHECK THAT, BLONDIE. I'M NOT SUPERMAN.

THAT GUY'S SUPERMAN

THE ONE AND ONLY!

Key issues

June–October 1993

Action Comics #687–691

Superman: The Man of Steel #22–26

Superman #78–82

Adventures of Superman #500–505

Green Lantern #46

Batman: Knightfall

May 1993–September 1994

The 1990s found a comics industry besieged by speculation-driven sales. Many companies used attention-grabbing cover enhancements, sparking a gold rush among fans and profit-conscious outsiders. While embracing print innovations, DC continued to rely on strong, event-based storytelling, as clearly evidenced in the unforgettable landmark *Knightfall*, collaboratively devised by editor **Dennis O'Neill** and Batman writers **Chuck Dixon**, **Doug Moench**, and **Alan Grant**.

Breaking the Bat
After pushing Batman to his limits, Bane applied a psychological death blow by ambushing Bruce Wayne in the place where he had always felt safest.

The 1990s saw nihilistic antiheroes increasingly challenge traditional superheroes. Across the medium, stories took on darker, more violent tones. DC responded with their own antiheroes and minor character reboots but also used major crossover events to remind the world why the likes of Superman, Wonder Woman, and Batman have endured since the Golden Age.

Concurrent but unconnected with plans to kill and resurrect the Man of Steel, Batman's writers drafted shocking blueprints to make the Dark Knight unmissable again. They began with debuts for steroid-addicted criminal mastermind Bane and the religious vigilante Azrael. They were soon to become key players in an overlapping cycle of tales tracing the fall, replacement, and return of Bruce Wayne as the one true Batman.

Under pressure

A period of frantic activity saw Batman and Robin (Tim Drake) swamped—facing Black Mask, Metalhead, Sharpshooter, the General, Riddler, Killer Croc, and The Joker in swift succession. They also had to foil plots against James Gordon and Lucius Fox while coping with the recent death of Superman (as seen in *Superman: Funeral for a Friend*).

Overworked and pushed to his limits, Bruce Wayne consulted holistic healer Shondra Kinsolving. She had been treating Drake's father, who had been left disabled by one of Gotham's criminal

Body blow
Bane craved a living reminder of his own superiority over the greatest warrior on earth, but his arrogance only laid the groundwork for his eventual humiliation.

> "You will know my name one day. And on that day you will beg for mercy."
>
> **Bane** | *Batman: Vengeance of Bane #1*

Batman no more
Alfred was a superb field medic who had doctored Batman for years, but he knew these injuries called for a brilliant physician... and a major miracle.

Knight errant
As Bruce Wayne lay incapacitated, the renewed war on crime soon showed Robin that his new partner, Jean-Paul Valley, was a competent Batman but hardly a team player.

lunatics. Sharing his workload, Bruce entrusted Tim with the deprogramming and retraining of the young warrior Azrael. Student Jean-Paul Valley had no idea he had been brainwashed from birth by ancient warrior-cult the Order of St. Dumas, who used "the System" to make him their assassin. Realizing his potential, Batman hoped to turn Azrael into a crime fighter, but the escalating caseload could not be ignored.

Wayne was unaware that Bane and his allies Trogg, Zombie, and Bird were surveilling him, even after they had liberated Arkham Asylum's most deranged inmates, forcing the Dark Knight into three months of unrelenting combat. Pushed beyond reason, Batman ordered Robin to continue training Azrael while he single-handedly tackled their enemies. Batman faced the Mad Hatter, Maxie Zeus, the Ventriloquist, Film Freak, Amygdala, Killer Croc, and more. So when Victor Zsasz attacked a girls' school, Batman snapped and GCPD patrolwoman

Renee Montoya could barely stop him from beating the villain to death.

Wayne seemed set on self-destruction. Ignoring pleas from Alfred, he prevented Jim Gordon's murder by cannibal Cornelius Stirk and allowed Tim to tackle Firefly while Batman hunted deadlier prey. With the Cavalier, Poison Ivy, Riddler, and Two-Face accounted for, the impatient Jean-Paul took to the streets on his own, eager to contribute, and used a makeshift mask to hide his identity. Unsanctioned vigilante Huntress also secretly joined them, before an exhausted Batman confronted Scarecrow and The Joker. Only after their defeat did Bane strike, ambushing Wayne in his own home.

Broken

Bane showed no mercy, snapping the Dark Knight's spine in a savage demonstration of physical superiority. He then dismissively dumped Batman's body in the middle of Gotham, declaring himself the new boss. Alfred and Robin

intercepted the ambulance carrying their shattered friend, but saving his life proved tricky. Wayne regained consciousness only to find himself paralyzed and paraplegic and revealed an even greater wound—his fighting spirit was gone.

Tim and Alfred consulted Dr. Kinsolving, as Bane tightened his grip on Gotham City's gangs and rackets, recruiting Catwoman as his personal thief and retrieval service in this new criminal paradise. Tim followed Bruce's wishes, offering Jean-Paul the mantle of the Bat. Despite their inexperience, the new Batman worked with Robin to quickly make criminals fear the night again, but only under strict instructions from Wayne to avoid major threats. However, Valley soon began unraveling, using excessive force and chafing to test himself against Bane.

When demoralized, wheelchair-bound Bruce Wayne witnessed the kidnap of Kinsolving and Tim's father, his distraction allowed Valley to overstep his orders. Hunting Bane, he clashed with Scarecrow and Anarky. In the fight, Valley was exposed to fear gas but believed his programming made him immune. He was wrong...

The Scarecrow's chemicals heightened Valley's savagery and paranoia, driving an irreparable wedge between him and Robin. In the Batcave, Jean-Paul realized he was still subject to the deep programming of the System. Waking from a trance, he discovered that he had designed deadly high-tech gauntlets to augment his war on crime. Until now, Bane had ignored the impostor, but when a ferocious raid by Batman and Robin netted his lieutenants, he reassessed.

Alienated and deeply troubled, Tim sought Bruce's input. However, oblivious to the situation in Gotham City, a freshly rededicated and driven Bruce Wayne used the skills of an extraordinary lifetime to trace Shondra Kinsolving's kidnappers to Santa Prisca. Robin was alone now, as Bruce and Alfred had flown out after them, unknowingly accompanied by stowaway Selina Kyle. It left Tim Drake on his own to work with the new and increasingly brutal Batman.

The final showdown began with the lawless new Batman breaking Trogg, Bird, and Zombie out of jail and following them back to Bane, only to fall before the villain's sheer power and ferocity. Somehow escaping certain death at Bane's hands, Valley retreated to the Batcave, submitted to his submerged programming and emerged utterly changed.

In a fugue state, he had devised a fully armored suit that transformed his Batman into a veritable human war machine. It was the final straw for Tim Drake, but Valley did not care. All that mattered was beating Bane.

The master of Gotham City wanted the fight, too, challenging "the impostor" to a duel in the center of what Bane considered "his" city. Their catastrophic clash comprehensively crushed Bane and publicly proclaimed a new, Darker Knight who cruelly left Bane a broken, humiliated living trophy. Robin—who had saved a train full of innocent bystanders from becoming collateral casualties—finally accepted that a different but equally appalling shadow had fallen over Gotham City.

The fall and rise of Batman

Knightfall had covered the worst three months in Bruce Wayne's life and the rise of a new Batman in one narrative. The sequel arc also occurred across a number of Bat-titles but was actually two parallel storylines. *Knightquest* was divided into *The Search,* which followed Bruce Wayne's hunt for and rescue of Shondra Kinsolving and Jack Drake, and *The Crusade*, which exposed Jean-Paul Valley's descent into madness.

Wayne's recovery, rehabilitation, and return to Gotham City followed. The story saw him travel from the Caribbean to Great Britain, the revelation of Kinsolving's metahuman powers, and Bruce's battle against the prospective mass murderer Benedict Asp. It ended with Bruce Wayne's spine psionically healed, brain-damaged Shondra Kinsolving institutionalized, and Alfred Pennyworth's resignation.

THE CITY IS STILL NEW TO HIM.

HE'LL LEARN ALL THE SECRETS SOON ENOUGH.

DIFFERENT JUNGLE.

SAME RULES.

CHUCK DIXON • writer
GRAHAM NOLAN • penciller
SCOTT HANNA • inker
ADRIENNE ROY • colorist
JOHN COSTANZA • letterer
DARREN VINCENZO • asst. editor
SCOTT PETERSON • editor

BATMAN *created by* BOB KANE

Impostor syndrome
Changes started slowly, but soon the point where the Batman substitute ended and medieval assassin Azrael began was impossible to see.

Reclaim the knight
Ultimately, it needed the original Caped Crusader and all his surviving apprentices to defeat the System and save brainwashed Valley from himself.

Meanwhile, in Gotham City, the resurgent System fueled Batman's war against the city's villains, including Tally Man, Trigger Twins, two Clayfaces, Mr. Freeze, Gunhawk and Gunbunny, The Joker, and even the neutral Catwoman. Driven to prove his superiority to Bruce Wayne, Valley's programming drove him to excessive violence and greater dependence on lethal gadgetry. During one harrowing clash, the new Batman allowed serial killer Abattoir to die, consequently alienating Commissioner Gordon, Robin, and other former allies.

Battle of the Bats
The concluding story arc *Knightsend* was published over two months (July–August 1994) as DC prepared for company-wide continuity reboot *Zero*

Gotham City Knights
Knightfall was subdivided into parallel storylines *The Breaking of the Bat* and *Who Rules the Night*, written by Alan Grant, Chuck Dixon, Doug Moench, and Denny O'Neill, and illustrated by Jim Aparo, Graham Nolan, Eduardo Barretto, Norm Breyfogle, Jim Balent, Tom Mandrake, Bret Blevins, Mike Manley, and Klaus Janson. Writer Jo Duffy and artists Barry Kitson and Ron

Wagner joined the team for the second and third parts of the trilogy.

The epic tale spanned 86 Batman-related titles and spilled over into many more unofficial participants. The editorial team also used trade dress to subtly augment the story. Although each branch of the trilogy carried banners and reading order badges, certain issues—such as *Robin #1*—deliberately omitted the graphics to avoid having spoilers impact the unfolding story.

Hour. It saw Wayne back in Gotham City but failing to convince the new Batman to stand down. Valley was now seeing his dead father in hallucinations driving him to greater excesses against evildoers. Still subpar, Wayne convinced martial-arts assassin Lady Shiva to retrain him before joining with Robin, Catwoman, and Nightwing in toppling the now truly unhinged Dark Knight.

The trilogy *Knightfall*, *Knightquest*, and *Knightsend* were a spectacular success from the old guard, confirming the true value and unshakable power of Batman. It also held one final shock

Truth hurts
Robin was utterly overwhelmed by his new partner's rapid descent into brutal resentment and inadequacy-fueled overreaction.

for fans. In the aftermath, Wayne refused to become Batman again, instead convincing Dick Grayson to assume the role in the sequel story arc *Prodigal*, which immediately followed *Zero Hour*. ∎

Key issues

Knightfall Prelude (September 1992–April 1993)
Batman: Sword of Azrael, Batman: Vengeance of Bane #1, Batman #484–491

Knightfall (May–October 1993)
Batman #492–500, Detective Comics #659–666, Showcase '93 #7–8, 10, Batman: Shadow of the Bat #16–18

Knightquest: The Crusade/The Search (October 1993–July 1994)
Detective Comics #667–675, Justice League Task Force #4–6, Batman: Shadow of the Bat #19–28, Robin #1, 7, Batman #501–508, Catwoman #4–7, Batman: Legends of the Dark Knight #59–61, Showcase '94 #5–7

Knightquest tie-ins (October 1993–July 1994)
Batman Annual #17, Detective Comics Annual #6, Batman: Legends of the Dark Knight Annual #3, Batman: Turning Points #4, Outsiders #7–9, Superman #83, Bloodbath #1–2, Chain Gang War #5–6, 10–12

Knightsend (July–August 1994)
Batman #509–510, Batman: Shadow of the Bat #29–30, Detective Comics #676–677, Batman: Legends of the Dark Knight #62–63, Robin #8, Catwoman #12

Batman: Knightfall Aftermath (August–September 1994)
Catwoman #13, Robin #9, Showcase '94 #10

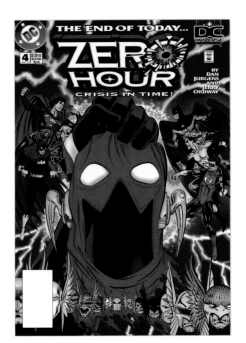

Flashback

History repeated itself as another Crisis began with a second Scarlet Speedster sacrificing himself to buy the universe a little more time.

Zero Hour: Crisis in Time

July–August 1994

Crisis on Infinite Earths reduced limitless possibilities into a manageable singular universe, but the unbridled creativity of so many storytellers working over the following decade created contradictions, sparked continuity paradoxes, and simply filled this reality with too many characters. Intending to rationalize this state of affairs, writer/artist **Dan Jurgens** and embellisher **Jerry Ordway** crafted a course-correcting clash to reignite the DC Universe via a fateful *Zero Hour*.

The universe born from the *Crisis on Infinite Earths* was compact but overflowing with creative opportunity. In the decade that followed, many new stars debuted and a wealth of vintage heroes (some from other companies acquired by DC) were reimagined and relaunched. Nurtured by a shared continuity that actively encouraged change and innovation, the process proclaimed that, regardless of whether they were born, reborn, or repackaged, all DCU characters faced the future together.

The fix is in

Generating landmark, blockbuster reboots, such as *Superman* and *Wonder Woman*, and launching fresh stars like Booster Gold and a new Captain Atom, DC sustained a period of experimentation that delivered cutting-edge print formats, alternative publishing imprints, different styles of comics, and ever innovative ways to tell stories. This boom time was possible thanks to the creative freedom granted to writers and artists, but, within the mainstream continuity, it was also difficult to manage.

Over an expansive, success-filled decade, experimentation delivered remarkable relaunches for many of DC's beloved characters, such as the Justice Society of America and Hawkman. However, many storylines

Calling time

Summoned from all regions of space and time, there was no shortage of volunteers willing to face a lethally uncertain future.

Past tense

Beginning quietly in assorted titles, oddly familiar alternate visions visited Super Heroes. Some of these strange visions included different kinds of Batman and Superman, futuristic Roman hero Alpha Centurion, forgotten Justice Leaguer Triumph, and a Barbara Gordon never paralyzed by The Joker who still battled evil as Batgirl. In a clever, sublimely nostalgic gesture, many of these earlier "past lives" were rendered in the style of their original publications, channeling iconic character moments, reproduced in tribute to those who made DC great.

The catastrophe began in *Showcase '94* #8–9 (Jul.–Aug. 1994) by scripter Dan Jurgens and artists Frank Fosco and Ken Branch. At Vanishing Point—the Linear Men's stronghold at the end of time—self-appointed guardians of reality Matthew Ryder and Waverider were outwitted by time-meddler Monarch, whom they had held previously captured.

increasingly contradicted and even clashed with concurrent ones. The DC universe was filling up and feeling a little cluttered. In an era where epic company crossover events were commonplace and demanded by readers, the elegant solution was to trigger a new all-encompassing crisis to once again reset the playing field.

> "I say we need a new start. A fresh beginning. Done **right**."
>
> **Hal Jordan (Parallax)** | *Zero Hour* #1

Formerly the Super Hero Hawk, Monarch had accidentally killed his partner Dove and slipped into guilt-driven madness. After killing all other Super Heroes and conquering Earth—thereby creating an alternate timeline—he was ultimately defeated when he followed Waverider back to the predivergent present of 1991, where he battled massed champions and his own previllainous self during the *Armageddon 2001* event. Now, after stealing Waverider's power to travel in time, Monarch reinvented himself as Extant, intent on remaking history to his advantage. He was not the only one.

The first inkling of what might imperil reality came at the End of Time, where a wall of weaponized entropy cut through history, eradicating existence. From outside reality, solitary New God Metron became aware of this and resolved to end the emergency by any means. His quest brought him to 1994 and the Age of Heroes, where he initially raised the alarm with Superman and Batman.

Time to kill

The two heroes were already consulting each other to determine the origins of the bizarre doppelgängers and other chronal anomalies increasingly occurring, unaware that their first champion had

NEW YORK CITY. 60 SECONDS AGO.

GREEN LANTERN!

NOT GREEN LANTERN, ARROW. NOT ANY- MORE.

I'VE TAKEN THE NAME PARALLAX.

I'VE SEEN THE UNIVERSE FROM MANY DIFFERENT DIRECTIONS, AND I KNOW HOW TO FIX IT--EVEN IF IT MEANS DESTROYING IT!

MY GOD!

No time for heroes
No one doubted that disgraced Green Lantern Hal Jordan was powerful and determined enough to kill all his old friends if it meant achieving his goals.

slate for one particularly troubled mind to overwrite and replace with his own idealized conception.

Changing the guard

With his purloined power, Extant continued unmaking all of time, with history vanishing from both its beginning and end—twin entropic waves converging on the late 20th century. With chaos everywhere and everywhen, Superman and Metron organized Earth's empowered defenders into an army of resistance to deflect time-triggered incidents at home and hunt the cause of the catastrophe within the timeline itself.

The crisis prompted the remnants of the legendary Justice Society of America— who possessed vast experience of chronal conflicts—to gather and

already fallen. When third Flash Wally West and the Linear Men headed toward the great white wave, their plan to disrupt the all-consuming, entropic wall failed. The Flash vanished and the wave continued traveling back in time, deleting all in its path. It would continue on to the birth of creation, excising all possible futures and leaving a blank

pursue Extant into the timestream. From 1994, they tracked him to Vanishing Point, but mightiest member, the Spectre, refused to join them, declaring he must not contest a "natural disaster." For many of the World War II veterans, the brutal battle against Extant was their last.

With history catastrophically unraveling, Waverider led another team of champions to the earliest moments of reality, but their relative youth was no defense, and casualties mounted. In the heat of battle, Extant absorbed Waverider, becoming virtually unstoppable. The far end of time was now the 30th century, which bore witness to the demise of the Legion of Super-Heroes. As one wave continued

> "What's **wrong** with us? Why do **we** keep living out our years... while the **young** keep **dying**?"
>
> **Jay Garrick (The Flash)** | *Zero Hour #3*

Time for action
Reincarnating warrior Hawkman was particularly susceptible to temporal anomalies before his many iterations were cruelly bound into one form.

Too little too late
This time, the modern Super Hero cavalry arrived too late to save history's original masked mystery-men from the inescapable consequences of their own valor and nobility.

backward, future-born champions Bart Allen and Booster Gold faded away once their home eras were unmade.

On learning of his comrades' fall, the Spectre finally acted. However, as he sought out his foe, another vagrant band of heroes had already toppled Extant. The hollow victory was not the end—it simply forced the true hidden mastermind behind the plot to emerge. Working to unmake and rebuild creation had not solely been Extant's dream but also that of fallen Green Lantern Hal Jordan.

When his hometown Coast City was destroyed, Jordan rebelled against the Guardians of the Universe and shattered the Green Lantern Corps. Gradually gathering incalculable power, he had quietly worked in

Extant's shadow and as Parallax was now primed to reduce reality to a single spark before restoring time and existence according to his carefully crafted design. Every lost moment would be restored, everything would be perfect, and everyone would be happy forever. Or else.

Time is running out

With a few old friends and heroic strangers trapped in his wake, Jordan succeeded. The white wave consumed everything and reality paused, waiting to be reborn. That moment was repeated in every participating title, ending with characters fading away and blank white pages closing every issue. One month later, each title began again with a new rebooted origin story. New features started in "Zero Month," some titles were retooled and modified, and, for a few, issue #0 was their last hurrah and they did not return. It heralded a new start across DC's line.

Right here, right now
The Spectre's conceptions of justice and retribution even appalled his allies, and the sinister spirit's arrival provoked a frantic scuffle, with tragic consequences.

End times
Jordan's apparent doom signaled the end of a cleaner, simpler Age of Heroes. Nothing would ever be the same again.

The core series had a countdown numbering system, beginning with issue four and appearing weekly until a concluding issue #0. The last moments of reality had passed, but before Parallax could build his dream reality, Superman's team and the vengeful Spectre arrived to stop him.

As Teen Titan Damage began absorbing all the potential energies of creation, the other heroes struggled with Jordan, whose honeyed words of paradise waiting were disproved by his willingness to kill anyone in his way. At the critical moment, his best friend Oliver Queen was forced to shoot him in the heart with a green arrow.

Averting the crisis allowed the Spectre to restart existence, with Damage acting as a substitute Big Bang. Existence past, present, and future returned, almost exactly as they had been before Extant and Parallax intervened. Later tales would prove that both beings survived to strike again, before finding very different paths to rehabilitation and redemption.

Times after time
Zero Hour was conceived to rationalize DC's continuity and reinvigorate the Super Hero line. It stemmed from the notion that *Crisis on Infinite Earths*—when myriad alternate realities became one singular universe centered on a New Earth—had triggered Multiversal aftershocks that were still settling. This served as the basis for Zero Hour to course-correct New Earth's history in a wave of character reboots combined with a mass launch of new titles. This plotline would be frequently referenced in future large-scale crossovers.

With stylistic fashions in comic books rapidly evolving and diverging in the early 1990s, many new titles showcased strong, forceful characters who were closer to antiheroes and exploited a more aggressive brand of storytelling. A rebooted Hawkman consisting of all his previous incarnations mystically merged into one godlike yet savage being was supported by a revolutionary and scary Manhunter who was more mythological beast than human hero.

The reimagined Doctor Fate stemmed directly from the "death" of the Justice Society in *Zero Hour*. When Fate was erased from time in the narrative, his mystic paraphernalia was wrecked and shredded. The fragments eventually found their way to glorified tomb raider Jared Stevens, who was reluctantly yet inexorably drawn into situations of mounting sorcerous peril.

There was also renewed emphasis on super-heroic youth. Troubled kid and potential delinquent Damage was the heroic spark who detonated himself to recreate the Big Bang as an unlikely savior of creation. Silver Age—and presumably middle-aged—Professor Ray Palmer was de-aged during the Crisis, becoming a coolly insecure yet approachable teen Atom. Bart Allen (Impulse/Kid Flash) had debuted two

The beginning of tomorrow

Zero Hour was a monumental shake-up and course correction. In many ways it was more dramatic and radical than *Crisis on Infinite Earths*, which was, at its heart, a rationalization and downsizing exercise.

Every in-universe title participated, with some series ending and some debuting as issue #0s. All of them offered fresh or revised origins for the characters they featured, with the new universe's history strictly detailed.

The end of *Zero Hour #0* depicted the universe reborn and that fateful last issue came with a fold-out back cover that carried a complete pictorial timeline of approved DC history and key events expected to be regularly referenced in all titles going forward. The addendum was

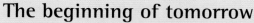

designed to give readers all they needed to know about DC at that moment in time. With supreme practicality, many older elements like the sinking of Atlantis, World War II, and the formation of the Justice Society of America were given fixed dates, while others such as Superman's costumed debut were classified as occurring in an ever-adjustable "10 years ago."

Advanced print technology was incorporated into the event, which was divided into *Zero Hour* and *Zero Month*. A silver metal ink was included in the trade dress and all promotional materials carried an exploding clock icon to mark the event and give all relevant issues higher visibility in comic book stores.

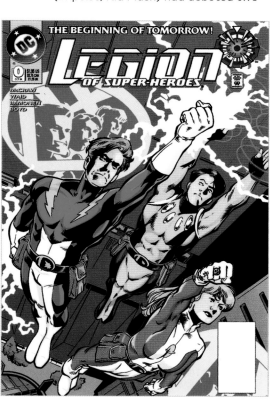

One more time
The Legion of Super-Heroes had been reinvented and repositioned many times, but now promised to be a far more open and diverse experience.

months before *Zero Hour* (in *The Flash #92*, Jul. 1994) and played a major role in the time tribulations before becoming a key component of The Flash family and winning his own popular title.

Future consequences

The biggest concession to youthful initiative had always been the Legion of Super-Heroes, and following Zero Hour, the 30th-century champions received a major makeover and a fresh start. Wound back to a younger, less experienced age and status, the juvenile team was awarded two series running alternately every month, in the manner of Superman. *Legion of Super-Heroes* and *Legionnaires* became, in essence, one continuous biweekly serial that would develop close links to the heroes of the present.

The effects of Zero Hour were extensive and long-lasting. Although the event occurred in 1994, the in-universe concept of time travel lent itself to later officially recognized additions. In 2008, reluctant chronal

custodian Booster Gold finally experienced his own long delayed Zero Month. In keeping with the now historical event, his reboot enjoyed all the trade dress and enhancements that graced the landmark reboot. ▓

Key issues

Zero Month

Series beginning with issue #0 (October 1994)

Fate, Manhunter, Primal Force, R.E.B.E.L.S., Starman, Xenobrood

Issue #0s (October 1994)

Action Comics, Adventures of Superman, Anima, Aquaman, Batman, Batman: Legends of the Dark Knight, Batman: Shadow of the Bat, Batman, Catwoman, Damage, Darkstars, Deathstroke the Hunted, The Demon, Detective Comics, Fate, The Flash, Green Arrow, Green Lantern, Gunfire, Guy Gardner, Warrior, Hawkman, Justice League America, Justice League Task Force, Legion of Super-Heroes, Legionnaires, Lobo, Manhunter, New Titans, Outsiders , The Ray, Robin, The Spectre, Starman, Steel, Superboy, Superman, Superman: The Man of Steel, Wonder Woman

Later additions

Extreme Justice #0 (January 1995)
Booster Gold #0 (April 2008)

Worlds Collide: The Fall of Metropolis

May–August 1994

In the 1990s, DC worked with competitor companies in collaborative crossovers that were always entertaining—but it was a team-up with a new and unique publishing partner that promised permanent change. Superman's writing-team joined Milestone Media's authors **Dwayne McDuffie**, **Robert L. Washington III**, and **Ivan Velez Jr.**, and a host of illustrators to craft the crucial moment two similar yet utterly different realities overlapped in *Worlds Collide*.

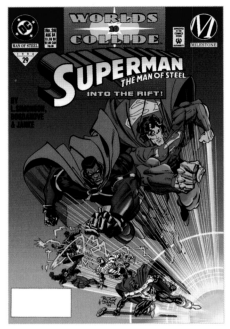

Border crossing
Barely believing in each other's existence, the champions of two Earths resolutely united against a petulant being claiming to have invented them all.

DC has always led the way with trailblazing tales. After publishing the first Super Hero with Superman, the company followed up with generations of iconic characters, while also acquiring some of the best from other publishers. DC's Multiverse includes properties purchased from Fawcett (Shazam!), Quality (Plastic Man, Blackhawks), Charlton (the Question, Peacemaker, Blue Beetle) and WildStorm (Stormwatch, Grifter, the Authority). Copublished properties have included *The Spirit*, *T.H.U.N.D.E.R. Agents,* and Archie Comics' superhero line, the latter branded as Impact Comics.

Building bridges
DC also founded specifically themed imprints and supported independent ventures. In 1993, they partnered with Milestone Media, marketing and distributing a comic book line of culturally diverse characters. Milestone was founded by African American creators Dwayne McDuffie, Denys Cowan, Michael Davis, and Derek T. Dingle. The new company was formed to address comics' general lack of diversity, in comic book characters as well as the editors, artists, and writers who brought them to life.

DC agreed to publish Milestone Comics without editorial management (but could veto releasing specific episodes that ran counter to DC's editorial standards). In essence, DC licensed Milestone's characters, resulting in a landmark line of superhero stories that would reshape the industry.

The target audience was considered to be a different demographic to regular comic fans and a crossover with one of DC's biggest stars was seen as mutually beneficial. *Worlds Collide* occurred just as the Superman titles concluded an epic story tracing the exposure and downfall of Lex Luthor. After years of secret manipulation, the sinister genius had been revealed as a serial murderer and racketeer, but had retaliated by destroying "his city" in a wave of destructive booby traps not even Superman and his allies could stop.

Insecure omnipotence
Able to eradicate worlds on a whim, Rift was obsessed with making his inferior "creations" acknowledge his superiority.

Getting a grip
Dragging their hastily constructed counterweapon out of hyperspace with their bare hands, the heroic alliance swiftly put Rift to sleep for good.

> "I would never have destroyed them had they had been **real**."
>
> **Rift (Fred Bentson)** | *Superman: The Man of Steel #36*

Dated May to August 1994 and spanning Superman Family events "Battle for Metropolis" and "Fall of Metropolis," the saga concluded in intercompany crossover "Worlds Collide." It left Metropolis in ruins, with Hobsneck Bridge, the city's main artery cut in half.

Despite the chaos, mailman Fred Bentson continued his seemingly dull, ordinary life. It was anything but. The moment Fred went to sleep every night, he awoke in the Midwest city of Dakota to start another day delivering mail. Fred unknowingly traversed universes while slumbering, believing each city to be a dream while asleep in the other.

On a painfully familiar alternate Earth, Dakota was a city rife with poverty, social inequality, and street gangs. Most of the latter preyed on the slum district, Paris Island, which was connected to the main conurbation by a suspension bridge. When rival gangs clashed in a battle dubbed the "Big Bang," authorities responded with experimental tear gas that killed hundreds and mutated the survivors.

Fred was a "Bang Baby," a survivor who had developed strange and, in his case, unsuspected superpowers. When he began suffering sleep disorders, Bentson consulted specialists in each reality, unaware that both Rainforest Technologies in Metropolis and Alva Technologies in Dakota were run by criminal super-geniuses. Both discovered that Fred could travel across dimensions and sought to control his power, triggering a shocking metamorphosis.

Not a dream!

The severed bridges in both realities formed a nexus point between them and, as walls between their worlds began to crumble, heroes from each started to switch realities. This was a particularly unsettling experience for the likes of Icon, Rocket, Hardware, and Blood Syndicate, since Superman and his allies were well known in Dakota—as fictional comic book and movie characters.

Driven into psychosis, Fred Benton became the reality-shredding monster Rift, believing he had created everything that existed. Noting "redundant" similarities between the two worlds he began editing, altering, and eventually merging the twin Earths and their heroes, until a last-ditch alliance with villains Edwin Alva and Hazard turned Rift's power against him, trapping Bentson in dreamless sleep. ∎

Deal of the century

Intercompany crossover *Worlds Collide* was editorially curated like an in-house event with uniform trade dress for both companies. As well as event-specific chapter numbers on the cover, issues also carried an advisory on the first interior page indicating in which title the previous chapter had taken place.

In many ways a standard "meet, greet, and defeat" event, the tale found time for social commentary and satirizing current comics trends. The midpoint of the storyline was a double-length one-shot that was

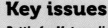

polybagged with premium adhesive stickers of participating characters as a bonus. They also depicted Fred Bentson's transformation into egomaniacal Rift and his subsequent battle with DC and Milestone's heroes.

As 2008 ended, a transdimensional clash with the JLA (#27-28, Jan.–Feb. 2009) formally repositioned the Milestone universe as part of mainstream DC continuity on New Earth. Latterly, youthful hero Static joined the Terror Titans and Teen Titans while Icon's alien race were revealed to be beyond the jurisdiction of the Green Lantern Corps.

Key issues

Battle for Metropolis
May–June 1994
Action Comics #699; Superman: Man of Steel #34; Superman #90; Adventures of Superman #513

Fall of Metropolis
June–July 1994
Action Comics #700–701; Superman: Man of Steel #35; Superman #91; Adventures of Superman #514

Worlds Collide
July–August 1994
Superman: Man of Steel #35-36; Hardware #17–18; Superboy #6–7; Icon #15–16; Steel #6–7; Blood Syndicate #16–17; Worlds Collide #1; Static #14

Underworld Unleashed

November 1995–January 1996

In an era when publishers reassessed and radically reworked their comics stars, **Mark Waid** and artists **Howard Porter**, **Dan Green**, and **Dennis Janke** took a hard look at DC's heroes and villains. They realized what they needed was fresh motivation, an expanded environment, and a more modern look. *Underworld Unleashed* extended the DCU into new narrative territory to deliver more of the old magic.

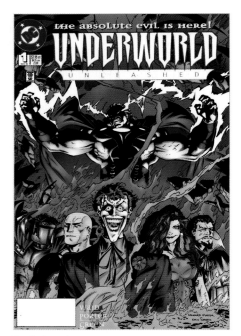

Dark victories
Earth's most cunning, wicked, and arrogant malcontents seemed oblivious to the true cost of making a deal with the devil.

Since the Silver Age, the DC universe had been largely a place of scientific rationalism with magic occupying its shadowy fringes. Despite publishing mystically derived champions like Wonder Woman, Zatanna, The Spectre, and Amethyst, Princess of Gem World, and frequently pitting Super Heroes against supernatural foes, the universe remained one where physics and logic were dominant.

Shock treatment

The Bronze Age saw a gradual shift with the debut of Madame Xanadu and revivals of The Spectre and Phantom Stranger, the 1980s saw DC respond to significant changes in reader tastes with edgy horror tales for an older, more sophisticated audience and in 1993, a separate "mature-reader" imprint—

Vertigo—was created. It removed iconic favorites like *Swamp Thing*, *Animal Man*, and the *Doom Patrol* from the general population of Super Heroes. Largely supernaturally themed, Vertigo also reinvented older characters like Black Orchid, Kid Eternity, Shade the Changing Man, and the Sandman, while adding new stars such as Hellblazer John Constantine.

An unexpected consequence was editorial acceptance that the darkest aspects of mystical horror could also work in the broader DCU. This led to reassessing villainous

Self-improvement
The Super-Villains accepting Neron's black candle enhancements contributed to Earth's aura of panic, but were merely stepping stones to his true target.

devil-analogues Nebiros, Satanus, and Blaze, as well as damned heroes such as the Demon Etrigan or Blue Devil Daniel Cassidy. This radical realignment would eventually

> "I didn't **believe** in my **soul** until I **lost** it... and **now** I want it **back**!"
>
> **Blue Devil (Daniel Cassidy)** | *Underworld Unleashed #3*

Chronicles of Chaos

According to author Mark Waid, Neron was designed as a one-shot nemesis, but his presence caught the imagination of many and he continued to be a major menace long after his debut. *Underworld Unleashed* crossed over into almost every DC title. A three-issue limited series was supported by four one-shot specials, 40 officially badged tie-ins, and a number of unofficial continuations, which, over three months, upgraded a host of Super-Villains.

Supplementary specials *Apokolips: Dark Uprising*, *Abyss: Hell's Sentinel*, *Batman: Devil's Asylum*, and *Patterns of Fear* added perspective to the story. The first traced Neron's efforts to destabilize succession on Apokolips after Darkseid's demise, while Alan Scott's sojourn in Hell presaged mystic super-team the Sentinels

of Magic. Changes were tracked in *Patterns of Fear #1*, which used the narrative device of Neron offering to repair Barbara Gordon's broken spine to obtain Oracle's data on the villains' transformations. And Batman's restrained crushing of an Arkham riot showed that, despite Neron's attempt to sow chaos and evil, reason and justice always triumphed.

---

culminate in a fully integrated continuity that incorporated science and magic, light and dark.

The transformation began in a company-wide event that highlighted Super-Villains. *Underworld Unleashed* revealed Hell had been taken over by ancient entity Neron—an obsessive dealmaker who always cheated and misinformed. The demon lord turned his eyes to Earth, offering increased power to super-criminals in return for their souls. However, this was simply the first move in a grand scheme that eventually drove humanity into paroxysms of anxiety and emotional chaos.

Neron induced five members of The Flash's Rogues Gallery—Captain Cold, Heat Wave, Captain Boomerang, Mirror Master II, and Weather Wizard—to summon him to Earth. They had no conception that their actions would cost their lives. Once Neron walked the world, he targeted traditionally solitary magic-based defenders while distributing his diabolical black candles. His greatest triumph was ending Primal Force, the latest incarnation of mystic militia the Leymen. His biggest mistake was tricking and killing Dan Cassidy, triggering Blue Devil's metamorphosis into a far more dangerous being.

The devils you know

Neron not only seduced criminals and monsters but also heroes such as Hawkman, Triumph, the Ray, Cassidy, and former Batgirl Barbara Gordon.

They were beguiled by offers to satisfy their "greatest desire" but only one succumbed to temptation. Neron's black candles also caused collateral casualties. When Alan Scott refused a deal, his aging wife, Molly, expressed her own wish for youthful vigor, compelling Scott, as the newly named Sentinel, to gather a team, invade Hell, and reclaim her soul.

To increase his client pool, Neron orchestrated a mass jailbreak from supermax penitentiary (and Suicide Squad HQ) Belle Reve. And back in Hell, he recruited Lex Luthor, The Joker, Circe, Doctor Polaris, and Abra Kadabra as his inner circle of advisors. Neron also counted on the villains' overarching

ambitions to sabotage each other and aid his own hidden agenda but didn't count on the wiles of conman James Jesse. The Trickster always knew that if something felt too good to be true, It probably was.

Even more than the massed resistance of Earth's heroes, Jesse's actions foiled Neron's plan to attain infinite power by corrupting a truly pure soul—Billy Batson, the boy who became Captain Marvel by shouting "Shazam!" As a result, Neron was defeated but most of his "improvements" remained. Jesse resolved to reform and lead a better life, because he now knew what was waiting for him if he died evil and unrepentant. ▪

Key issues

November 1995–January 1996

Underworld Unleashed #1–3
Aquaman #14
Underworld Unleashed–Apokolips: Dark Uprising #1
Azrael #10
Manhunter #21
Damage #18
Guy Gardner, Warrior #36–37
Extreme Justice #10–11
The Flash #107
Primal Force #13
The Spectre #35–36
Starman #13
Robin #23–24
Hawkman #26–27
Justice League America #105–106
R.E.B.E.L.S. '95 #13

Steel #21
Green Lantern #68–69
Green Arrow #102–103
Impulse #8
Detective Comics #691–692
The Ray #18–19
Fate #13
Underworld Unleashed–Patterns of Fear #1
Adventures of Superman #530
Superman: The Man of Tomorrow #3
Underworld Unleashed–Abyss: Hell's Sentinel #1
Batman #525
Underworld Unleashed–Batman: Devil's Asylum #1
Catwoman #27
Justice League Task Force #30
Legion of Super-Heroes #75
Legionnaires #32
Lobo #22
Superboy #22

The Flash: Dead Heat

December 1995–May 1996

The Golden Age concept of speedsters became intrinsic to Super Hero comics when a reinvented Flash kick-started the Silver Age. Heralding a new style of drama, he was the epitome of self-sacrifice before writer **Mark Waid** and illustrators **Oscar Jimenez**, **José Marzan Jr.**, **Humberto Ramos**, and **Wayne Faucher** showed how his successor might be the greatest to carry the name in *The Flash: Dead Heat.*

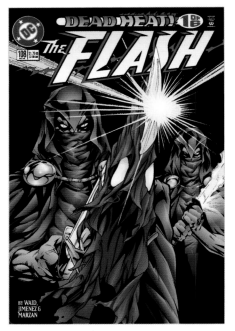

The quick and the dead
Savitar's fanatical followers included junkies addicted to speed drug Velocity-9 and former hero Lady Flash.

The universe seemed to be tumbling from Crisis to Crisis, but each event also brought greater knowledge of reality's true nature. Having helped defeat demonic tempter Neron, the third Flash, Wally West, had no time to rest, finding himself at the center of imminent universal catastrophe generated by the extradimensional source of his own powers.

Original Golden Age crime buster Jay Garrick was the very first Scarlet Speedster. "The Fastest Man Alive" inspired imitators as disparate as DC's own Johnny Quick and Merton McSnurtle, the Terrific Whatzit. Max Mercury also joined them. The hero had originally been known as Quicksilver and was originally a Quality Comics hero in the 1940s before joining the DC stable, where he became a mentor to several Speedsters.

Speed kills

When the second Flash, Barry Allen, spearheaded the Silver Age superhero revival in 1956, he was always a front-runner. Following decades of valiant service, Allen perished heroically saving all life during *Crisis on Infinite Earths*. The averted catastrophe rationalized and standardized DC's continuity, and the speedster vacancy was promptly filled by his apprentice Wally West. The young hero stepped up from the role of Kid Flash to fill his mentor's golden boots.

Struggling at first, unable to access the velocities or match the uncanny endurance of his mentors, Wally persevered, eventually overcoming his self-imposed restrictions. Key to his advancement was learning that all speedsters drew "fuel" from the same source—a cosmic energy field touching all of creation. This "Speed Force" generated energy and strength needed for extreme acceleration, but later adventures proved that it was also shaped and driven by an emotional component. Moreover, all who tapped it were doomed to be trapped within the Speed Force after reaching a critical velocity.

In a desperate battle against ruthless terrorist Kobra, Wally moved too fast. A brush with the time stream changed his body and now, if

Speed forces
Generations of energized speedsters united to confront self-styled god of speed Savitar, racing to destruction for humanity and their fast friends.

Go into the lightning
Would-be god Savitar's hunger for dominance was no match for Wally West's capacity to mainline Speed Force energy.

Speed trap
The third Flash beat Savitar by giving him his greatest wish: entrance to the ineffable, inescapable Speed Force dimension.

he moved too fast, he might devolve into raw speed energy. It was only a matter of time before he slipped, turned to lightning, and was sucked into the Speed Force.

While battling Kobra, Wally almost succumbed to the Speed forces overwhelmingly seductive Light but was anchored to Earth by his love for journalist Linda Park. That strength

helped again when Savitar, a Speed Force savant, sought to seize and monopolize the field's total energies through his devoted speed cult. Savitar would not share the force and was determined to become the god of speed and master of reality.

Race against time
Many speedsters congregate in the twinned metropolis of Keystone and Central Cities, and when his hometown became ground zero for speed cult attacks, Wally reluctantly accepted the aid of WWII speedsters Jay Garrick and Johnny Quick, legacy hero Jesse Quick, Max Mercury, Legion of Super-Heroes member XS, and Barry Allen's grandson Bart.

Bart had arrived from 1,000 years in the future, afflicted with hyper-aging and in desperate need of speed-

training. When Wally couldn't cope, he placed Bart, who later took the Super Hero name Impulse, with master mentor Max Mercury. However, now all the speedsters were targets for Savitar.

Crossover epic *Dead Heat* saw crazed cult disciples trying to pick off other Speed Force users. When that failed, Savitar started remotely absorbing speed energy into himself. After defeating and dispatching veterans and newcomers alike, he failed at the last moment when The Flash stopped running fast and started running smart. The gambit imprisoned the would-be god beyond the Speed Force barrier, but now tragically, so was Wally West. His place temporarily taken by future Flash John Fox of the 27th century, Wally's fight to return would change the world's image of speedsters forever! ▪

> ## "What's **gone**? Our **powers**. We don't have **super-speed** anymore."
>
> **Jesse Quick** | *The Flash* #108

Key issues
December 1995–May 1996
The Flash #108–111
Impulse #10–11

Cold, dead fingers
Slow, freezing Armageddon gave humanity and its champions plenty of time to ponder and despair.

The Final Night

October–November 1996

Following decades of astounding victories in numerous crisis events, Earth's Super Heroes finally faced defeat from a catastrophe that had no malign villain at its core, but simply cosmic misfortune. Scripter **Karl Kesel** and illustrator **Stuart Immonen** explored humanity's response to gradual, inescapable doom and, as the sun died, offered a last chance to one lost hero in *The Final Night*.

Like crossover predecessor *Invasion*, *The Final Night* took inspiration from cinema blockbusters, depicting Super Heroes as first responders to an incomprehensible natural disaster that threatened humanity's end. The story began in a free promotional premium, with new character Dusk failing to convince New Tamaran refugees to evacuate their newfound home and flee from an interstellar phenomenon that consumed suns. Arrested, Dusk escaped with the help of the hero Starfire, even as the horror made the former Teen Titan an orphan of space once again.

Dark days ahead

By the time Dusk reached Earth, the Sun-Eater was already at work on Sol, and her attempts to warn humanity were too little, too late. As the Super Hero community mobilized, the uncanny interstellar predator began absorbing heat and energy, and, even with the help of super-genius Lex Luthor, there seemed little hope of survival. Earth slowly froze, its ecology fatally compromised while those heroes dependent on solar energy started to lose their powers. Despite his gradually fading strength, Superman maintained a frantic pace to save his friends and adopted planet, aided by time-transplanted teens the Legion of Super Heroes and apprentice newcomer Ferro.

Supernatural guardian the Spectre was unable to intervene and declared he could not work against "God's will," even as he covertly provided sustaining energy to keep the embodiment of the planetary life force—Mother Earth—alive. The Gods of New Genesis and other alien visitors also failed to destroy, repel, or elude the hunger of the transdimensional devourer. The world seemed truly doomed.

Darkness falls
As heroes gather, the lights go out all over the world and the City of Tomorrow succumbs to crushing shadows.

With heroes occupied policing the global crisis or attempting ever more desperate solutions, other embattled champions weighed their options. They could fight on, preserve fragments of civilization where possible, or simply surrender with dignity. As Firestorm, the Ray, Fire, and more strove without hope to keep pockets of humanity alive, Etrigan the Demon offered the heat of Hell to mankind in return for all their souls, but was thankfully refused.

As weary scientists discover the Sun-Eater's feeding will cause a supernova to propel it to another star,

> ## "Mankind's **darkest night** approaches. I can do **nothing.**"
>
> **The Spectre** | *The Final Night* #1

Cosmic consumption
Even all the power accumulated by Hal Jordan paled before the hungry void of the Sun-Eater.

one last glimmer of hope comes as Green Lantern Kyle Rayner tracks down his despised predecessor Hal Jordan. The once-lauded ring-wielder had broken all his oaths, destroyed the Corps to which he had devoted his life, and even killed fellow Super Heroes after his hometown Coast City was destroyed by Mongul and Cyborg Superman during the "Reign of the Supermen" event.

Survival strategy

Driven insane by tragedy and having become a mass murderer many times over, Jordan was later revealed to have been possessed by universal fear entity Parallax. This absolved him of most of the atrocities he had perpetrated, but he was desperate to make amends. Moved by Rayner's entreaties, Jordan resolved to save and restore the frozen, broken Earth and use his energies and life force to reignite the sun.

Two years later, *Green Arrow* #137 (Oct. 1998) disclosed that Jordan also used his last day on Earth to trigger the resurrection of dead friend Oliver Queen, beginning a wave of original Super Hero revivals. This selfless act of redemption also began Jordan's own protracted path back to the

Light up the sky
Hal Jordan's indomitable willpower was the crucial spark that saved the solar system.

light and life as one of DC's first rank of costumed champions.

A drama of human determination built from a tapestry of personal stories and character-led incidents, all deftly interwoven with a central narrative of courage under fire, *The Final Night* was a breakthrough saga that laid the groundwork for deeper, darker epics to come. ◼

Final choice

Award-winning and one of the most popular limited series of the year, intercompany crossover "The Final Night" was another weekly event whose repercussions echoed across the DCU. The event was heralded by a free monochrome preview, given away at comic book stores, which acknowledged the growing power of the independent retailers. The promotional story was later colored and added to a collected trade paperback edition as part of the increasingly popular graphic novel market.

As usual, the tie-ins were badged (with an eclipsed sun DC logo and title banner), but the true innovation was the absence of an evil, scheming antagonist. As the core limited series dealt with saving the world, 22 individual crossover issues found heroes dealing with mankind in its worst moment and finding as much hope and faith as despair, despondency, and self-inflicted destruction—a message of hope underscored by the ultimate sacrifice of Hal Jordan.

Genesis

October 1997

Since launching in 1970, Jack Kirby's Fourth World concept had become a fundamental component of DC continuity, its characters and scenarios seamlessly assimilated into one vast and accommodating cosmos of homegrown and acquired Super Heroes. With crossover events now a crucial component of comics, writer **John Byrne** and artists **Ron Wagner** and **Joe Rubinstein** revealed the true nature and divine *Genesis* of all those empowered individuals.

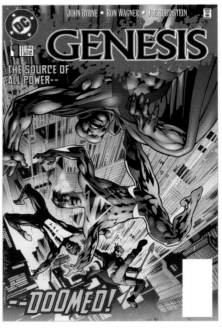

Powers cut
The sudden effects and abrupt reversals of the Godwave were random, unpredictable, utterly inescapable, and potentially fatal.

By the 1990s, Jack Kirby's trailblazing *Fourth World* mythology was completely assimilated into DC's cosmology of astounding heroes, mighty villains, and incomprehensible wonders. Over many years, in every manner of title, previous stories and events had explored the origins of Kirby's creation, seeking to explain the how and why of super-beings—everything from magical endowment to genetic aberration and enhancement—before John Byrne devised an elegant solution in a crossover saga that seemingly held all the answers.

Probing questions

A fresh era of *Fourth World* exploits had begun in October 1995 with *New Gods* #1, and when Byrne, Superman's Post-*Crisis* redesigner, took over writing and penciling the series with #12 (Nov. 1996), he had big plans. That title ended with #15 and was relaunched as *Jack Kirby's Fourth World* (#1, Mar. 1997) where Byrne and A-List collaborators like Walter Simonson delved deep into aspects of the celestial drama that had shaped civilization from the beginning.

The weekly limited series *Genesis* took that bold, breakthrough

proposition and, by inviting other creators to contribute one-off personal tales, held the very notion of super-humanity up to scrutiny.

It started simultaneously across creation as scientific principles suddenly became wildly unreliable. On Earth, The Flash could not attain previous velocities and Green Lantern rings began to malfunction. Recently converted into living energy, Superman's abilities were proving a liability, and the magically empowered Captain Marvel was reduced to helplessness.

The planet's ancient pantheons were forced into action after centuries of noninterference in human affairs. Everywhere, humanity was plagued by emotional imbalance, with anger, fear, and despondency attacking like plagues. With chaos mounting, an alien armada arrived, threatening to destroy the world.

Answers came from New Genesis patriarch Highfather, who revealed that the calamity was the result of history and higher physics. After eight billion years since the start of reality, a primal GodWorld populated by incredible beings fell

Reasoned response
Darkseid's disciples believed violent attacks were the solution to every problem, but Earth's heroes also knew how to negotiate the Apokolips way.

Unstable alliance
Temporarily smashed together by cosmic forces, the remerged world of Apokolips and New Genesis was physically unstable and primed to destroy everyone on it.

into war and was destroyed in a violent detonation. Eventually, its cindered remains evolved into Apokolips and New Genesis, and the cycle of life continued. However, the far-reaching repercussions of that cosmic catastrophe drove ever onward across the universe.

Broken barrier
The Source Wall enclosed all of creation but sundered like glass when faced with the rampant energies of the Godwave and manipulations of Darkseid.

Divine reckoning

Genesis was supported by trade dress cover banners that announced each title's participation in the event, but as every tie-in dealt with individual responses to the crisis, chapter numbering was absent. However, in a move to increase clarity and enhance cross-selling, an editorial supplement in each issue of the core limited series briefed readers on "what has gone before." It also listed—with cover reproductions—each week's participating

Youthful endeavors
Genesis and its fallout affected a large number of DC titles starring young heroes, such as the *Legion of Super-Heroes.*

titles and previewed upcoming issues and crossovers/tie-ins.
Although endangering all of reality, rewriting the source code of existence, and spanning the entire history of space-time, *Genesis* was a comparatively low-key crossover event, and creators were allowed to balance cosmic drama and soul-searching angst with dark humor.

A mix of magic, rationalistic energies, and mysteries was disseminated as a field of potency and potential, affecting planets, creating gods, and leaving a spark of untapped divinity everywhere it touched. Over ten billion years, the Godwave reached the very edge of reality and rebounded inward again. This second pass installed a potential for change— metahuman superpowers—in the denizens of many worlds.

Bouncing back

Rebounding again, the Godwave now canceled out the benefits of previous journeys. Yet its effect on gods and mortals was simply a by-product of the true threat. The real dilemma was that as the waves

intersected, the resulting resonance produced intolerable stress on the structure of existence. And if gods, heroes, and villains could not unite and reverse the phenomenon, reality would shatter and be replaced by a new and terrible Fifth World.

With everything at stake, Highfather and the once human New God Takion conducted an army of heroes beyond the ineffable Source Wall to repair the damage. However, they were almost thwarted by Darkseid's hunger to possess the Godwave's power, the intervention of war god Ares, and the machinations of rival survivors of the original GodWorld explosion.

Ultimately, imminent Armageddon was averted by Super Heroes linking all universal life into one irresistible force to repair reality, reconstruct the sundered Source Wall, and summarily dispatch all the power-hungry tyrants to their just fate. ▨

> "There has been a new **genesis**. All is changed, yet all remains **the same!**"
>
> **Metron** | *Genesis #4*

Key issues

All titles October 1997

Genesis #1–4, Adventures of Superman #551, Aquaman #37, Azrael #34, Batman #547, Green Lantern #91, Impulse #30, Jack Kirby's Fourth World #8, Legion of Super-Heroes #97, Lobo #44, The Power of Shazam! #31, Resurrection Man #6, Robin #46, Starman #35, Steel #43, Superboy and the Ravers #14, Supergirl #14, Superman: The Man of Steel #72, Superman #128, The Spectre #58, Teen Titans #13, Wonder Woman #126, Xero #6

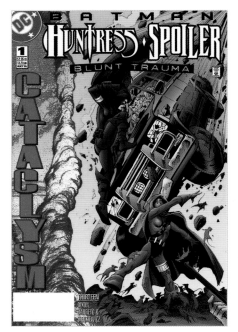

Sudden impact
Old grievances and hurt feelings were forgotten as the world turned upside down and sudden death rained down on Batman's unsanctioned allies.

Batman: Cataclysm

March 1998–February 2000

At a time when the Batman franchise seemingly jumped from one crossover event to the next, the end of the 20th century proved to be truly exceptional. There is no other place like Gotham City, or heroes like its benighted champions, so when Batman group editor **Jordan B. Gorfinkel** laid out an epic scenario for his writers and artists, the result was two years of matchless drama in the aftermath of *Cataclysm*.

After *Knightfall*, Batman's family frequently faced further daunting emergencies endangering their city and themselves. Human-scaled threats like *Contagion* and *Legacy* saw Gotham City decimated by plague. As the millennium approached, Batman group editor Jordan B. Gorfinkel upped the ante, with a devastating scenario.

Shock treatment
The result was *Cataclysm*, as Gotham City was shattered by a massive earthquake with its epicenter less than a mile from the Batcave. Super Heroes, vigilantes like Huntress, Spoiler, and Catwoman, irredeemable villains such as the Penguin, and thousands of civilians all battled to stay alive as buildings collapsed and fires raged through the destruction.

Although Bruce Wayne had previously hired seismologist Dr. Jolene Relazzo to map out the likelihood of quakes, when the moment struck, he was too busy to take her call. Scattered and caught off guard, the assorted Knights of Gotham responded as best they could. Batman was swept away by underground floods erupting into the Batcave, Alfred fell through the mansion floor, and Oracle Barbara Gordon was trapped in her communications center before linking up with her father. Ultimately, it was Commissioner Gordon who truly rose to the disaster, rallying his surviving forces, just as aftershocks began to hit.

Nightwing helped whoever he could, and Batman's roving agent Jean Paul Valley (Azrael) returned, having just captured Bane again. However, when Bane escaped, killing bystanders, the Azrael had to suspend lifesaving activities to stop him. Everywhere else, crime fighting took a back seat to preserving life. Robin (Tim Drake) saved

Elemental extremes
Bruce Wayne survived toppling rocks, asphyxiation, premature burial, and sudden drowning only to helplessly watch Gotham burn.

ultimate assassin Lady Shiva and Catwoman stopped Poison Ivy from exploiting the carnage by dumping super plant fertilizer into Gotham City's remaining water supplies.

When a tsunami hit the island on which Blackgate Prison perched, dozens of convicts perished but many more escaped, utilizing a temporary land-bridge thrown up by ground disruptions.

> ## "That's the structural alarm... the seismic sensors!"
>
> **Batman** | *Batman: Shadow of the Bat #73*

Critical list

Cataclysm ran for most of 1998, generating 34 crossovers into regular Bat-titles, ties-ins, and one-shots, all carrying trade dress that displayed collapsing skyscrapers. The sequel event *Aftershock* featured above title banners and 1999's *No Man's Land* and prologue *Road to No Man's Land* employed a spine strip simulating yellow and black emergency incident tape. The epics were mapped out by Batman Assistant Editor Jordan B., Gorfinkel, with *Cataclysm* scripted by Chuck Dixon, Alan Grant, Doug Moench, Dennis O'Neill, Devin Grayson,

and Kelly Puckett, and written and drawn by Chris Renaud, Rick Burchett, Klaus Janson, and illustrated by Jim Aparo, Flint Henry, Mark Buckingham, Scott McDaniel, Roger Robinson, Graham Nolan, Jim Balent, Staz Johnson, Marcos Martin, Alex Maleev, Eduardo Barreto, and Dave Taylor.

No Man's Land encompassed a further 80 associated monthly issues plus four specials and the *Batman: Harley Quinn* graphic novel. These came courtesy of writers Bob Gale, Greg Rucka, Ian Edginton, Janet Harvey, Bronwyn Carlton, Steven Barnes, and Larry Hama, and

artists Damion Scott, Dan Jurgens, Greg Land, Sergio Cariello, Mat Broome, Pablo Raimondi, Paul Ryan, Paul Gulacy, Jason Temujin Junior, Rafael Kayanan, Dale Eaglesham, D'Israeli, Frank Teran, Mike Deodato Jr., Gordon Purcell, N. Steven Harris, and more.

Close call
Born to soar in the air, Nightwing was forced to crawl through the wreckage to save Barbara Gordon and other entombed survivors.

Only the late intervention of Batman stopped the situation from becoming a bloodbath. Tragically, the facility was also being used to hold Arkham Asylum inmates. The tremor unleashed many of the asylum's frenzied patients on the broken city and its terrified and troubled citizens.

Just as the cataclysm seemed to be over, someone calling himself Quakemaster delivered a tape to the GCPD demanding $100 million or he would unleash another, bigger shock on the city. Various Batman associates tracked him down, just in case his threat was real, but he was revealed to be a human puppet of Arkham escapee The Ventriloquist. The crisis seemed over but the worst was yet to come.

In the following weeks, Bruce Wayne and other Gotham City elites sought

federal funds to rebuild their demolished city but were refused. Instead—in chilling anticipation of what occurred six years later when hurricane Katrina devastated New Orleans—the US Government ordered all citizens to leave the disaster zone. Officially evacuating the entire city, the authorities declared it uninhabitable, blew up all the bridges, and set an armed perimeter to stop anyone from entering or exiting the city.

No man's land

Although almost entirely devastated, Gotham City lived on as many of its denizens refused or were unable to leave. Criminal gangs and Super-Villains carved and ruthlessly defended territories, and James Gordon and police diehards did the same, refusing to let the city fall to the most despicable people it harbored. Batman and his allies prowled the ruins and protected whoever they could, aided by new Batgirl Cassandra Cain.

Despite the increasing depredations of The Joker, Penguin, Two Face, and others, Lex Luthor attempted to procure and reconstruct the city, which prompted a fierce public backlash outside "No Man's Land." Ultimately, the government bowed to local pressure, reversed its decision, and allowed Gotham City to rebuild just as a new year dawned. ■

Key issues

Cataclysm (March–May 1998)

Detective Comics #719–721, Batman: Shadow of the Bat #73–74, Nightwing #19–20, Batman #553–554; Azrael #40, Catwoman #56–57, Robin #52–53, Batman: Blackgate–Isle of Men, Batman Chronicles #12, Batman: Huntress and Spoiler–Blunt Trauma #1, Batman: Arkham Asylum–Tales of Madness #1

Aftershock (June–October 1998)

Batman: Shadow of the Bat #75–79, Batman #555–559, Detective Comics #722–726, Robin #54, Batman Chronicles #14

Road to No Man's Land (November 1998–February 1999)

Azrael #47–49, Batman: Shadow of the Bat #80–82, Batman #560–562, Detective Comics #727–729

No Man's Land (March 1999–February 2000)

Detective Comics #730–741, Batman: Shadow of the Bat #83–94, Nightwing #35–39, Batman #563–574, Azrael #50–61, Catwoman #72–77, Robin #67–73, Batman: Legends of the Dark Knight #116–126, Batman: Harley Quinn OGN, The Batman Chronicles #16–18, Batman: Day of Judgment, Batman: No Man's Land, Batman: No Man's Land Secret Files and Origins, Young Justice: No Man's Land

DC One Million

November 1998

All fantastic fiction and DC continuity depend upon a willing suspension of disbelief, with the audience accepting some underlying premises on faith to further the unfolding story. Following a mind-expanding run on *Justice League of America*, author **Grant Morrison** joined penciller **Val Semeiks** and inker **Prentiss Rollins** in taking that principle to the ultimate extreme. They introduced unsuspecting readers to Super Heroes who were still starring in DC comics *One Million* months into the future.

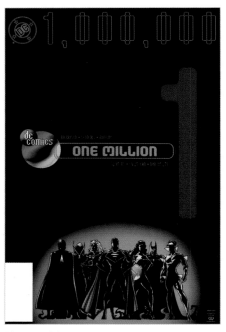

Time sensitive
No matter how well meaning the intentions of the heroes, it seemed that every chronal excursion was destined to end in calamity and catastrophe.

With crossover events now embedded in superhero lore, ever bigger blockbusters frequently failed to deliver the requisite thrills. Writer Grant Morrison addressed the problem in a smart, time-bending yarn packed with whimsy, wonder, humor, and math, which proved that possible futures need not be doom-laden.

Shiny happy prospects
Morrison figured out that if DC maintained its regular publishing schedule, the 853rd century would see the millionth issues of many titles. He further extrapolated that the legacy of the 20th-century Justice League and 31st-century Legion of Super-Heroes would inspire imitation, expansion, and proliferation.

Introduced in *Justice League of America* #23 (Oct. 1998), Justice Legion Alpha was the most prestigious of 24 heroic coalitions safeguarding the cosmos. All sprang from the example of Superman and his contemporaries. The saga began with them visiting the distant past, wanting to invite a number of the Justice League to an historic celebration. In that distant tomorrow, analogues of historical heroes thrived, as did daily threats and menaces, but now immortal Kal-El (Prime Superman One Million) was

about to end 15 millennia of self-imposed exile inside the sun. Justice Legion Alpha felt the celebration wouldn't be complete unless his earliest self and comrades were in attendance on the big day.

The future solar system was crowded with new terraformed worlds and warmed by a second sun, Solaris. This was originally a malevolent computer intelligence bent on destroying all life, until defeated and reprogrammed by one of the Man of Steel's many descendants.

Meanwhile in the present, undying villain Vandal Savage had nuked the Uruguayan capital city, Montevideo. After defeating Supergirl, Jesse

Quick, Arsenal, and Tempest, Savage loaded them into atomically powered Rocket Red suits aimed at Washington DC, Singapore, Brussels, and Metropolis, but had not expected superpowered time travelers to wreck his plans.

Infinite variety
The true legacy of the Man of Tomorrow and the Justice League was a universe where almost anybody or anything could be a Super Hero.

> ## "Send me your Super Heroes from past, present **or** future. I'll kill all of them."
>
> **Vandal Savage** | *DC One Million #2*

Time wasters

Unknown to all, the Justice Legion harbored a traitor, later revealed as Starman, who was working with a resurgent Solaris. Starman had brought a virus from the future that attacked machines and drove organic beings into violent paranoia. The virus affected the entire world and sent Vandal Savage's Rocket Red suits astray. Although the heroes inside the suits had escaped, the suits themselves became makeshift missiles that killed over one million people. In the aftermath, Savage declared all-out war on the Justice Leaguers and those Justice Legionnaires who remained in the past. The grudge match would continue into the 853rd century where Savage ultimately allied with a revived and vengeful Solaris.

Sun and heir
Thanks to the paradoxes of time travel and immortality, far-future allies Solaris and Vandal Savage were the cause of each other's demise.

In an inevitable time loop, the 20th-century heroes and their chronal guests were compelled to invent and construct Solaris to destroy the virus ravaging Earth but afterward were unable to stop it before it escaped to become Superman's future nemesis. In the future, Superman Prime's arrival was ruined as the evil sun attacked, slaughtering hundreds of Super-champions before being defeated. Thinking to escape, Savage fell into a snare laid over eons by 20th-century Justice Leaguer Huntress and a string of assistants carrying on her work over the ages. Savage paid for his countless crimes by being snatched back through time and space to arrive in Montevideo seconds before it was atomized.

The upbeat, utopian sensibilities of *DC One Million* would also inform Grant Morrison and Frank Quitely's 2005–2008 landmark reappraisal of the mighty Man of Steel in *All-Star Superman*. ■

Heritage of heroes

The core *DC One Million* limited series was released weekly with symbolic covers designed in the manner of prose science-fiction novels. The event incorporated 34 one-shot tie-ins that participated to varying degrees. All issues sported new uniform title logos replacing the usual ones, and the unifying trade dress included creator credits on the cover.

The content varied from the creation of offbeat and wild reinventions of present-day heroes like Superboy and Robin to glimpses of strange new worlds, as well as introductions to new characters and key revelations that advanced the main plot. The most crucial was when future Starman sought out his ancient ancestor Ted Knight. Deeply conflicted, Farris Knight followed Starman's legacy down the centuries before confessing to being a traitor who would betray his comrades and two eras to Solaris. Other titles used the event to conclude hanging plotlines, while *Hitman #1,000,000* sharply—and violently—satirized the entire affair.

As with other large-scale events, DC allowed chapters to be added to the official canon months or years later. *DC One Million 80-Page* Giant (Aug. 1999) offered further glimpses of the everyday future, while in Sep. 2008 *Booster Gold #1,000,000* saw the Time Master meet his descendant Peter Platinum. *Superman/Batman #79–80* (Feb.-Mar. 2011) featured the return of Kal Kent and Robin the Toy Wonder, as a World's Finest team from many eras battled the time villain Epoch.

Key issues

Prelude (October 1998)
JLA #23

November 1998
DC One Million #1–4

November 1998 and numbered #1,000,000

Action Comics, Adventures of Superman, Aquaman, Azrael, Batman, Batman: Shadow of the Bat, Catwoman, Chase, Chronos, Creeper, Detective Comics, The Flash, Green Arrow, Green Lantern, Hitman, Impulse, JLA, Legionnaires, Legion of Super-Heroes, Lobo, Martian Manhunter, Nightwing, The Power of Shazam!, Resurrection Man, Robin, Starman, Superboy, Supergirl, Superman, Superman: Man of Steel, Superman: Man of Tomorrow, Young Justice, Wonder Woman

August 1999
DC One Million 80-Page Giant #1,000,000

September 2008
Booster Gold #1,000,000

February–March 2011
Superman/Batman #79–80

Ghost of a chance
Earth's defenders met their greatest challenge when humanity's most powerful guardian ran amok.

Day of Judgment

November 1999

A cornerstone of DC's shared universe since 1959, Hal Jordan was the greatest Green Lantern of all before tragedy, madness, and worse drove him to destroy everything he valued as universal nemesis Parallax. Scripter **Geoff Johns** and illustrator **Matthew Dow Smith** continued the disgraced hero's rehabilitation via the magically themed *Day of Judgment*, an event that would reposition Super Heroes and supernatural saviors for the next millennium.

O ne of DC's earliest stars and most resilient characters was the Spectre. Created by Jerry Siegel and Bernard Baily, he debuted in *More Fun Comics* #52 (Feb. 1940) and was originally the alter ego of police detective Jim Corrigan, who had accepted a divine offer of power to punish the gangsters who murdered him on his wedding day.

The ghostly guardian was the only Earth-Two character to win his own title during the Silver Age (*The Spectre* #1–10, Dec. 1967–Jun. 1969). Disappearing when supernatural anthologies started outselling Super Heroes, he arose again in *Adventure Comics* #431 (Feb. 1974) for a short, career-redefining run as a true spirit of retribution, spectacularly stopping evildoers.

He resurfaced after *Crisis on Infinite Earths* and maintained an unchanged presence until John Ostrander and Tom Mandrake's 1990s series revealed the Spectre was the Spirit of Divine Wrath, an agent dispensing holy punishments and bound over millennia to various flawed mortals by divine command of (universal creator) the Presence. The quest for salvation of each of the Spectre's mortal hosts was key to controlling the raging fury of the spirit.

Divine interventions
Since 1940, Corrigan had steered the Spirit's relentless hunger for justice, mitigating its capricious inclination to punish, with excessive force and macabre irony, any wrongdoers it encountered. Countless rogues and thugs suffered ghastly judgments, but the power was also a potent tool of true salvation. With Corrigan in control, the Spectre repeatedly saved Earth, the universe, and all reality from arcane abomination and cosmic calamity.

Spirit guide
Merged with the Spirit of Wrath, outcast angel Asmodel was beyond the capabilities of humanity's heroes and strong enough to challenge Heaven itself.

Ultimately, the weary cop attained personal atonement and moved on to a heavenly reward. The Spectre Force was left ungoverned and pilotless, giving infernal upstart Etrigan the Demon a chance to make deadly mischief for Hell's latest overlord, Neron. Hell was at that time torturing fallen King Angel Asmodel after his attempt to destroy humanity, and when Etrigan orchestrated the Asmodel's merging with the Spectre, the corrupted

> ## "...But I've only begun to make up for what I've done."
>
> **Hal Jordan** | *Day of Judgment* #2

Arcane overwatch
Escalating mystical emergencies inevitably forced solitary heroic adepts to forsake their natural biases and form a team to tackle magical menaces.

king gained incalculable power. Freezing the infernal pit, Asmodel drove its demons and devils to Earth, with Etrigan in gleeful pursuit.

With Super Heroes outmatched, Earth's mystic defenders reluctantly united to battle the invasion. Proven champions like Doctor Occult, Phantom Stranger, Zatanna, Ragman, Deadman, Raven, and former Green Lantern Alan Scott—now dubbed Sentinel—allied with previously neutral Madame Xanadu and the evil Enchantress and Sebastian Faust to turn back the ravening hordes and Asmodel.

Phantom force
Hal Jordan's dead Green Lantern Corps comrades were proud to offer their spectral support to his rehabilitation and return to duty.

Spectre of doubt

As DC's shared universe grew ever more closely connected, cross-company events escalated and intersected with a selection of different titles. Some of the crises generated relatively few tie-ins or spin-offs, while others proved to be historical turning points that reshaped the destiny of characters and changed the entire continuity's direction, requiring confirmation in every DC title.

Day of Judgment was a relatively low-key event with minimal trade dress and no reading order on tie-in covers, but its ramifications were many and far-reaching. It saw the formation of a magical team, foreshadowing both

Shadowpact and two iterations of *Justice League Dark*, the resurrection of fan favorite Blue Devil, and presaged forthcoming mega-events *Day of Vengeance* and *Blackest Night*.

Moreover, when Jordan returned to life in *Green Lantern: Rebirth* (Dec. 2004–Jul. 2005), the Spectre was left directionless until murdered Gotham City cop Crispus Allen merged with it. The lengthy vacancy between Allen's death and Spectral merger, plus his cautious, methodical nature, sparked a degree of autonomy in the Force. This allowed the Spectre and its new host the luxury of debate and consultation before delivering their interpretations of Divine Judgment as a Spirit of Closure and Renewal.

Magic tricked

While a team of heroes worked to reignite the flames of Hell and a "home front" team battled demonic ravagers on Earth, a third contingent traveled to Heaven in search of Corrigan, hoping he would desert paradise to again command the Spectre. The mission failed, but an angelic prompt sent the assembled sentinels to Purgatory, where those who have yet to be judged wait. Here, among many dead heroes, Hal Jordan's soul convinced the questers he was ready, willing, and able to command the Spectre's measureless fury.

After almost destroying existence as Parallax, Jordan had sacrificed himself to reignite Earth's failed sun. He was offered a second chance and bonded to the Spectre by convincing the Force to choose him over Asmodel. Jordan's willpower spearheaded the angel's defeat, the punishment of

hidden manipulator Neron, and restoration of Earth. Left to wander the world, the new Spectre explored situations where its fearsome power could change, not extinguish lives, repurposing revenge to fuel a new Spirit of Redemption. ▧

Our Worlds at War

August–October 2001

Accustomed to summer's end bringing epic comic book crossover events, readers were primed for something truly special in a world where Lex Luthor had beaten the odds and defied all logic to become America's President. Scripted by Superman writers **Jeph Loeb**, **Mark Schultz**, **Joe Casey**, and **Joe Kelly**, and illustrated by **Ed McGuinness**, **Mike Wieringo**, **Doug Mahnke**, **Leonard Kirk**, and **Ron Garney**, the manifold terrors of humanity under ruthless attack proved to be shocking and timely as DC unleashed *Our World at War*.

United front
Imperiex threatened everything that lived, but the coalition confronting it could barely stop squabbling for long enough to care or respond.

The saga had actually started months before in *Superman* #153 (Feb. 2000) when Superman and sworn enemy Mongul briefly joined forces. The monstrous tyrant needed help confronting Imperiex, Destroyer of Galaxies, after the cosmic colossus casually crushed the villain's mobile planetary weapons platform Warworld.

Who goes there?
The unlikely allies' ill-tempered strike against the armored enigma was accomplished only with some impromptu assistance and signature violence from interstellar bounty hunter Lobo. However, what no one realized after the stardust settled was that their herculean efforts had been directed against a simple probe-drone. Sadly, the true galactic obliterator was now aware of their existence… and location.

Time passed and new American President Lex Luthor began reshaping the country to his agenda, pressing several Super Heroes and villains into his service. However, emergencies were constant, with his sworn enemies Superman, Batman, and Wonder Woman particularly hard-pressed. Following an attack from future terror Brainiac-13, Metropolis had been transformed into a vast computerized City of Tomorrow and Luthor's daughter Lena was possessed by hostile code, becoming the computer-despot's puppet avatar.

Boiling point came after Brainiac-13 converted dwarf planet Pluto into his own Warworld. When Superman investigated the astral alteration, it led to a massive coalition of alien refugees led by Darkseid, Massacre, Mongal (the daughter of Mongul), and former comrades Maxima and Adam Strange. Forcibly establishing a bunker-base on Earth, and seizing Metropolis, they interned its human population in

Home guard
The Destroyer of Galaxies had never experienced the sheer resolve and tenacity of heroes like the Last Son of Krypton.

> ## "This is war. And you should consider yourself **drafted**, Superman!"
> **President Lex Luthor** | *Adventures of Superman* #594

Outraged by a controlling cabal that included Luthor, Kryptonian arch-villain General Zod, and Darkseid, Superman fought the invasion apart from Earth's armed forces, but after Imperiex bombarded the planet, the hero was forced to work with the administration. Topeka, Kansas, was eradicated and brutal damage done to Atlantis, Gotham City, and other major population centers, but Superman was kept in the dark about President Lex's secret pact with Brainiac-13, trading knowledge of imminent events for future favors. The Commander-in-Chief had his own plans and a unique notion of what constituted "acceptable losses."

Working wounded

With a Justice League force floundering in space and alien boots on the ground across the planet, Luthor called in the reserves, including youthful heroes like Young Justice, to fight for their world. Robin, Wonder Girl, Superboy, Impulse, and the rest went much farther than that, ultimately making their own last stand on Apokolips.

In constant combat that cost countless lives, especially those of his comrades, Superman got closer to discerning Imperiex's motives and origins. The destroyer was drawn to Earth because it was the center of the Multiverse-rending *Crisis on Infinite Earths*. That was key to the plan devised to save everything. Of course, the alliance of devious masterminds had schemed to take advantage of even this desperate situation, unaware that Superman and the surviving heroes had other ideas.

War no more

The greatest minds and most evil souls of the galaxy had conceived a way to end the threat of Imperiex, but it depended upon cracking the beast's armor. The marauder was

Counterstrike
Reinforced with the life force of cosmic energy avatar Strange Visitor, and propelled by Green Lantern Kyle Rayner's willpower, Superman became a speeding bullet aimed at Imperiex.

a space ark and offered an alliance with Earth's leaders against an existential threat.

Adam Strange explained that they were all fleeing Imperiex, who had stopped deleting galaxies wholesale to specifically target Earth. Unlike the mechanistic armored thug Superman had previously defeated, this Imperiex was an implacable universal abstract—the literal embodiment of entropy. And it was preparing to erase and restart reality in a new Big Bang, because it had detected a temporal anomaly contaminating the current universe. With an infinite army of probes, the cosmic consciousness ripped its way across creation, while survivors of its rampage decided Earth was where life would make its final stand.

General orders
The adage "keep your friends close and your enemies closer" took on new meaning when Darkseid allied himself with the joint task force to stop Imperiex.

OUR WORLDS AT WAR: CASUALTIES OF WAR

The RED BADGE of COURAGE

JEPH LOEB writer · ED McGUINNESS penciller · CAM SMITH inker · special thanks to: BILL SIENKIEWICZ · TANYA & RICH HORIE colors · RICHARD STARKINGS letters · TOM PALMER jr ass't editor · EDDIE BERGANZA editor · SUPERMAN created by: JERRY SIEGEL & JOE SHUSTER

Cosmic ceasefire

Swallowing justified suspicions and deep disgust, Earth's Super Heroes had no choice but to work with and not around the villains they used to battle.

further empowered by the spiritual faith and force of Tempest (formerly Aqualad), the surviving Atlanteans, and the Themysciran Amazons who had lost so much and so many, Superman drew on the power of John Henry Irons' last invention. The Entropy Aegis Henry had built from Imperiex probe armor was used to push Brainiac-13's Warworld through a time portal that had been opened by Lex Luthor, which utilized Darkseid's Boom Tube to move the unmovable.

The weaponized planet, which held the computer tyrant's consciousness and the sentient energies of Imperiex, reentered reality 14 billion years previously, just as the original Big Bang detonated, destroying both. Imperiex's last realization was that the temporal anomaly he had scoured the cosmos to find had always been his own existence.

a mass of sentient energy, fueled by the destruction it wrought. If the shell could be penetrated, those collected energies could be taken and used to restore previously destroyed galaxies—instantaneously redistributed via Darkseid's Boom Tube technology.

The strategy started well but required more sacrifice. With Imperiex's armor being impenetrable even to the Superman's solar-charged strength, Earth's last chance came from an unexpected source. The geomagnetic being Strange Visitor surrendered all her power to imbue the Man of Steel with measureless might before he was launched like a projectile into Imperiex.

However, when Darkseid then sought to transfer the Imperiex's now leaking energies to rebuild lost galaxies, he found that Brainiac-13 had secretly co-opted those roiling forces for his new Warworld. The malign computer intelligence had chosen to conquer and rule whatever remained after the destruction of the Galactic Obliterator rather than return to its never-ending conflict with organic life for dominance.

In a desperate gamble, Superman plunged into the sun, once again supercharging his overtaxed cells as Earth's other champions united through the telepathic gifts of Martian Manhunter J'onn J'onzz. Linked and

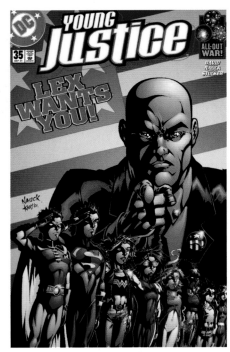

To serve and protect

With more than eight million already dead, the planet's youngest champions were ready and willing to join the fight.

Calling all heroes

The war impacted Earth on many fronts and brought out the hero in most. Even unconventional and unpredictable criminals like Harley Quinn were moved to outlandish acts of heroism in the name of love and honor, albeit because she was showing off for journalist Jimmy Olsen.

After being drafted as medical retrieval staff and ordered to bring wounded metahumans back to hospital facilities, Young Justice was briefly catapulted through history to different epochs. They met the Legion of Super-Heroes and Robin (Tim Drake) on their travels and also inadvertently prompted Imperiex and Brainiac-13 to battle each other in other eras, before the young heroes reached home again.

While saving a new iteration of the Suicide Squad from death and defeat on the moon, Young Justice also encountered the Apokoliptian

Black Racer. An independent ambassador of Death, the Black Racer was taking the soul of fallen Super Hero John Henry Irons to the Source. The Black Racer allowed the young heroes to retrieve the spirit of Steel. This subsequently preserved all life as the inventor's Entropy Aegis turned the tide against Imperiex. However, their efforts ultimately marooned Young Justice on Apokolips, where every moment was a manic struggle for survival and escape.

With the crisis averted, the weary heroes finally found time to honor the dead. Aquaman was still missing, so

> "It's **over**, Superman! It's every planet for itself! The first who takes Warworld wins... and devil take the losers!"
>
> **Maxima** | *Superman: Man of Steel #117*

No surrender
No matter their experience or power level, every hero on Earth gave their all to repel the invasion and crush the enemy.

the Justice League of America erected a maritime beacon on the poisoned site where Atlantis once lay, while their venerable forebears, the Justice Society of America, commemorated their dead comrade Queen Hippolyta of Themyscira (the WWII Wonder Woman) with a quiet, contemplative poker game. Everywhere, survivors regrouped and turned toward another uncertain tomorrow.

Warworld
With survival assured and victory in sight, the combined commanders raced to reap the postwar rewards but did not anticipate Brainiac-13's digital ambush.

Family at war

The bombardment of Earth shattered families. With Wonder Woman severely wounded in the struggle, her mother came out of retirement to fight in her stead.

Casualty report

The collateral damage of the war was world-changing and long-lasting. Clark Kent's beloved Kansas was slow to recover from the destruction and Superman's failure to save Topeka

War room

Admitted into the inner circle of Earth's defense command, Superman was ordered to abandon his principles and assassinate Imperiex-Prime.

remained a wound he carried for years. Many regular characters were reported killed—including, briefly, Ma and Pa Kent, General Sam Lane, and Guy Gardner—but while inventor John Henry Irons was quickly resurrected as a new kind of Steel, WWII veteran General Rock remained dead.

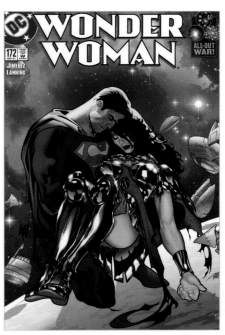

> "Gotta... keep it together... can't... pass out... Actually... guess I... **can** pass out..."
>
> **Supergirl** | *Supergirl #60*

Servant of the people

Servant of the people
After being Wonder Woman during WWII, Hippolyta returned to action to save Athens from annihilation—and paid the ultimate price.

Wonder Woman's mother Queen Hippolyta perished tragically and heroically, while Strange Visitor's unflinching sacrifice was the key to victory. Many minor and supporting characters would be later found alive and resume an active role. Others had to wait for later continuity revisions to resurface. Some, like alien mass-murderer Massacre, have never returned to DC pages.

Aquaman and his entire race of Atlanteans were seemingly eradicated and the seas of Earth left severely damaged. These particular consequences would eventually be resolved in the epic Justice League story arc "The Obsidian Age" (*JLA* #68–75, Sep. 2002–Jan. 2003), while the destruction wrought on Metropolis and Gotham City were simply adapted into the unfolding storylines. Both Keystone City and New York were targeted by Darkseid's Parademons, who were ultimately defeated by former Teen Titans Cyborg and The Flash (Wally West). ∎

Skirmish lines

By the turn of the century, large-scale events had become essential reading for comics fans, delivered in a variety of formats. *Our Worlds at War* was primarily a Superman crisis that was so big it could not help but impact the rest of the DCU. Instead of a core limited series, major incidents transpired in the Man of Steel's regular titles, with crossover stories—individually badged as successive monthly milestones "Prelude to War," "All-Out War" or "Casualties of War"—drawing in other Superman family stars like *Steel*, *Supergirl*, and *Superboy*, and other A-listers, particularly "Trinity" partners Batman and Wonder Woman.

Supplementing the action, nine character-themed one-shots were released, exploring the progress, costs, and repercussions of the

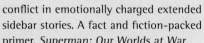

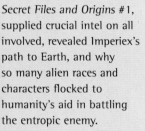

conflict in emotionally charged extended sidebar stories. A fact and fiction-packed primer, *Superman: Our Worlds at War Secret Files and Origins #1*, supplied crucial intel on all involved, revealed Imperiex's path to Earth, and why so many alien races and characters flocked to humanity's aid in battling the entropic enemy.

The creative contributor roster was huge, but the narrative thrust came primarily from *Superman* team writers Jeph Loeb, and Joe Casey, Mark Schultz, Joe Kelly, and Peter David and Phil Jimenez with their illustrative collaborators Ed McGuinness, Mike Wieringo, Doug Mahnke, Ron Garney, and Leonard Kirk.

Key issues

(August–October 2001)

Superman #171–173, Adventures of Superman #593–595, Superman: The Man of Steel #115–117, Superboy #89–91, Action Comics #780–782, Supergirl #59–61, Wonder Woman #171–173, Young Justice #35–36, Impulse #77, Batman #593–594

One-shot specials (August–October 2001)

Green Lantern: Our Worlds at War #1, Batman: Our Worlds at War #1, Young Justice: Our Worlds at War #1, Superman: Our Worlds at War Secret Files and Origins #1, JLA: Our Worlds at War #1, Nightwing: Our Worlds at War #1, JSA: Our Worlds at War #1, Wonder Woman: Our Worlds at War #1, The Flash: Our Worlds at War #1, Harley Quinn: Our Worlds at War #1, World's Finest: Our Worlds at War #1

Additional untold story (March–June 2010)

Superman/Batman #68–71

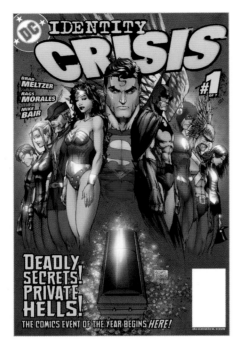

Identity Crisis

August 2004–June 2005

Superhero comics often mine real-world scenarios to bestow authenticity. In the long, deliberate, and clandestine buildup to the ambitious mega-event *Infinite Crisis*, tensions were ratcheted up across many DC titles. In that fevered atmosphere, writer **Brad Meltzer** and artists **Rags Morales** and **Michael Bair** created a truly shocking and controversial story that would shake the ethical underpinnings of all DC's Super Heroes and trigger a devastating *Identity Crisis*.

Death of the dream
By killing a loved one rather than a costumed enemy, a mystery villain struck terror into every hero's heart and sparked catastrophic consequences for the entire world.

Although readers were kept in the dark at the time, *Identity Crisis* was an opening shot in a barrage of events and story arcs designed to pave the way for a monumental undertaking— *Infinite Crisis*. It would be followed by more remarkable tales; many—but not all—crafted to frontload a major revision in DC continuity.

Comparatively low-key and human-scaled, *Identity Crisis* played out as a murder mystery with far-reaching implications that changed the tone of DC's Super Hero comics, forcing heroes to reassess their careers and actions as they hunted a murderer. This time it was very personal as the victim was Sue Dibny, wife of Justice Leaguer Elongated Man. Super-Villain Doctor (Arthur) Light was the prime suspect, revealed to have savagely assaulted her in the JLA satellite years previously, before being caught by The Flash (Barry Allen).

Newer JLA members such as The Flash Wally West and Green Lantern Kyle Rayner were appalled at the disclosure, and Light's boasting that he would do the same or worse to all the heroes' loved ones. In response, their

Rite of passage
The grief and solemnity of Sue Dibny's funeral would be followed by a superpowered war that tore America apart.

mentors The Atom, Green Lantern Hal Jordan, Green Arrow, Black Canary, and Hawkman convinced Barry to let sorceress Zatanna alter Light's mind. They did not stop there, but also intellectually lobotomized him, turning Light into an ineffectual buffoon.

The junior heroes were further shocked when they discovered that the late-arriving Batman had attempted to stop the mind-wipe intervention, but the conspirators had edited his memories too. As years passed, the iron-willed Dark Knight began to recall

vestiges of the incident. He became increasingly cautious around his allies, ultimately trusting only those he had personally trained. As a result, Batman carefully drew up contingency plans to take down his Justice League allies if they ever "went rogue" and led to him building the Brother Eye satellite for surveilling all of Earth's metahumans.

It transpired that this was not the first time the heroes had overstepped

Grave consequences
Batman's resistance to the League's mind-wipe solution and their response signalled the end of a golden age of trust and cooperation between heroes.

legal and ethical boundaries. When the Secret Society of Super-Villains (Wizard, Floronic Man, Reverse-Flash, Blockbuster, and Star Sapphire), swapped minds with Superman, Batman, Black Canary, Zatanna, and Hal Jordan, they learned the secret identities of the entire Justice League but were stripped of this knowledge by Zatanna after being defeated. Green Arrow even implied there had

Paid in full

Trade dress for *Identity Crisis* was sporadic, with many tie-ins omitting cover badges and banners. However, the story was expanded with great effect during and after the limited series' run. The Flash would suffer as the Rogues' outrage over Captain Boomerang's death grew. The Teen Titans assembled their greatest roster ever to crush Doctor Light in unbadged, supplementary story arc *Identity Theft/Lights Out*. The Justice League ran a parallel storyline

Crisis of Conscience, which depicted the team falling apart over the terrible revelations, while the final chapter (*JLA* #119, Nov. 2005) carried a banner announcing "*Infinite Crisis* is here!"

Identity Crisis was DC's top-selling title of the period, and issue #1 was the bestselling comic book for June 2004. The controversial series also garnered critical approval. In 2007 the collected story was added to the Young Adult Library Services Association recommended list of Great Graphic Novels for Teens.

been other times when sheer practical necessity triumphed over morality.

The revelation spread far and wide as enraged heroes hunted Light, who had regained his memory of what the League did. Villains went wild in the knowledge that their enemies would compromise their principles just like any bad guy. Brutal battles occurred everywhere, and the notion of a serial offender gripped the heroes after The Atom's ex-wife Jean Loring was almost strangled to death. She could not describe or identify her attacker, and soon after Lois Lane received a death threat from someone who knew the identity of her husband.

Betrayal

The death toll mounted when an unknown party used the Calculator to hire Captain Boomerang to kill Robin's father, Jack Drake. The plan was doubly successful, as the mystery manipulator had provided Drake with a gun and the victim killed Boomerang before dying himself. In a savage clash

with irate and terrified super-criminals, Firestorm was stabbed with a magic sword and fatally detonated in the stratosphere after reaching an unstoppable critical mass.

When an autopsy revealed tiny footprints across Sue's brain and that her death was caused by a cerebral infarction, the awful truth was clear. There was never a criminal mastermind, only lonely, mentally unstable Jean Loring who used The Atom's technology in hopeless attempts to win back the husband she had cheated on and then divorced. Her scheme spiraled tragically out of control, driving her to improvise ever more excessive threats to keep her hopes and deluded dream alive. As Batman, Doctor Mid-Nite, and Mister Terrific closed in, Ray Palmer also realized the horrifying truth for which he was indirectly responsible. After committing Jean to Arkham Asylum, the despondent hero cast himself forever into the Microverse, unaware of what was coming for Earth. ▪

> ## "Anyone who puts on a costume paints a bullseye on his family's chests."
>
> **Elongated Man (Ralph Dibny)** | *Identity Crisis* #1

Key issues

August 2004—February 2005
Identity Crisis #1–7

Tie-ins (July 2004—June 2005)
The Flash #213–217, *Firestorm* #1–6, *JLA* #115–119, *Manhunter* #2–5, *JSA* #67, *Teen Titans* #20–23

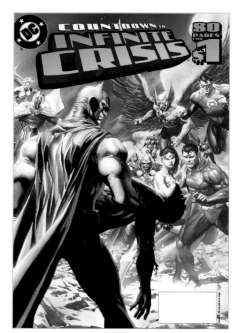

Countdown to Infinite Crisis

May–June 2005

Somehow, the world had changed. Constant peril and catastrophe had always loomed, but now incidents came without letup—as if a vindictive intelligence was behind it all. With instability growing every moment, writers **Geoff Johns**, **Greg Rucka**, and **Judd Winick** and artists **Ed Benes**, **Phil Jimenez**, **Rags Morales**, **Ivan Reis**, **Jesús Saiz**, and **Michael Bair** exposed part of the answer in a *Countdown to Infinite Crisis*.

Cry for Justice
The callous execution of a beloved hero reunited warring friends in readiness for the greatest struggle of their lives.

The revelations of *Identity Crisis* opened wounds that festered. The deaths of Elongated Man's wife Sue, Robin's father Jack Drake, and even Digger "Captain Boomerang" Harkness, plus the self-imposed exile of Ray Palmer (The Atom) had exposed deep-seated problems.

The disclosure of immoral acts by heroes drove apart the previously inspirational trinity of Superman, Wonder Woman, and Batman. Without their spiritual leadership, the Justice League, Outsiders, Teen Titans, and the Justice Society of America, all written by Geoff Johns, struggled to move on.

Finest hour

Third Flash Wally West demanded the Justice League come clean and tell Batman they had altered his memories.

When all finally agreed, Martian Manhunter discovered that the Dark Knight already knew (seen in story arc *Crisis of Conscience*, JLA #115–119, Aug.–Nov. 2005). A grim situation was about to get worse. Alien archenemy Despero restored the memories of mind-wiped criminals, readying an aggrieved and vengeful Secret Society of Super-Villains to attack the JLA.

Batman had taken a darker path by then, establishing precautions and protocols to counter former Justice League allies and building a satellite-monitoring system to watch them and all metahumans. Another subtler player also worried about super-beings, and used Batman's innovations for his own purposes.

Out of the blue
Despite Kord's suspicions, it was a shock seeing his life on a screen and realizing his friends had targets on their backs.

> "This is why I want you, Ted. You **never** back down."
>
> **Maxwell Lord** | *Countdown to Infinite Crisis #1*

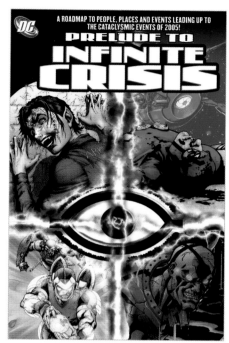

Eye spy
DC gathered relevant material from *Superman Secret Files and Origins 2004* (Aug. 2004), *The Flash #219* (Apr. 2005) and *Wonder Woman #214* (May 2005) into a special edition.

Sign of the times

The buildup to *Infinite Crisis* was slow and initially covert. After the event's conclusion, it was clear that the saga had been building since 2004—signaling a return to mass, intercompany participation in wide-scale sagas.

A first sly hint came with the updating of the company colophon. The hallowed "DC Bullet" (designed by acclaimed designer Milton Glaser and used since 1976) was replaced by a swirling, kinetic "DC Spin" symbol, starting with August 2005 cover dates and proudly adorning the cover of *DC Special: The Return of Donna Troy #1*, incorporated into the limited series' title.

Carefully planned and calculated to deliver maximum shock and revelation, many precursors to *Infinite Crisis* had no identifying trade dress. Limited series

Adam Strange: Planet Heist concluded with a cover date of June 2005 but gave no hint of the *Crisis* event that would begin one month later. Even pivotal launch title *Countdown to Infinite Crisis* carried only a title logo and not the iconic multipurpose headline banner that would soon adorn and inform DC's comic books in the months ahead.

Countdown to Infinite Crisis was a huge commercial hit. An all-new material 80-Page Giant with a $1 cover price, it swiftly went into a second printing with an amended cover clarifying that the body being carried by Batman was Ted Kord.

Trouble was brewing everywhere. Occasional ally Adam Strange scoured the universe for his adopted homeworld Rann, which had been apparently destroyed by a supernova. Desperate to reunite with his wife and child, and solve the mystery, he enlisted (or clashed with) the Omega Men, Thanagarians, Vril Dox's L.E.G.I.O.N., draconian peacekeeping Darkstars, cosmic vampire Starbreaker, and Superman. Eventually, Strange realized that some hidden force was methodically destabilizing the political power balance of the universe.

The realm of magic was also in turmoil. The all-powerful Spectre had no human host and was being seduced toward evil by a new Eclipso. The tempter had recently possessed the ostracized and increasingly unstable Jean Loring, whose murder of Sue Dibny triggered the converging crises. Now the Spectre was being slowly convinced that the way to end evil on Earth was to kill all magic users.

On Earth, only one man questioned the state of affairs to ask how and why.

Blue Beetle Ted Kord was valiant and brilliant but considered even by his friends something of a clown. It was an act he loved and a role he deliberately fostered. Largely inactive and semi-retired after several serious injuries incurred in service to the Justice League, the strictly human adventurer began considering the way the world was heading and reached conclusions even, the admittedly distracted, Batman missed.

Enemy action

The conclusive factor was a slow but steady embezzling of his fortune, but the inventor didn't care about money, only answers. With best friend Booster Gold and Oracle (Barbara Gordon), Kord investigated, redoubling his efforts after being attacked by minor villains the Madmen. Booster was blown up while using Kord's computer and, despite being humored, patronized, and ignored by major Leaguers such as Superman, Batman, and Green Lantern, Kord continued undeterred.

Encouraged by (lukewarm) support from Wonder Woman and J'onn J'onzz,

and determined to prove that his concerns were justified, Kord finally deduced the only possible solution. Infiltrating intelligence agency Checkmate's headquarters, Ted was shocked to discover that his friend and former Justice League International boss Maxwell Lord was behind it all. He had used Kord's cash and connections to gather deadly intel, including secret identities and details of loved ones, of every Super Hero on Earth.

In a chilling confrontation, Lord confirmed that, despite being metahuman himself, he planned to eliminate every unnatural being alive and make the planet safe for real humanity. When Kord refused to join him, Lord executed him and ordered his agents and robotic OMAC warriors to begin the next stage... ◼

Key issues

November 2004–June 2005

Adam Strange #1–8, Countdown to Infinite Crisis #1, Prelude to Infinite Crisis #1

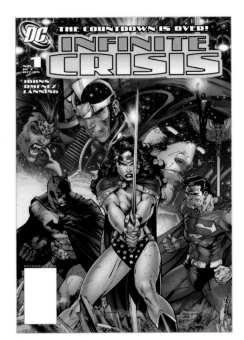

Three-way split
The hidden schemers' plan depended upon not just moving planets but also destroying the friendship of Superman, Batman, and Wonder Woman.

Infinite Crisis

May 2005–June 2006

At last, multiple strands coalesced into a clear assault upon existence, sowing discord and destruction. DC writers and artists, steered by core creators **Geoff Johns**, **Phil Jimenez**, **George Pérez**, **Ivan Reis**, and **Jerry Ordway** unpicked the mystery, revealing the tragic motivations of heroes driven to distraction and retaliation. Resolved to repair the damage they had done and mistakes they had made, the heroes triggered an *Infinite Crisis*.

In the buildup to *Infinite Crisis*, DC released four 6-issue limited series (each later supplemented by a one-shot), setting the scene and amplifying the sense of chaos and catastrophe. The *Rann-Thanagar War*, *Day of Vengeance*, *Villains United*, and *The OMAC Project* counted down (literally on the cover trade dress) to *Infinite Crisis*, as did a crossover in Superman titles intended to warm up readers for the big event.

Driven to distraction

Villains United followed the creation of an army of evildoers, by focusing on those who wouldn't join Lex Luthor's Secret Society of Super-Villains. While The Flash's Rogues and a misfit gang named the Secret Six fought back, Luthor's Society grew in strength, destroying the Justice League satellite and waging a battle for Metropolis against hard-pressed Super Heroes.

Day of Vengeance saw an increasingly unstable and apocalyptic Spectre beguiled by Eclipso. Intent on destroying all magic, the Spirit of Vengeance shattered the Rock of

Big sky thinking
For Luthor Jr., a cosmic puncture in the fabric of creation was just a useful way to keep potential nuisances occupied while he made modifications to the universe.

Eternity, freeing countless malign mystic creatures and eradicating the ancient system of rules controlling supernatural forces, before attacking Earth's greatest magical heroes. In the clash, an unlikely alliance of minor mages and heroes banded together as Shadowpact to stop the Spectre. When the Rock of Eternity detonated, the transformative scarab of original Blue

Beetle Dan Garrett landed in El Paso, Texas, attached itself to schoolboy Jaime Reyes, and created a new kind of hero and a new Blue Beetle.

Watchers from beyond
After the Crisis on Infinite Earths, the last survivors of perished alternate worlds watched in dismay and growing horror at dark developments on New Earth.

Returned from death and apparent paradise New Cronus, Donna Troy recruited a team of heroes to help seal a rip in reality. Not all survived, and no one knew that the deadly anomaly had been created by Alexander Luthor, Jr. as a diversion. Galaxies were already in uproar as the Rann-Thanagar War spread. Deviously orchestrated, it took experienced space heroes Adam Strange, Hawkman, Hawkgirl, Captain Comet, the Omega Men, and Green Lanterns Kilowog and Kyle Rayner out of the picture.

Exposed as a calculating schemer sworn to save humanity from metahumans, Maxwell Lord suborned Checkmate, stole Batman's technology (corrupting the AI of his Brother Eye satellite) to create The OMAC Project. Unleashing a terrible nanite plague, Lord transformed humans into Super Hero-hunting cyborgs but faced mounting resistance from the Dark Knight and others.

Running through *Superman* #218–219 (Aug.–Sep. 2005), *Adventures of Superman* #642–643 (Sep.–Oct 2005), *Action Comics* #829 (Sep. 2005) and *Wonder Woman* #219 (Sep. 2005), the story arc "Sacrifice" revealed that Superman had been systematically mind-controlled by Maxwell Lord, becoming his secret weapon against metahumanity. During a brutal struggle against her friend, Wonder Woman was forced to kill Lord to free Superman. The impromptu execution was streamed live around the world and Diana became a pariah in the aftermath.

Boiling point

Crisis on Infinite Earths saw all alternate universes not destroyed by the Anti-Monitor merged into one. Despite some continuity aftershocks, life was saved and reality returned to its natural progress. Four valiant survivors from Earths that now had never existed—Earth 2's Superman (Kal-L); his wife, Lois Lane; Alexander Luthor Jr. from Earth-3; and Superboy from Earth Prime—exiled themselves from a new reality that had no room for them. They now dwelt in a nebulous paradise found or perhaps created by Luthor Jr.'s dimension-warping powers. From there they watched the new universe unfold.

Descending disorder

While the lead-up to *Infinite Crisis* was heavily foreshadowed in participating titles during the core limited series run, not all crossovers and tie-ins were badged or bannered. DC was judicious in promoting the major event, and trade dress title banners acted as both identifiers and a countdown clock announcing "4 months to…" and ultimately "*Infinite Crisis* is Here!"

The core series carried two covers per issue, one set by George Pérez and the other by Jim Lee and Sandra Hope, which probably contributed to both the first and second issues being the top-selling preordered titles of their respective release months.

Years passed. New Earth faced perils and was defended by its Super Heroes. It was an exceedingly dark and dangerous place. Superman was killed by Doomsday and resurrected—opening death's doorway to other returnees. More heroes died, were maimed, or

Key issues

Prelude and Crisis

May–November 2005

Countdown to Infinite Crisis #1, Prelude to Infinite Crisis #1, Day of Vengeance #1–6, The OMAC Project #1–6, Rann-Thanagar War #1–6, Villains United #1–6

Tie-ins (June–December 2005)

Action Comics #826, 829–831, Adventures of Superman #639, 641–644, Superman #216–217, 219–222, JSA #73–78, Batman: Gotham Knights #66, Birds of Prey #83, JLA #115–119, Nightwing #109–110, DC Special: The Return of Donna Troy #1–4, Breach #7, Wonder Woman #219–221, Blood of the Demon #6–7, Manhunter #13–14, Firestorm #17–18, Aquaman #35

December 2005–June 2006

Infinite Crisis #1–7

> "Activate Project: **OMAC**… it's time to save the **world** from **itself.**"
>
> **Maxwell Lord** | *Countdown to Infinite Crisis #1*

became evil. Hawk became Monarch and Extant. Hal Jordan sought to remake the universe in his image. Heroes were indistinguishable from villains. In their perfect pocket universe, the survivors of *Crisis on Infinite Earths* looked on at this merged and seemingly corrupted New Earth with horror.

From their detached vantage point, Kal-L, Lois Lane-Kent, Superboy-Prime, and Alexander Luthor Jr. increasingly despaired at the disturbing world they had sacrificed everything to create. Earth-2's first Super Hero was especially distressed, but this was driven by his concern for his wife. Lois was elderly and dying, and her husband remained convinced that if their Earth still existed, she would live. So they all resolved to rectify the situation.

Passion play
Kal-L agreed to Luthor Jr.'s plan to replace New Earth with a gentler one. The exiles had been secretly editing reality, creating opportunities for change. Kal-L just wanted happiness with Lois and never realized his allies had more selfish motivations. Troubled observation had at some point become clandestine destabilization. Superboy-Prime had become obsessed with Conner Kent (New Earth's cloned

Family fortunes
Kal-L was so delighted to see his lost cousin again, he never questioned why exactly Luthor Jr. needed her so badly.

Superboy) and hungered to be the best and only Boy of Steel, while Luthor Jr. had succumbed to madness, furtively working to create the perfect Earth by plundering portions of pre-*Crisis on Infinite Earth* realities he discovered in Hypertime. His arrogant meddling would eventually reverse the great

> "You're just an imitation! Everyone **knows** that! I'm the **real** Superboy!."
>
> **Superboy Prime** | *Infinite Crisis #5*

Iconic action
As the Golden Age Superman pummeled his New Earth successor, he unconsciously reenacted the most memorable feat of his epic career.

dissolution of worlds and unlock a new Local Multiverse of 52 Earths.

As years passed, the quartet started to unpick and reweave the fabric of a universe they deemed faulty. Luthor Jr. and Superboy-Prime often excluded Kal-L and Lois and secretly went further and faster. The results of their covert actions, however, soon became unmanageable. Jointly manufactured crises *Day of Vengeance*, *Rann-Thanagar War*, *Villains United*, and *The OMAC Project* had been preceded by the *Identity Crisis* and *Seven Soldiers* incidents. Even problems prior to *Zero*

Earthshock
As Luthor Jr.'s plans spiraled out of control, his meddling sparked the return of the Multiverse and too many Earths.

Hour potentially had Luthor Jr. and Superboy-Prime's fingerprints on them.

Initially it was enough to simply nudge events and let their subjects' natural instincts lead them into disaster, but eventually direct action was needed. Luthor Jr. had crossed over and impersonated his New Earth counterpart to found the Secret Society, unleashing atrocities as awful as any he had observed. His organization murdered the Freedom Fighters and used the monstrous Chemo to reduce Blüdhaven to smoking, toxic ruins. For his part, Superboy-Prime had stealthily shifted entire planets to further their schemes.

After Kal-L crossed over, he tried to recruit his cousin Power Girl (who had migrated to and integrated on New Earth) and a now-isolated Batman. Luthor Jr. needed beings connected to vanished Earths to power an enormous dimensional tuning-fork built from the Anti-Monitor's corpse. Combined with Luthor's own powers, it would rewrite reality.

When Power Girl refused to join their misguided and malign efforts, Superboy-Prime defeated her and plugged the hero into the machine before going on a murder spree across New Earth. His attack on Conner Kent triggered an army of Teen Titans rising up to defend Conner. At the height of

Superboy-Prime's slaughter, Kid Flash (Bart Allen) pushed the murderer into the Speed Force, aided by his ghostly grandfather Barry Allen, Johnny Quick, and Max Mercury.

A deafening silence
By the time Superboy-Prime escaped the kinetic dimension, attended by a fully grown Bart Allen, Luthor Jr. had restored Earth-2, just in time for Lois to die there. It was devoid of life, an empty ghost world where Kal-L's grief translated into a brutal clash with New Earth's Superman until Wonder Woman pacified them both.

Kal-L then joined the fight against the totally deranged Superboy-Prime. His capture cost many more lives—including 32 Green Lanterns, Conner Kent, and Kal-L himself—but the real damage had already been done. Luthor Jr. had unleashed the chaotic forces of fractured reality, restoring New Earth but also accidentally restoring a Multiverse.

New Earth's problems had not ended either. Batman destroyed Brother Eye with the aid of a new Blue Beetle, but the OMAC virus was still loose in the population. Many heroes were lost in space and more simply dead, killed by Superboy-Prime and the Secret Society in savage battles across the planet. The events

Missing in action
The world might have lost it greatest heroes, but not its desperate daily need for them.

In the end
The return of the Earth's champions was tinged with tragedy and came at a heavy price.

left New Earth reeling and in their wake recovery was slow. The demoralized Trinity, however, started to talk to each other again, outlining shocking plans.

Moreover, after the interconnected crises subsided, reality had once more been clearly altered, with very few knowing how or why. There were major changes for all to see—Superman, Wonder Woman, Batman, Robin, Nightwing, The Flash, Aquaman, Green Arrow, and others were gone. Missing in action. The Trinity and their allies had abandoned costumed personas for personal reasons. Some veterans—like The Flash Jay Garrick in Keystone City—tried holding the line, but it would be a long time before Earth had Teen Titans or a Justice League again.

As humanity mourned and rebuilt, ordinary mortal Clark Kent fought crime with journalism. Mayor of Star

City Oliver Queen tackled greed from behind a desk. DEO agent Diana Prince worked with a gun and computer files, while Bruce Wayne and his wards had disappeared. Booster Gold patrolled Metropolis, courting sponsors, while the enigmatic Supernova reminded the world what true heroism was. John Henry Irons (Steel) clashed with niece Natasha. She wanted powers and sought them from Lex Luthor's Everyman Project, even though the process had mutated Irons into solid metal. On New Year's Eve, the Project reached a grim and bloody conclusion.

Flavor of the week
Still mourning his wife, Ralph Dibny probed a resurrection cult targeting Wonder Girl, who could not accept Connor Kent's death. Soon Dibny abandoned rationalism for magic. Gotham City saw a new Bat-masked avenger terrorizing crooks, a Bible of Crime converting mobsters into

fanatics, and ex-cop Renee Montoya chasing Intergang thugs before being chosen by Vic Sage (the Question) as his disciple. Their journey led Renee to the ends of the Earth and a future full of questions.

Rip in time
After solving the mystery of 52, Time Master Rip Hunter and his protégé Booster Gold had to save this new Multiverse from eradication.

> "It's time for heroes who don't just patrol the world... they change it!
>
> **Black Adam** | *52 #3*

When survivors of Donna Troy's mission to repair a tear in space returned mutated, maimed, and exhausted, nobody knew that Animal Man, Starfire, and sightless Adam Strange were still marooned light-years from anywhere. Being found by Lobo, the deadliest bounty hunter in the universe, did not (initially) help them. And everywhere bizarre occurrences of the number "52" were appearing.

Across the world, mad scientists vanished, congregating on Oolong island in the China Seas with unlimited resources and encouraged to let their creativity run wild. One such was Metal Men inventor Will Magnus, craving to prove himself and return to rationality and heroic ways. In Kahndaq, Shazam-powered despot Black Adam found love and a new family. His transformation into a force for good was cruelly ended by an unforgiving American intelligence agency who deployed the Suicide Squad to bring tragedy and disaster back into his life. This sparked Black Adam's declaration of war on the world.

Supernova's true identity obsessed Metropolis and was later revealed as a ploy by Booster Gold and his mentor Rip

Unjustice league
Firestorm's dream of leading a new Justice League died due to a lack of suitable talent and motivation.

Playtime

After *Infinite Crisis*, DC reset its timeline, offering stories set "One Year Later." This fresh start offered a jumping-on point for newcomers and fascinated fans eager to know how reality had changed. Regular titles carried current events as usual, while yearlong weekly series *52* unveiled how everyone got there, employing new or minor players in a saga devoid of crossovers—because it happened "a year ago."

Everything built toward another momentous spectacle at the end. Maxi-series *52* unfolded in real time—a day-by-day diary systematically detailing what happened between *Infinite Crisis #7* and current DC releases, in a rolling flashback that concluded where One Year Later began. Contributing titles all carried a cover symbol and the company-wide shake-up led to flood of new series.

Cowritten by Geoff Johns, Grant Morrison, Greg Rucka, and Mark Waid, *52* was a unique publishing landmark proving the power of forward planning and solid editing. Pages were roughed out by Keith Giffen, for stellar illustrators to finish, and each issue boasted spectacular covers by J. G. Jones and Alex Sinclair that integrated image, logo, trade dress, and reading order.

Pencillers Ken Lashley, Shawn Moll, Todd Nauck, Chris Batista, Joe Bennett, Eddy Barrows, Tom Derenick, Jamal Igle, Phil Jimenez, Drew Johnson, Dan Jurgens, Patrick Olliffe, Joe Prado, Dale Eaglesham, Andy Smith, Giuseppe Camuncoli, Mike McKone, and Darick Robertson delivered the astounding serial in weekly installments.

Hunter, who had uncovered a dire threat to existence and needed to distract everyone while they dealt with it.

At long last, heroes reappeared. Batman, Robin, and Nightwing resurfaced far from home, Clark Kent's Kryptonian cells were finally recharged enough to make him a Superman again, and Donna Troy inherited the mission and title of Wonder Woman.

Whose counting?

Starfire and Adam Strange eventually returned to Earth, the inventors of Oolong Island reaped just rewards for their manic inventiveness, and Booster Gold and Rip Hunter learned the fateful secret of "52." The Time Masters had covertly scoured space-time for a mastermind behind New Earth's woes and found the end of creation imminent. With time running out, they defeated the chrono-devouring cosmic predator Mister Mind only to discover the incredible truth—New Earth was only one of 52 alternate realities in an enclosed Multiverse.

As the planet caught its collective breath, a countdown began... ∎

Key issues

One Year Later

July 2006–July 2007

52 #1–52, World War III #1–4

Tie-ins (November 2005–July 2006)

Firestorm #17–22, Green Arrow #17–18, Adventures of Superman #645, 648–49, JSA #79–80, 82, JSA Classified #4, Birds of Prey #87–90, JLA #120–125, Outsiders #29–33, Gotham Central #37, Hawkman #7–18, Superman #223–226, Aquaman #37, Green Lantern #7–18, Wonder Woman #224, Robin #146–147, Teen Titans #32–33, Annual #3, Nightwing #116, Action Comics #836, Infinite Crisis Special: Day of Vengeance #1, Infinite Crisis Special: Rann–Thanagar War #1, Infinite Crisis Secret Files and Origins #1, Infinite Crisis Special: The OMAC Project #1, Infinite Crisis Special: Villains United #1

Spin-offs (June 2007–September 2010)

Infinite Crisis Aftermath: The Battle for Blüdhaven #1–6, Infinite Crisis Aftermath: The Spectre #1–3, Secret Six #1–6, Ion #1–12, Checkmate #1–31, Shadowpact #1–25, DCU: Brave New World #1, All–New Atom #1–25, Creeper #1–6, Martian Manhunter #1–8, OMAC #1–8, The Trials of Shazam! #1–12, Uncle Sam and the Freedom Fighters #1–8, Booster Gold #1–47, Black Adam: The Dark Age #1–6, Infinity Inc. #1–12, 52 Aftermath: Crime Bible–Five Lessons of Blood #1–5, 52 Aftermath: The Four Horsemen #1–6, Metal Men #1–8, The Great Ten #1–9

Seven Soldiers

April 2005–December 2006

In an era of innovative and complex, interwoven storytelling, one of DC's oldest properties received a 21st-century makeover in a compelling two-issue prestige limited series conceived and scripted by **Grant Morrison** and illustrated by **J. H. Williams III**. The tip of a creative iceberg with most of its material lying just below the surface waiting for later events to reference, *Seven Soldiers* introduced DC readers to the concept of nonteams in an epic crossover event.

Seven for a secret
Brilliantly manipulated, a group of heroes and villains carried out a universally critical mission without ever being aware of the cause or cost of failure.

A coproduction between DC and All-American Comics, the Justice Society of America's 1941 launch altered the budding comics industry forever, but the game-changing innovation was slow in spreading. While a few competitors compiled hero-groups during the 1940s, it would be decades before the notion became an industry standard. In the meantime, scant months after the JSA debut, DC doubled down, launching their own proprietary squad of solo stars who hadn't made it into the co-produced Golden Age team. They joined a growing battalion of other groups—Kid Gangs like Newsboy Legion and Boy Commandos and military groups like Ghost Patrol and Red, White & Blue.

Editors never settled on a name for their second team. Non-superpowered mystery men Crimson Avenger and Wing, Star-Spangled Kid and Stripesy, Sir Justin, the Shining Knight, Vigilante, and Green Arrow and Speedy (who premiered as a team in *Leading Comics* #1) were retroactively and alternatively dubbed the Law's Legionnaires or the Seven Soldiers of Victory. They joined forces 14 times without ever gaining a title logo, simply grouped together on spectacular covers, before vanishing as World War II closed.

Lucky sevens

The heroes were rescued from obscurity—and exile in different time eras during the 1970s—thanks to the combined efforts of the Justice Society and Justice League of America, but

Never to be told
Despite being inextricably linked, the victorious Seven Soldiers never once simultaneously occupied the same time or space.

somehow never achieved their true potential. In 2000, another seven-strong team (Adam Strange, Mento, Batgirl, Metamorpho, Blackhawk, Shining Knight, and Deadman) briefly convened to face alien terror Agamemno, but it required a threat to existence itself to see the soldiers reach full potential. All it took was a wildly ambitious, self-contained event that proved some teams work better apart than together.

At the fringes of reality lurked existential threats to humanity.

> "We weren't hunting **it**. They were hunting **us**, all along."
>
> **I, Spyder** | *Seven Soldiers: #0*

Perhaps the worst was the Sheeda, predators who periodically voyaged from the end of time to harrow humanity and destroy its greatest heroes. The winged horrors and their ghastly queen were acutely sensitive to the number seven—targeting combat and heroic groups with that number of operatives, such as the Ultramarine Corps (*Justice League Classified* #1–3, Jan.–Mar. 2005).

This was due to a prophecy handed down through time that their defeat would come at the hands of seven soldiers, and it shaped the Sheeda's tactics over successive waves of assaults across eons. That there were so many was due to the subtle machinations of the marauding horde's greatest opponents—a self-perpetuating cadre known as the Seven Unknown Men of Slaughter Swamp. They were tasked by equally unknown masters with safeguarding universal continuity. They were never combatants but rather administrators tirelessly organizing forces against the Sheeda, but recent efforts had been failing. When their seventh teammate—Bulleteer—missed the rendezvous, the Unknown Men's most recent unit (Vigilante; the Whip; Gimmix; Dyno-Mite Dan; Boy Blue; and I, Spyder) fell to a Sheeda ambush and were easily butchered.

Seven soldiers strike

Aware of imminent disaster for the present era, the Unknown Men orchestrated situations to set another seven on personal quests and into solo battles that could imperceptibly advance their covert war against the Sheeda. Each unsuspecting combatant had an indirect connection to the previous group but ostensibly pursued their own agenda. Zatanna, Bulleteer, Manhattan Guardian, witch boy Klarion, second Mister Miracle Shilo Norman, monster-hunter Frankenstein, and time-displaced Sir Ystin, Shining Knight from an obscure primordial Camelot, each encountered Sheeda incursions singly and overcame them.

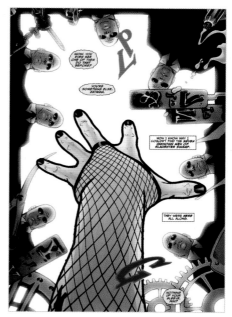

Mystery men
If the situation demanded, the Seven Unknown Men of Slaughter Swamp might intervene, but not if it meant taking any significant action.

Thanks to Zatanna's instinctively uttered spell "ekirts sreidlos neves," each reached New York City just as S.H.A.D.E. agent Frankenstein brought Castle Revolving (the Sheeda's floating fortress) back from the future. Joined by Vigilante (secretly an undying werewolf) and recently resurrected I, Spyder, they separately, but in unison, subverted the Queen's mystical Cauldron of Rebirth and inflicted a crushing defeat on the terrors out of time. ∎

Magical surrealism

Seven Soldiers was a bold storytelling experiment as writer Morrison told individual stories in parallel while moving the core narrative arc through each limited series in a modular manner. This delivered a startling epic of doomed heroes simultaneously but separately fighting a futile final battle. Morrison termed their experiment—comprising 30 issues in total—a "megaseries" or "metaseries." In 2006, it won the Eisner Award for Best Finite/ Limited Series.

The seven sub-series were bookended by *Seven Soldiers* #0 and #1, offering the beginnings and conclusion while the nested features showed how heroes who never met had worked together to save humanity. The stories employed a range of design and typographic styles, emphasizing mood and depicting psychedelic

sensibilities. Each component series carried a (seven) starred spangled banner above its title.

The seven soldier tales were powerfully and distinctively illustrated by Simone Bianchi (*Shining Knight*), Cameron Stewart (*Manhattan Guardian*), Ryan Sook (*Zatanna*), Frazer Irving (*Klarion*), Doug Mahnke (*Frankenstein*), Yanick Paquette (*Bulleteer*), and Pasqual Ferry and Freddie Williams II (*Mister Miracle*), and stylistically looked like nothing else on the market at the time.

Seven Soldiers was retroactively announced to have occurred one week before the events of *Infinite Crisis*, and few of its stars appeared after the conclusion of that major event, aside or a brief transdimensional clash with the teleporting teen hero Sideways in 2018-2019.

Sinestro Corps War

August 2007–February 2008

Cornerstones of DC continuity, the Green Lantern Corps and Guardians of the Universe had spent decades largely sidelined. Writer **Geoff Johns** was determined to restore their preeminence, and with cowriter **Dave Gibbons** and artists **Ivan Reis**, **Patrick Gleason**, and other artists reinvented cosmic physics and the history of creation during a terrifying assault on Earth in the *Sinestro Corps War*.

Force majeure
Sinestro rebelled against the Guardians because they would not do what was needed to compel universal order. His new corps would ensure perfect peace through total terror.

Hal Jordan of Earth saved existence countless times in service to the Guardians of the Universe but, after being corrupted by primal fear entity Parallax, killed most of his comrades. Jordan attempted to unmake reality, but ultimately redeemed himself, giving his life to save his homeworld. After years of atonement as the human conscience guiding the Spectre, Jordan was reborn as part of a restored Green Lantern Corps.

Following Jordan's rebirth (*Green Lantern: Rebirth* #1–6, Dec. 2004–May 2005), Geoff Johns continued his mission to make the emerald warrior a cornerstone of DC's Universe, crafting increasingly ambitious storylines and major events. This culminated in transgalactic war in *Green Lantern* and *Green Lantern Corps* (written by Dave Gibbons), with tie-ins and spin-offs in other space-themed titles.

Here be monsters!

The star-spanning epic began in *Green Lantern: Sinestro Corps Special* #1 (Aug. 2007) in *Prologue: The Second Rebirth*. This saw Sinestro reinventing himself after retreating to planet Qward in the anti-matter universe. Taming the yellow light of the emotional spectrum, the obsessive seeker of order mass-produces yellow rings to arm his own corps. Recruiting from the most heinous beings in existence, Sinestro orders an army of ring-wielding warriors to destroy the peacekeepers of the Guardians of the Universe.

One of the Oans' longest-suppressed secrets was that emotions generated by sentient life are energies to be harnessed and manipulated. The phenomenon separates feelings into visible wavelengths, capable of affecting the material world in astonishing ways. Green Light is concentrated will, Blue is hope, Red embodies rage, and Yellow

Ion deficient
Paragon Green Lantern Kyle Rayner was brutally deprived of willpower to become the latest host of Fear entity Parallax.

> "I have been to every corner of every sector of the universe, and I have learned one thing. The universe **needs** to change."
>
> **Sinestro** | *Green Lantern: Sinestro Corps Special* #1

Prime numbers
Sinestro's dread and diverse assembly of evil included ruthless rivals Cyborg Superman and a now fully mature malevolent Superboy-Prime.

absolute security and total terror hits Earth after Sinestro's forces carve a bloody swathe through the galaxies. Here, they finally flounder when a last stand of Green Lanterns unite with Earth's Super Heroes, and immortal Guardians pay a fateful final price to snatch a victory of sorts from the jaws of defeat. Sinestro, however, has played a deeper game all along, in expectation of even greater terrors to come.

Themes, portents, and characters incorporated in *Sinestro Corps War* originated in "Tygers," a 1986 Green Lantern Corps tale crafted by writer Alan Moore and artist Kevin O'Neill, and Geoff Johns further built on them in the subsequent months.

All of creation was shaken by the revelation that Green was not the only color of power. Emotional Spectrum energies underpinned new, audacious storylines. Johns and his co-creators developed disciples of each hue, and unleashed forces that transformed DC's continuity, signaling the fall of the Guardians under the weight of their own secrets. This escalating situation would lead inexorably to major crossover events *Blackest Night*, the sequel *Brightest Day,* and even more momentous milestones in the coming decades. ▪

channels fear. Reborn through his own determination, Sinestro uses the reanimated corpse of the Anti-Monitor as his battery of power and scours the universe for beings capable of "instilling great fear," whose subsequent acts of terror constantly fuel their rings. Co-opting Parallax to his cause and having it possess Kyle Rayner (the Green Lantern dubbed Ion), Sinestro convinces many Super-Villains—such as Cyborg Superman, the robot Manhunters, Mongul, and Superboy/Superman-Prime—to join his assault on everything good and safe and decent.

Attacking across creation, the Yellow horde decimates Green Lanterns, subverting where they do not destroy outright. Their final goal is Earth, where the heroes making ready for a last stand cannot know that Sinestro's entire campaign has been a huge bluff. His real intentions have been to force the Guardians to rewrite the sacred Book of Oa and their Green warriors' rules of engagement, thereby triggering a long-prophesied cosmic cataclysm.

Shoot to kill
With the Green Lanterns' stricture against lethal force removed, the universe-shaking battle between

Night falls
In the aftermath of Sinestro's war, Nekron used the Anti-Monitor's remains to make Black Lantern rings to bring about the Blackest Night.

Key issues

Green Lantern: Sinestro Corps Special #1 (August 2007)

Green Lantern #21–25 (September 2007–January 2008)

Green Lantern Corps #14–19 (September 2007–February 2008)

Tales of the Sinestro War: Parallax #1, Cyborg Superman #1, Superman-Prime #1, Ion #1 (November 2007–January 2008) Tie-ins.

Blue Beetle #20 (December 2007) Tie-in.

Green Lantern/Sinestro Corps Secret Files and Origins #1 (February 2008)

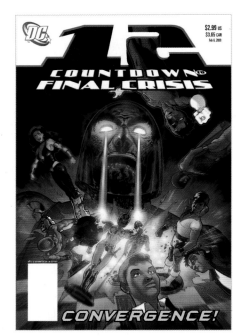

Countdown to Final Crisis

July 2007–June 2008

Something big was happening. Once again hints, signs, and limited series detailing portentous major changes were appearing. As concluding serial *52* reconciled past and present, the future looked increasingly grim. Lead writer **Paul Dini**, coplotter and breakdown artist **Keith Giffen**, and team scripters **Justin Gray**, **Jimmy Palmiotti**, **Tony Bedard**, **Adam Beechen**, and **Sean McKeever** had some answers and more questions revealed in the *Countdown to Final Crisis*.

Pawns in the game
Darkseid believed he was controlling the game, unaware that he was simply one of the pieces in play.

Beginning as *Countdown*—and retitled *Countdown to Final Crisis* at midpoint issue #26—the successor to *52* was another weekly serial generating a tightly woven braid of parallel and interlinked stories all moving to a single conclusion—invasion from Apokolips and subjugation of humanity.

Challenging times

The anthology saga was released in reverse order from #51 (May 2007). However, unlike its predecessor, *Countdown* was not a stand-alone series but crossed over into many titles during its run. The concluding issue was entitled *DC Universe* #0 (Jun. 2008). Primarily written by "showrunner" Paul Dini and a number of scripter/artist teams, it detailed a large cast of characters undergoing transformative adventures, all unwittingly advancing the devious schemes of Darkseid. The Fourth World was changing and an unknown force was systematically eliminating New Gods.

Since time was reordered and reality fractured into 52 universes, each has had its own Monitor, who safeguarded it and enforced Multiversal isolation. Now one rogue Monitor started killing "jumpers"—beings who migrated from their origin reality to another Earth. The resulting debate fractured the Monitors' previous solidarity and set them on a deadly path to civil war.

On New Earth, the killing of Duella Dent (The Joker's Daughter) by a Monitor prompted a Multiversal quest

Appointment in Samarkand
The crisscrossing paths of assorted heroes and villains was inescapably destined to end in death, destruction, and more mystery.

by Donna Troy, Jason Todd (Robin/ Red Hood), Green Lantern Kyle Rayner, and "Bob" the Monitor, in search of missing hero Ray Palmer (The Atom). The questers called themselves "Challengers of the Unknown," and as they roamed the Multiverse, their ranks grew to include many others.

Since the Bart Allen incarnation of The Flash had been murdered by the Rogues, innocent-but-implicated Pied Piper and Trickster had been running from Super Heroes and villains alike.

> ## "We came to serve notice! We're out there! Watch yourselves!"
>
> **The Atom (Ray Palmer)** | *Countdown to Final Crisis #1*

Mission creep

Following a weekly serial told in real time, DC's second narrative breakthrough was a yearlong buildup to the third stage of an epic trilogy. Like *52*, *Countdown* incorporated its title (decreasing by one every issue) into the cover design, with identifying trade dress restricted to some, but not all, tie-ins. This was to ensure the "big reveal" at the end would not be diminished or surprise revelations of later installments compromised. Issues contained context-supplying backup features—beginning with a post-*Infinite Crisis* history of reality,

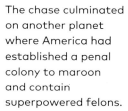

told (by Dan Jurgens and Norm Rapmund) from the point of view of the 52 individual and increasingly at-odds Monitors who each oversaw one of the universes comprising the Multiverse. On completion, the backup was replaced by brief tales outlining the origins of characters who appeared in that issue's main feature.

Companion titles such as *Countdown: Arena #1-4* (Feb. 2008) and *Countdown to Mystery #1-8* (Nov. 2007–Jun 2008) all shared the distinctive logo, and tie-ins such as *Captain Carrot and the Final Ark #1-3* (Oct.–Dec. 2007) or *All-New Atom #15* (Nov. 2007) were badged

with a banner strap line indicating participation. However, connected series like *Amazons Attack!*, *Salvation Run*, and *Death of the New Gods* were devoid of cover indicators, ensuring narrative disclosures were not given away too soon.

Countdown was subject to late revision and the plot shifted somewhat from the original aims, often while individual issues were being produced. Even the concluding #0 was altered and retitled *DC Universe #0* (Jun. 2008) to better emphasize the broad, far-reaching changes anticipated in the imminent event—*Final Crisis*.

The chase culminated on another planet where America had established a penal colony to maroon and contain superpowered felons.

Meanwhile, Jimmy Olsen developed unpredictable superpowers that manifested only when his life was endangered. Mary Marvel sought her lost Shazam powers and, after sharing the magical energies of Black Adam, was progressively corrupted until she became a pawn of Eclipso and Darkseid, despite the intervention of Zatanna and other magical champions.

Harley Quinn and Holly Robinson (Catwoman's sidekick) both craved redemption and fell under the sway of goddess Hera. They did not know the true deity had been secretly replaced by Granny Goodness of Apokolips, who triggered an Amazon attack on America.

Exiled from the future, Karate Kid and Una (Triplicate Girl) hunted for a cure to the Morticoccus virus killing the super-martial artist. Their search took them to Earth 51, where they met Al

Fathers and sons
At no stage did Darkseid believe that he would be the loser in the long-prophesied final showdown with his ungrateful firstborn.

Brother Eye, Buddy Blank/OMAC, the Great Disaster, and the boy who would one day be Kamandi. In space, as the Fourth World disintegrated, the debased alternate Superboy-Prime grew up, embracing true evil, destroying worlds, torturing Mr. Mxyzptlk, and joining the growing legions of Monarch.

The murderous tyrant was exactly the kind of threat the disunited, increasingly warring Monitors should have tackled. Monarch gathered the worst examples of super-killers from across the Multiverse, building a formidable army of conquest.

Crisis point

As more New Gods died, Jimmy Olsen arrived on Apokolips where, thanks to insectoid Forager, he learned he was a "soul-catcher" inadvertently storing dead deities' life forces. It was all part of Darkseid's plan, but it went awry

when Ray Palmer destroyed the soul tech and Orion arrived to fulfill an ancient prophecy by killing his sire.

However, this act was a beginning, not an end. As Earth 51's Monitor Nix Uotan ended the war between his fellows and Palmer, Donna Troy, Forager, and Kyle Rayner appointed themselves watchmen overseeing the Monitors continued good behavior, all were unaware that the *Final Crisis* had already begun. On New Earth, Darkseid's inner circle were paving the way for their master's arrival and accession. ■

Final Crisis

July 2008–March 2009

Worlds lived and died again as an ambitious program of renewal concluded with continuity reconfigured in advance of fresh mega-events and stories starring DC's greatest heroes. Scripted by **Grant Morrison** and illustrated by **J.G. Jones**, **Carlos Pacheco**, **Marco Rudy**, and **Doug Mahnke**, the death of Jack Kirby's Fourth World and advent of a crueler, more complex Fifth World on Earth was the goal of the *Final Crisis*.

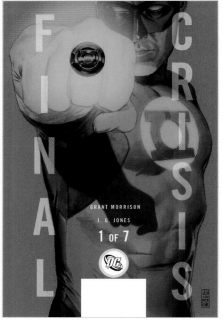

Green screen
The first phase of Darkseid's convoluted plan was accomplished by removing Hal Jordan, Earth's most effective Green Lantern.

It began with the death of gods, assassinated by the Source because their time was done. Darkseid, however, was killed by his son Orion, and his spirit tumbled through space time. His passing disrupted reality, creating a singularity at creation's center that began drawing in everything.

His minions' essences were drawn to Earth. Rescuing Darkseid's personality, they possessed humans, while agent Libra propounded a religion of crime, gathering an army of Super-Villains whose first triumph was murdering the Martian Manhunter.

As Darkseid burned through the form of New York gangster Boss Dark Side, an intergalactic emergency was declared when Orion was shot and killed. The Green Lantern Corps claimed jurisdiction but their agent Kraken was possessed by Granny Goodness, who framed Hal Jordan for the crime.

Submit

Accused of dereliction of duty, Nix Uotan was reduced to humanity and sentenced to Earth by his fellow Monitors. Darkseid possessed police officer Dan Turpin but found the cop's will as resolute as his own. Attacks on Earth's heroes mounted. Wonder Woman was infected with the Morticoccus Virus and Lois Lane nearly died when the *Daily Planet* was bombed. Mary Marvel, possessed by Desaad, brutalized Earth.

Barry Allen, the second Flash, escaped the Speed Force. Pursued by the Black Racer (New God personification of Death), Allen recruited Wally West to run beside him back through time. The bullet that killed Orion had been fired from the future, and reality might be saved if they caught it before it killed him.

Superman won a chance to save Lois, joining Monitor Zillo Valla's posse of Multiversal heroes exiting reality to fight the source of all evil, Monitor

Mandrakk. The clash took the Man of Steel into the future, where the Legion of Super-Heroes shared plans for a wish-granting Miracle Machine.

Without Superman to help humanity, Darkseid's forces won. When The Flashes left the time stream, Earth was paralyzed by the Anti-Life Equation via the Internet. Those still possessing free will resisted, but corrupted Super Heroes controlled by Anti-Life imposing Justifier helmets became Darkseid's shock troopers. In space, Green Lanterns were prevented from helping by an impenetrable wall of time distortion.

Yet, there was still hope. In the dawn of humanity, New God Metron had entrusted caveboy Anthro with a symbol that would negate Anti-Life. Now it

Quest for fire
Divine forward planner Metron left the key to Darkseid's defeat with a primitive blessed with the power of imagination and resilience of a hero.

was revived and disseminated by minor Super-Villain the Tattooed Man; Sonny Sumo; Japanese heroes Super Young Team; and Shilo Norman (apprentice of Mister Miracle Scott Free) as part of a concerted counterattack. Lex Luthor and Dr. Sivana disrupted commands sent to the Justifier helmets, while the Ray painted Earth with the ancient liberty symbol.

Resist

The timing was perfect. Earlier in Darkseid's scheme, Batman had been abducted to be a template for cloned soldiers. He escaped and shot Darkseid with the bullet intended for Orion, before being killed himself. The distraction allowed the Flashes to draw both the Omega Force and the Black Racer to Darkseid. The villain was finally destroyed when recently restored Wonder Woman used her Lasso of Truth to banish Darkseid's soul from Turpin's body. At that moment, Nix Uotan resumed his true form and joined the fight...

Crisis management

Final Crisis unfolded in seven extra-length issues over nine months, with supplemental but interlinked limited series and one-shots—such as *Superman Beyond #1–2* and *Final Crisis: Legion of 3 Worlds #1–5* (Oct. 2008–Sep. 2009)—running in parallel but woven into crucial points of the saga. Writer Morrison later announced his suggested reading order was *Final Crisis #1–3*, *Superman Beyond #1–2*, *Final Crisis: Submit*, *Final Crisis #4–5*, *Batman #682–683*, and *Final Crisis #6–7*.

The core saga offered two styles of covers, printed on enhanced glossy card stock and providing luxurious quality for the last chapter of the "Crisis Trilogy." The conclusion set up years of successive Batman storylines, as seen in *Battle for the Cowl* and 2010's *Blackest Knight* (*Batman and Robin #7-9*), and *Batman: The Return of Bruce Wayne #1–6*.

Official one-shots *Last Will and Testament, Requiem, Resist, Secret Files,* and *Submit,* plus miniseries *Superman Beyond* and *Rogue's Revenge,* were designed as key parts of the saga and intended to be read at specific junctures in the narrative (such as *Last Will and Testament* between *Final Crisis #3* and #4).

Otherwise unbadged, early tie-in issues carried DC's "Sightings" banner, signifying content especially worthy of readers' attention. Unofficial, unbadged, limited series *Terror Titans* (Dec. 2008–May 2009) was set during the early stages of *Final Crisis,* with young metahumans cage fighting at New York's Dark Side Club and Apokolips' invasion HQ prior to conquering Earth.

Darkseid's essence eroded reality's core and summoned Mandrakk from his realm beyond. Existence faded into darkness, but the champions of countless Earths united against him, as Superman returned to deploy the Miracle Machine—saving everything and granting reality a happy ending. In the aftermath, it was discovered that the Monitors were gone, leaving Nix Uotan sole Superjudge of existence and leader of a pan-dimensional League defending Multiversity everywhere.

Batman's "death" and Bruce Wayne's eventual return sparked epic tales. His absence inspired many seeking

Requiem
The grieving heroes could not know the corpse was a clone and the true Batman now dwelt with Anthro at the dawn of history.

a worthy successor to keep predators at bay, but a "Battle of the Cowl" ended the only way it could, with Dick Grayson becoming Batman until the original returned. ■

Key issues

July 2008–March 2009

DC Universe #0, Final Crisis #1–7, Terror Titans #1–6

Tie-ins (July 2008–March 2009)

Final Crisis: Requiem #1, DCU: Last Will and Testament #1, Final Crisis: Submit #1, Final Crisis: Resist #1, Final Crisis: Rage of the Red Lanterns #1, Final Crisis: Secret Files and Origins #1, Final Crisis: Revelations #1–5, Final Crisis: Rogues Revenge #1–3, Final Crisis: Legion of 3 Worlds #1–5, Final Crisis: Superman Beyond #1–2

Crossovers (January 2009–October 2010)

Batman #682–683, 701–702, Justice League of America #21–27, Superman/Batman #76, Superman #670, Action Comics #866, Superman: New Krypton Special #1, Reign in Hell #4, Birds of Prey #118, The Flash #240, Infinity Inc. #11–12, Teen Titans #59–60

Aftermath (May 2009– April 2010)

Battle for the Cowl #1–3, Final Crisis Aftermath: Run #1–6, Final Crisis Aftermath: Dance #1–6, Final Crisis Aftermath: Escape #1–6, Final Crisis Aftermath: Ink #1–6, The Flash: Rebirth #1–6

> ## "Don't push your luck with the Judge of All Evil!"
>
> **Nix Uotan, the Superjudge** | *Final Crisis #7*

Blackest Night

June 2009–May 2010

After years of foreshadowing, a long-building terror finally assaulted existence on all fronts. It targeted heroes, villains, and their loved ones—not just the living but even those who had died. No one was safe. Writer **Geoff Johns** and artist **Ivan Reis**'s core series touched every corner of DC continuity, while reanimated characters in resurrected titles and new limited series all endured the agony and horror of the *Blackest Night*.

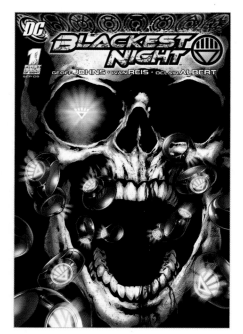

Face of death
Black Lantern power rings sought out and reanimated the dead, magnified all the anger, pain, and resentment of their lives and programmed them to kill.

For all their power and an apparent revolving-door of death for Super Heroes, the toll of the lost and the fallen in the DCU is vast. This underpinned *Blackest Night*, when the dead returned, charged by a malign manifestation of mortality with inflicting the agonies of the damned on the living.

The premise was simple and brilliant. Previously, whenever someone had returned to life—like Hal Jordan or Barry Allen—it was no miracle, but part of Nekron's malignant plan to abolish the very notion of Life. Superman, Green Arrow, Red Hood Jason Todd, Bart Allen (Impulse/Kid Flash/Flash IV), Donna Troy, and many more were resurrected as links in a chain of incidents to replace the light of Life's emotional spectrum with the black gleam of all-encompassing Death.

Hand of death

The Guardians of the Universe were reeling under successive, long-dreaded, prophesied crises when Nekron struck. Previous attempts had failed due to the Green Lantern Corps, but now the Lord of the Unliving acted through an avatar. Black Hand targeted heroes across creation, unleashing ruthless revenants of fallen loved ones who were animated by Black Lantern power rings.

As seen in the limited series *Blackest Night* by Geoff Johns, Ivan Reis, Oclair Albert, Rob Hunter, Julio Ferreira, and Joe Prado—and in dozens of tie-in tales—cosmic catastrophe had been

Rainbow warriors
Led by Green Lanterns and Super Hero survivors, Blue, Indigo, Violet, Orange, Red, and Yellow champions of Life turned back Black Hand's raging hordes.

building since time began. When the deeply divided Guardians admitted their eons-long efforts to forestall the Blackest Night had failed, "Scar" announced her own corruption by killing a fellow Guardian.

This activated black rings across existence—seemingly resurrecting Green Lanterns, Super Heroes, villains,

> ## "Barry Allen. You owe me your life. You all do."
>
> **Nekron** | *Blackest Night #4*

and loved ones. On Earth, the dearly departed stalked their nearest and dearest, sparking terror, love, grief, compassion, and other emotions the zombies used to fuel their rings... and feed something else.

First responders Jordan and Allen spearheaded the fightback. The Flash (Barry Allen) knew bodies meant nothing—Black Lantern zombies were just power rings using downloaded memories. Programmed to act with murderous rage, and using familiar bodies to provoke emotional responses, the simulations fed on feelings until they could tear the hearts from the living—figuratively and literally.

However, black rings were not infallible. One unsuccessfully targeted Don Hall's grave. The original Dove stayed buried and at peace, unlike his brother Hank, revived as an even more savage Hawk. Boston Brand reeled in psychic shock after his long-buried corpse was reanimated. Seeking to repossess his own skeleton, Deadman suffered a torrent of stored memories and discovered how Black Hand brought about the Blackest Night.

Guardian Ganthet took drastic steps and exposed the Emotional

Grave ideas
Failed super-thief William Hand discovered his true destiny only after Nekron paroled him from death to be his agent among the living.

Spectrum's secret. Together, the seven wavelengths of the Spectrum formed a pure White Light of Life that reversed death—if the right people wore the component rings. Leading a task force comprising the entire Spectrum, Jordan battled Nekron as

Green Lanterns Guy Gardner and Kyle Rayner gathered ring-bearers of all hues for Life's last counterattack.

Buried treasure

At ground zero, hero Dawn Granger changed everything. The new Dove was an avatar of Peace and her touch obliterated Black Lanterns. Navigating the escalating chaos, she liberated Nekron's hidden power reservoir while he was occupied elsewhere, revealing a gleaming white Entity hidden beneath Earth for eons. Life's personification was always Nekron's true target. Every action he took over billions of years was simply to get him close enough to kill it. With all creation succumbing to eternal darkness, its least likely champion took on the White Lantern power to save everything and proved that even the likes of Sinestro had a place and purpose.

The climax of *Blackest Night* ended one threat, but its endgame left a dozen of the undead hordes fully restored to life. Their sudden return proved the universe wasn't out of the dark woods yet—and even greater deeds would be needed from those reborn in sequel event *Brightest Day*. ■

Resurrection shuffle

Blackest Night was part of an ambitious cycle of crossover story arcs devised by Geoff Johns and centered around Green Lantern. Following *The Sinestro Corps War* and part of the all-encompassing *War of Light* mega-event, the core series ran for eight months with all tie-ins carefully coordinated to conclude in May 2010. This was to capitalize on the last issue's shock ending and maximize interest in the sequel *Brightest Day*, which launched a month later.

The event highlighted powerful new costume and character designs by Ivan Reis, Joe Prado, and others, which participating issues adapted for the eerie

trade dress over-title banner. This included nine three-issue limited series examining the effects of the zombie apocalypse on major stars like Superman, Wonder Woman, and The Flash.

Another sidebar strand revived defunct comic book series *The Atom and Hawkman*, *Phantom Stranger*, *Green Arrow*, *Adventure Comics*, *Starman*, *The Question*, *Catwoman*, *Weird Western Tales*, and *The Power of Shazam!*, for a spooky last hurrah. All were carefully calculated to appeal to older fans and intensify the sense of impending, inescapable doom.

Brightest Day

June 2010–October 2011

After darkness comes the dawn, but that doesn't always bode well or bring contentment. *Blackest Night* revealed that the entity embodying universal life had hidden and hibernated in Earth but was now awake and exposed. Inspired scripters **Geoff Johns** and **Peter J. Tomasi**, and a host of top artists, spearheaded a yearlong, mass crossover event exploring the idea that after death comes birth, rebirth, and renewed purpose on the ***Brightest Day***.

Fight for your life
The risen dead were beyond the call of good or evil but were chosen to repair Earth in ways traditional Super Heroes could not fathom.

Blackest Night saw heroes, their enemies, and even loved ones reanimated by Black Lantern rings in a ghastly crusade ordered by death entity Nekron, seeking to eliminate his counterpart, the White Entity of Life. The champions of creation fought valiantly and the attempt ended with the slumbering vital spirit awakening from eons of hidden slumber in the depths of Earth.

Brightest Day found 12 Black Lantern zombies restored to life—Maxwell Lord, Captain Boomerang, Eobard Thawne, Jade, Hawk, Firestorm component Ronnie Raymond, Aquaman, Hawkman, Hawkwoman, J'onn J'onzz, Osiris, and Boston Brand. In the shining light of day, disembodied spirit Deadman found himself corporeal again yet still invisible to the majority of humanity.

Carpe diem

Brand had bonded to a white power ring that advised him to "live," and he now also demonstrated unexpected new gifts, accidentally resurrecting a dead bird. A mysterious voice screamed "Help me" and Brand was teleported away, arriving beside Super Hero Dove (Dawn Granger) and menaced by returned Hawk (Hank Hall). Hall once more attempted to bring back his deceased brother, Don, who was "at peace" during Blackest Night and remained so even after Hawk forced Deadman to attempt his "resurrection touch."

Other White Entity beneficiaries had no power rings but were given vague missions by the voice. The Entity's awakening had reshaped worlds and people—Star City was overwhelmed by a colossal forest, while Aquaman could now control only dead sea life.

The world soon learned of these "rebirths," and debate erupted over why these heroes—and villains such as

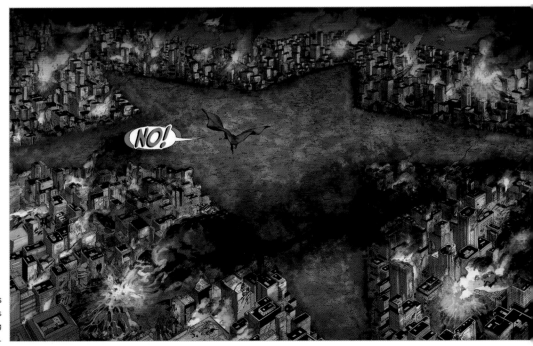

Reborn in flames
As Star City burned, the entity remade J'onn J'onzz as the world's new earth elemental, before sacrificing him against a Black Lantern Swamp Thing.

Brand awareness
From its place of concealment, the Life Entity selectively revoked the finality of death, psychically chaining reborn Boston Brand to the key players in its plan to rejuvenate creation.

Lord and cold-blooded murderers like Boomerang and Reverse-Flash—rather than gentle, good-hearted individuals such as Elongated Man and his wife, Sue, were recalled to life. Instead of providing answers, the voice doled out obscure tasks whose completion would ensure that those who had returned would remain alive. Many of these tasks would be completed in other related titles, not the core narrative.

Green dividend

Brightest Day unfolded in a twice-monthly core series over a year, beginning with issue #0 and concluding with #24. Like its predecessor *Blackest Night*, it carried a unified design for trade dress that also featured on 94 tie-in crossovers, and one-shots such as *The Atom Special*. Spin-off series *Justice League: Generation Lost* by writer Keith Giffen and artist Judd Winick also appeared twice a month, with issues published on alternate weeks.

The event was used to relaunch a number of regular series, such as *The Flash*, *Green Arrow*, and *Birds of Prey*, and these too carried the banners and badges of *Brightest Day* for as long as they tied in to the event, which was, in some instances, a full year. More than 40 additional assorted issues joined the event without carrying the *Brightest Day* logo banner.

The core limited series was written by Geoff Johns and Peter J. Tomasi, and penciled by Ivan Reis, Patrick Gleason, Ardian Syaf, Fernando Pasarin, Scott Clark, Joe Prado, and Rob Hunter, bringing DC's continuity to the moment *Flashpoint* began. The event closed with the limited series *Brightest Day Aftermath: The Search for the Swamp Thing* (#1–3 Aug.–Oct. 2011), bringing Vertigo characters Swamp Thing and John Constantine back into the DC fold, in advance of a root-and-branch reboot in *DC Comics: The New 52*.

> "I want to live. Do you hear me?
> I want my **second chance!**"
>
> **Boston Brand** | *Brightest Day #14*

Go into the light
Long reconciled to existing as a barely noticed, bodiless outsider, Deadman struggled to cope with being the prime player in a cosmic drama to literally fix the world.

Aquaman rescued Black Manta's son Jackson Hyde, preventing war between Atlantis and Xebel, while Firestorm stopped Black Lantern counterpart Deathstorm from killing the White Entity, before battling a revived Anti Monitor. Maxwell Lord's psychic power made (almost) everyone on Earth forget he ever existed. His task was to prevent demigod Magog from creating a generational Super Hero Armageddon (seen in alternate Earth tale *Kingdom Come*).

On the Red Planet, Martian Manhunter made the dead world bloom again before battling deranged survivor D'Kay D'razz and returning to Earth as its environmental defender. Jade had to "balance the darkness," Osiris freed his sister Isis (goddess of nature), and Eobard Thawne rescued his ancestor Bart Allen from the Speed Force.

Eternally reincarnating lovers Hawkman and Hawkwoman had died countless times since their murder in Ancient Egypt, but this time was different. When ancient enemy Hath-Set seized the planet Thanagar, he was empowered by hundreds of magically reactivated skeletons: centuries of the Hawks' remains previously acquired by the wizard. Despite this, the Winged Wonders fulfilled their individual tasks.

Elemental endgame
As a Black Lantern Swamp Thing imperiled all life on Earth, the White Entity's plan entered its final phase and its original planetary plant paladin bloomed again.

Night and day

The idea of an Emotional Electromagnetic Spectrum was first conceived by writer Geoff Johns in *Green Lantern: Rebirth #3* (Feb. 2005). His extrapolation of long-established powers of color—the green light of the Guardians of the Universe, Sinestro's yellow ring energy, and the Zamarons's violet light—was gradually expanded until it became a underlying aspect of DC cosmology. By the time of *Darkest Night* and *Brightest Day*, the concept had gelled into both rationalistic science and foreboding prophecy.

All Multiversal life forms generate emotions: tangible energies divided into seven distinct forms, recognized as a spectrum of colors. They comprise a near-infinite power reservoir that can be accessed through unique intermediaries—Entities. Living embodiments of each emotion, these avatars of colors represent its primal characteristics. Willpower is green and personified by Ion, while Fear is yellow, residing within sinister avatar Parallax. Hope, Compassion, Love, Rage and Avarice are blue, indigo, violet, red and orange, embodied respectively by Adara, Proselyte, Predator, The Butcher,

and Ophidian. Now the Emotional Spectrum embraces fundamental forces—Death (Black) and Life (White). Wedding past triumphs to modern innovation, Johns repurposed a forgotten villain into a governing Entity—Nekron.

Created by Mike W. Barr, Joe Staton, and Frank McLaughlin for *Tales of the Green Lantern Corps* (#1–3, May–Jul. 1981), Nekron ruled the dead, and sought to annex living realms. He was defeated when living Green Lanterns rallied their fallen comrades to revolution inside the death dimension. In *Blackest Night*, Nekron is a rapacious manifestation of Death, embodying the absence of all emotion but his own. Utterly discontented, he trespassed across the boundaries of existence, expanding his influence and triggering the *Blackest Night* in an attempt to finally destroy an as yet undisclosed eternal opposite.

First appearing in *Blackest Night #7* (Apr. 2010, by Johns and Ivan Reis, the Life Entity

Guiding lights
Even the implacable Guardians had to accept the dominance of Life's raw energy over all other colors and emotional forces.

is the pure white force of creation. Hidden beneath Earth for countless eons and sheltered by the Guardians, it is finally revealed as the spark that brought forth Multiversal life after an eternity of cold, interminable darkness. Enigmatic and inscrutable, the Life Entity's primordial glow was introduced into reality by Higher Powers, but fractured into seven sections when the darkness retaliated.

Having brought forth life, the Entity retreated, allowing unimpeded expansion and evolution for countless beings whose lives thereafter empowered it and the Spectrum. The Life Entity's modern-day exposure by Nekron prompted renewed activity and direct involvement with living and resurrected agents as it course-corrected Earth on the *Brightest Day*.

Hawkwoman defeated Hath-Set, while Hawkman sealed the interdimensional gateway to Hawkworld.

The voice's tasks ranged from profound to seemingly pointless. Digger Harkness was tasked to throw a boomerang at Dove that Hawk had to stop. However, these "simple" jobs invariably went awry, undoing the White Entity's original scheme and led to unforeseen divergence from it. Crisscrossing Earth, Deadman paved the way for the next guardian of life to emerge. His true assignment was to

reexperience humanity as a living being, not an invisible observer, while hunting the new White Entity. It was a task that let him physically interact with heroes such as Batman and Resurrection Man.

Death becomes him

Ultimately, Boston Brand died again after Hawk failed to catch Harkness's boomerang, and his white ring revived the dormant Swamp Thing. The elemental attacked the manifested, rampaging remnants of Nekron's touch and spectacularly cleansed the world.

A series exploring the idea of second chances and wasted opportunities, *Brightest Day* brilliantly reestablished the Super Hero status quo—just in time for everything to change forever.

> **"I suppose it was only a matter of time. Swamp Thing returns?"**
> **John Constantine** | *Brightest Day #24*

Key issues

June 2010–June 2011
Brightest Day #0–24

Tie-ins (June 2010–July 2011)
Adventure Comics #516–521, Birds of Prey #1–5, Brightest Day: The Atom Special #1, The Flash #1–7, Giant-Sized Atom Special #1, Green Arrow #1–12, Green Lantern #53–62, Green Lantern Corps #47–57, Green Lantern: Emerald Warriors #1–6, Justice League: Generation Lost #1–24, JLA #44–48, JSA #40–48, Titans: Villains for Hire Special #1, Titans #24

August–October 2011
Brightest Day Aftermath: The Search for the Swamp Thing #1–3

New Krypton

August 2008–August 2010

In an era of social unrest and economic uncertainty, comics had a tough time competing with real-world events. Relying on ambitious, epic storytelling, writers **Geoff Johns**, **James Robinson**, and **Sterling Gates** and illustrators **Gary Frank**, **Alex Ross**, **Renato Guedes**, **Jamal Igle**, and **Pete Woods** spearheaded a bold move that dominated Superman titles for two years as Earth confronted an immigrant crisis that began with the founding of *New Krypton*.

Brave new world
One of Superman's most ardent dreams finally came true, but only brought disillusionment, heartbreak, and catastrophe.

While destroying humanoid computer Brainiac, Superman discovered that 100,000 Kryptonians still lived. Contained in a bottled, controlled environment since before their homeworld exploded, they had carried on with their lives. Now their city of Kandor was released and stood on the site of Superman's Fortress.

To further complicate matters, during Superman's battle with Brainiac, his adoptive father, Jonathan Kent, died from a heart attack that the hero was powerless to prevent. This left Clark Kent to deal with loss and grief while discovering that his idealized notions of his lost people did not measure up to reality.

City of dreams
Hopes of brokering friendly relations between Earth and Kandor or securing peaceful integration soon faltered as the newly superpowered Kryptonians showed no interest in working with Earthlings. As they dismissively and arrogantly threw their weight around, it fueled the xenophobic suspicions of Lex Luthor, General Sam Lane, and others. Superman's father-in-law had led a murderous anti-extraterrestrial covert ops unit for years and redoubled efforts to destroy Superman and Supergirl, even using his youngest daughter Lucy as infiltrator—and ultimately assassin—Superwoman.

Led by Supergirl's parents Zor-El and Alura, Kryptonians began imprisoning potential threats, including Superman's old enemies such as Doomsday, in the Phantom Zone. When Earth police officers interrupted their capture of the Parasite, Kryptonian soldiers killed them. His suspicions confirmed, Sam Lane marshaled his "Project 7734." Luthor unleashed repurposed Brainiac robots in Kandor, and Lane's operatives Metallo and Reactron invaded the city, killing Zor-El. When the JLA and JSA demanded the Kryptonians hand over the cop killers who had seized the Parasite, grieving sole ruler Alura denounced humanity and war erupted, with Superman caught in the middle.

After an inconclusive clash, Alura ordered the city's relocation. Kryptonian and Brainiac technology positioned Kandor on the far side of the sun and built a new planet beneath it. After much indecision, both Superman and Supergirl officially relocated to New Krypto, but secretly maintained contact with Earth. Their place and roles on Earth were assumed by Daxamite Phantom Zone exile Mon-El and mysterious duo Flamebird and Nightwing (Kryptonians working undercover in the guise of mythological icons). The separation was particularly hard on Clark Kent's wife, Lois Lane, his adopted mother,

Hidden Jemm
Even the solar system's most reclusive isolationist culture felt compelled to register an unambiguous and warning for New Krypton not to make trouble.

Martha, and Lana Lang, who was Supergirl's new stepmother.

To ensure the security of New Krypton, Alura pardoned Phantom Zone criminals and controversially reinstated their leader, General Zod, as commander of the resurgent civilization's armed forces.

Kal-El made it his personal mission to monitor the mass-murdering tyrant, joining the Military Guild and rising to the position of second-in-command. He was kept busy as internal political strife and continued Earth covert-ops strikes destabilized the city-state. Other interplanetary empires, such as the Saturnians ruled by Jemm and the star-roving Thanagarians, put the solar system's newest inhabitants on notice to behave, before, eventually, Kal-El inherited full command after Zod barely survived an assassination attempt.

Never-ending saga

Not so much a story arc or crossover as a full repositioning of Superman titles, *New Krypton* affected virtually every aspect of Superman's life. Beginning in the prologue and the extended clash with Brainiac, the subsequent nested tales involved all the Man of Steel's allies—Supergirl, Superdog Krypto, Daxamite Mon-El (who inherited Superman's role as guardian of Metropolis while Kal-El lived on New Krypton), and new iterations of old allies Nightwing and Flamebird.

The mega-story unfolded in specials, limited series, and regular periodicals *Superman*, *Action Comics*, and *Supergirl*, featuring a huge cast of characters such as Steel, Superboy, and the Guardian. It was designed as an evolving event with a succession of crossover story arcs that seamlessly moved from *World of New Krypton*, *Codename: Patriot*, *Superman: Last Stand on New Krypton*, and *War of the Supermen*.

The saga's mutable nature demanded continuous revision of trade dress, reading-order badges, and banners. During the concluding arc, *War of the Supermen*, all other Superman family titles paused publication, with only associated series *Adventure Comics* and *Superman/Batman* continuing as normal.

Enemy of my enemy
So great was Kryptonian loathing of Brainiac, that it could make allies of Superman and General Zod.

Man of two worlds

Relations between the two planets— covertly sabotaged by General Lane's team—continued to deteriorate, igniting a "100 Minute War" when Reactron self-detonated to destroy the artificial planet. Zod's forces headed for Earth to wreak bloody vengeance, perishing in the thousands when Luthor turned the sun red. Flamebird used the power of Kryptonian deity Rao to restore it to yellow before also dying, but by then only 7,000 Kryptonians survived. Zod's last-ditch attempt to punish humanity was foiled by Superman, Superboy, and Earth's Super Heroes.

Zod was returned to the Phantom Zone, guarded by the new Nightwing (his own son in adult form) and Mon-El. Sam Lane committed suicide when confronted by his daughter Lois and Supergirl, leaving Superman with two monumental tasks—cleaning up Earth and regaining humanity's trust. ▨

Family fortunes
Kara Zor-El's joyous reunion would soon become a nightmare, with her father assassinated and her mother reduced to a vengeful, murderous tyrant.

Key issues

> "You know your targets. Let's use the day well. For Krypton!"
>
> **Zor-El** | *Superman #682*

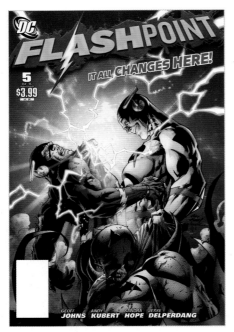

Flashpoint

July–October 2011

Behind the scenes, a major transformation was being completed to reshape DC's universe forever. As in the Silver Age, the key player was Barry Allen, whose actions would set continuity on a new course. Before that new beginning, however, writer Geoff Johns and illustrator Andy Kubert revealed The Flash as a devastating agent of change—tragically unmaking reality and triggering the end of everything in the speed-induced *Flashpoint.*

Velocity of vengeance
Reverse-Flash was happy to see history ended and the universe with it if it meant despair and defeat for his despised archenemy.

Since his resurrection during *Final Crisis*, Barry Allen had struggled to reconcile his role in a world that had moved on without him. However, a deadly and transformational duel through time seemed to end in his acceptance of his fate. Once again, the enemy was his most implacable foe—Eobard Thawne (Professor Zoom, Reverse-Flash)—but Allen triumphed with the support of other speedsters.

Barry Allen's life was haunted by memories of his murdered mother and dead father (who had died in prison, framed for her murder). In a publishing event that jump started The Flash's corner of the DC universe, the tragedy's repercussions grew to transform every aspect of existence, but only after starting with a dream and a mystery.

Nightmare scenario
After another night poring over cold cases, Barry Allen was roused from dreams of his many Super Hero allies to discover that his powers were gone. When his dead mother, Nora, arrived

Lead from the front
Barry Allen was not the first heroic speedster, but all his predecessors, peers, and descendants considered him the greatest and most driven.

for her birthday lunch, Barry was forced to question everything he believed. Careful research convinced him he was not crazy and that reality had changed. Trying to learn more about what had happened, he broke into the Batcave before being brutally set upon by a Batman who was not Bruce Wayne.

Years before, Thomas Wayne had witnessed his son, Bruce, gunned down.

> ## "You were like a bullet through a window. You shattered history."
>
> **Eobard Thawne (Reverse-Flash)** | *Flashpoint #5*

Flash of faith
Against the odds and all scientific sense, Barry endured incrementally more dangerous chemical baths and lightning strikes until his speed was restored.

The horror and loss drove him to hunt criminals dressed as a bat, while his wife was totally lost and haunted the city as deranged killer The Joker. Seeking to convince Batman of what has occurred, Allen tested the ring that stored his compressed costume, and a Reverse-Flash uniform erupted from it. The only logical conclusion was that Thawne had again changed history, preventing the Justice League's formation. Not so logical was trying to replicate the electrochemical accident that first granted Allen super-speed. Multiple failures almost killed him before he regained his speed powers. Wayne went along with the suicidal scheme, not from any conviction or moral imperative, but on the doomed hope that if the world could be changed again, his son might be reborn.

Earth was in a pitiful state, locked in a war between ancient powers that could destroy everything. The aliens and metahumans at large were mostly dark, selfish beings, resisting every effort of America's greatest Super Hero Cyborg to join a proposed team to end the conflict. Barry had even bigger problems. His memories of the previous existence were fading, replaced by new ones specific to this reality. With Allen's speed back, he and Thomas Wayne tracked down the heroes Allen remembered—Allen seeing what had become of them in this changed reality. Best friend Hal Jordan was still a jet pilot, while Wonder Woman and Aquaman were hell-bent on killing each other at any cost. Finally, decades-old reports of a crashed spacecraft led them to the being that should be Superman.

Fear factory
Probed, tortured, and deprived of yellow sunlight for 30 years, the Kryptonian was out of their reach until Cyborg lent a metallic hand. After uncovering even greater atrocities perpetrated by the military-industrial complex, the abused alien was freed from a hidden bunker only to disappear without a word into the beckoning skies.

Time ran out for the heroes and Earth plunged into full-scale war. As Atlantis and the Amazons intensified hostilities, threatening

Body chemistry
Thankfully, once Barry Allen reconnected with the Speed Force, his horrific, life-threatening injuries healed super-fast.

to obliterate Europe, America launched a conventional military assault, while Batman and The Flash joined Cyborg's superpowered militia to halt the madness. They all converged on a blood-soaked plain in the newly conquered Amazon territory of Great Britain—now called New Themyscira—and the slaughter escalated, until a sudden interruption made everyone pause. All action ceased as the true manipulator of events—Eobard Thawne—gloated at his successful stratagem. The scope and scale of his personal vendetta had driven an entire planet to disaster.

Dark deputies
The Flash's impromptu super-team was doomed to failure and harbored a murderous traitor in its midst, in the form of Amazon agent the Enchantress.

Butterfly effect

Preceded by prelude stories in *Time Masters: Vanishing Point #6* and *The Flash* (#9–12, Apr.–Jul. 2011), which signposted *The Road to Flashpoint*, Thawne's triumph was detailed in core series *Flashpoint* and supplemented by 61 ancillary issues, grouped in themed niches and published at the same time as *Flashpoint #2–4* (Aug.–Oct. 2011.

These prologue titles provided historical background for the new reality, in tales that were framed as questions, such as "Whatever Happened to Gotham City?" "Whatever Happened to the World's Greatest Super-Villains?" and "Whatever Happened to the Aliens?" They depicted familiar characters that were greatly changed and in darkly different situations, all spiraling into imminent Armageddon due to subtle tampering with the timeline.

This was a universe that was wholly altered thanks to the absence of the

Destiny denied
Thawne prevented Hal Jordan from becoming a Green Lantern but couldn't stop the hero from dying for what he believed in to stop the war in Europe.

Barry Allen Flash. However, some inhabitants—like teen witch Traci 13 and her precognitive mentor Madame Xanadu—felt echoes of a different, truer reality but couldn't find ways to repair the damage. Like everyone else, it was all they could do to simply stay alive, especially as Traci's father, Dr. Terrence Thirteen, was leading a cabal of human autocrats determined to end the globe-threatening war between Atlantis and the Amazons by destroying both adversaries with a satellite-based supergun.

In this changed reality, where there was never a Justice League and Superman had been imprisoned ever since crashing into Metropolis as an infant, aliens and metahumans lived a precarious existence. When a royal marriage between Aquaman and the Amazon Princess Diana was sabotaged by jealous family members, the tragedy escalated into war that wiped out Themyscira, forcing the women warriors to invade and conquer Great Britain. In retaliation, Atlantis overwhelmed western Europe but failed to drown the Amazon's new island fortress.

Africa had become a continent-wide charnel house where super-gorilla Grodd killed and conquered at will. In America, fighter pilot Hal Jordan never inherited Abin Sur's power ring and the alien Green Lantern instead rebelled against the Guardians. American authorities callously and covertly experimented on any aliens it captured, augmenting decades of monster-making by the military. Cyborg Victor Stone was the country's greatest hero, brokering tenuous deals with metahumans on both sides of the law to form a team able to avert the crisis. Batman Thomas Wayne was an obsessed vigilante little better than those he preyed upon, while Central City idolized charismatic bandit Len Snart—aka Citizen Cold—and lived in terror of his murderous former allies the Rogues.

Top journalist Lois Lane went undercover, gathering information for Cyborg as a member of the Resistance harassing the increasingly brutal Amazons—and their legion of female metahuman allies—in what remained of the United Kingdom. As a final battle loomed, many mystical and supernatural

Last writes

Flashpoint changed the entire DC universe and introduced—in teaser form—a wave of acquired and returning characters soon to be incorporated into continuity, while simultaneously triggering a complete reimagining of the company's pantheon of stars. The main *Flashpoint* series also primarily unfolded outside the established reality.

The core title generated 16 interlinked but self-contained three-issue limited series and four one-shots. These explored every terrifying aspect of an Earth that The Flash had inadvertently tipped into meltdown and imminent destruction.

Sidebar series generally took place in the middle of Barry Allen's search for answers and attempts to rectify the situation. They also all converged at a critical moment in *Flashpoint #5*. The entire event had been eerily foreshadowed at the end of *Time Masters: Vanishing Point #6* (Feb. 2011) as headings on an incident board in the chronal guardians' HQ predicted key events of *Flashpoint*.

Doom and board
The warnings on Rip Hunter's chalkboard echoed the *Infinite Crisis* when reality shifted to spawn 52 universes (*52* #1–52, May 2006–May 2007).

The warped world also spilled over into uniquely time-bending regular continuity series *Booster Gold* (#44–47, Jul.–Oct. 2011) with the timestream adjuster drawn into the war between Atlantis and the Amazons.

forces gradually convened in the ruins of Great Britain to bolster empowered operatives and human warriors hoping to stave off total annihilation.

Time out of joint

At the height of the conflict, Barry Allen absorbed and internalized the totality of the Speed Force, enduring a physical transformation that brought answers to all his questions and granted him knowledge to correct the appalling world he now inhabited. Answers came from the past and one possible future as Thawne—his greatest enemy—finally revealed himself, while his time-erased grandson Bart Allen from a dystopian alternate future "returned" to help reset reality.

Impulse control
As both Impulse and Kid Flash, young Bart Allen had fought evil and saved the world, but now he was expected to repair all of time and rescue his bad-tempered grandfather.

Long ago, Eobard Thawne recreated himself in his enemy's image and existed solely to torture and destroy The Flash, the hero who had once been his inspiration. Due to years of time travel, earlier versions of Thawne still tormented Barry Allen. Frustratingly, he was unable to kill Allen without deleting himself from existence, as his own existence depended on his early hero-worship of the Scarlet Speedster. Realizing that he couldn't eliminate Allen, Thawne, now calling himself Reverse-Flash, contented himself with making his enemy suffer. He targeted Barry Allen's entire extended family—speedsters and civilians—methodically rewriting the past to make The Flash's existence a living hell. Thawne's most successful ploy had been to deprive Barry of a happy childhood by murdering his mother, Nora, and framing his father, Henry, for the crime.

Flash of insight

When Barry awoke to find himself powerless and his mother still alive, he was troubled rather than joyous. He still retained jumbled but lingering memories of a different past and utter belief in a world where valiant Super Heroes were his friends. Now they were gone, somehow edited out of history and replaced by broken, bitter strangers.

With the battle between the Amazons and Atlanteans momentarily paused, Thawne, the cause of Barry's grief and anger stood triumphantly before him gloating that he had pushed Allen to the edge of madness while tormenting his Justice League comrades in a world rushing to self-destruction that he had manipulated Barry into creating.

Pause for thought
With his complex plan only moments from successful completion, Reverse-Flash ruined everything because he could not resist gloating.

"Have any of you actually thought about what's going to happen if Aquaman and Wonder Woman **aren't** stopped? No more pizza. No more anything."

Billy Batson (Captain Thunder) | *Flashpoint #4*

On Nora Allen's birthday, Barry had stood at her grave, burning with the recently acquired knowledge that Thawne had murdered her and that his life had been warped to satisfy the whims of a sadistic madman. Allen had snapped, using his super-speed in a

Speed of hate
Even with death and destruction all about them, the eternal enemies could see only each other and another chance to kill each other.

futile attempt to fix the travesty. Traveling back in time to save his mother from Thawne, Allen accidentally absorbed the entire Speed Force. This act distorted the timeline, resulting in every one of his super-heroic allies having very different lives. Crucially, It also made Thawne a living paradox who could now kill Allen without destroying himself. However, as Reverse-Flash maniacally boasted how his plan had come to fruition, Batman impaled the villain on a discarded broadsword.

Fighting soon resumed and Thomas Wayne was himself fatally struck down saving Barry from the sinister sorceress the Enchantress. Recently liberated Kal-El of Krypton finally joined the war, having found and lost his true love, Lois Lane. As the slaughter intensified, Batman used his final

Strange visitor
Captive and deprived of joy for his entire life, the last Kryptonian had seen enough and was going to stop the slaughter at all costs.

breaths to tell The Flash to restore the world, giving Flash a letter he had previously written to his lost son Bruce, if Allen made it back.

New world order

After a final heartfelt farewell with Nora Allen, her sadder, wiser son started running. Hitting the time stream, The Flash aimed for the point of divergence he had originally created. He saw amazing and prophetic sights—glimpses of strange days to come—before catching up to his earlier self. Merging with him, Barry aborted the *Flashpoint* reality before it could ever begin. And it was only days later, while delivering Thomas Wayne's last words to his son Bruce, that Barry remembered events and began to wonder whether everything was exactly as it used to be.

It wasn't. Reality itself had changed. With the trigger of *Flashpoint*, DC had rebooted its entire line, merging characters from different imprints (DC, WildStorm, and Vertigo) and their collective wealth of characters and concepts into one vast, cutting-edge, and uncompromising new continuity known as *DC Comics: The New 52*. ∎

Key issues

Road to Flashpoint (April–July 2011)
The Flash #9–12, Time Masters: Vanishing Point #6

July–October 2011
Flashpoint #1–5, Booster Gold #44–47

Flashpoint spin-offs (August–October 2011)
Batman: Knight of Vengeance #1–3, Deadman and the Flying Graysons #1–3, Citizen Cold #1–3, Deathstroke and the Curse of the Ravager #1–3, Legion of Doom #1–3, The Outsider #1–3, Abin Sur: The Green Lantern #1–3, Project Superman #1–3, Frankenstein and the Creatures of the Unknown #1–3, Secret Seven #1–3, Emperor Aquaman #1–3, Wonder Woman and the Furies #1–3, Lois Lane and the Resistance #1–3, Kid Flash Lost #1–3, The World of Flashpoint #1–3, Hal Jordan #1–3

Flashpoint one-shots (August 2011)
Grodd of War #1, Reverse-Flash #1, Green Arrow Industries #1, The Canterbury Cricket #1

The New 52

November 2011–June 2016

As the dust from *Flashpoint* settled, a new reality was revealed. The time-bending event had spawned a harsh, uncompromising Earth, and its corrective unmaking left something new and different—a reconstructed Multiverse incorporating both familiar and startlingly new characters and situations. Overseen by **Geoff Johns** and **Jim Lee**, a host of creators reinvented the DCU, preserving past legends while making a new mythology for the modern world—*DC Comics: The New 52*.

Call to arms
Despite complex backstory and revelatory clues to the nature of reality, this epic clash of heroes never stinted on blockbusting action and nerve-jangling suspense.

Primarily set five years after a global trigger event—invasion by Darkseid and his defeat by Super Heroes who would go on to form a universally accepted Justice League—*DC Comics: The New 52* was mass reinvention. Designed to appeal to long-term fans and newcomers, it merged characters from DC, Vertigo, Milestone Media, and WildStorm lines in a dangerously destabilized new world.

It began with *Justice League* #1, which reached stores on Aug. 31, 2011. A monster hit, the issue generated seven printings and was the bestselling comic book of 2011. Hard on its heels came 51 more titles, including *Batman*, *Superman*, *Wonder Woman,* and other classic DC characters.

United notions

These were supplemented by *Stormwatch*, *Grifter*, and *Voodoo*, Milestone Media's *Static Shock,* and experimental titles, including a new iteration of *The Blackhawks*, horror sensation *I, Vampire,* and medieval team title *Demon Knights*. It was a truly diverse offering that contributed to a fresh history and cosmology.

Editorially, the event was a "soft reboot," since many storylines from previous continuities, such as the murder of Robin (Jason Todd) by The Joker, were folded in as part of the new reality's history. However, even the most prestigious titles were included, and *Action Comics* and *Detective Comics* both began again at #1.

The relaunch was a bold experiment on many levels. One of the most attention-grabbing aspects was merging continuities from four separate imprints, while the most fundamental was the decision to henceforth publish printed comics and their digital editions on the same day.

Previously, electronic editions were released months after physical copies, which gave distributors and comic book stores an optimal and preferential sales window. Henceforth and once again, characters and stories became creators' primary consideration.

The lineup was compartmentalized as

Out of their league
Battling a force beyond reckoning or comprehension, the newly united heroes' incredible triumph reshaped humanity's attitudes to superhumans.

seven strands. "Justice League" contained titles related to the core team book, while "Batman" covered titles specific to the Dark Knight and Gotham City. The same principle underpinned "Superman" titles, while "Green Lantern" comics spanned space via assorted ring-wielders of the expanded Emotional Spectrum. "Young Justice" encompassed titles with teen heroes, and "The Dark" specialized in supernatural-themed characters previously accommodated by Vertigo and others, while "The Edge" focused on western, science fiction, crime-themed titles and former WildStorm properties. New try-out title *DC Universe Presents* gave fringe characters a shot at stardom, but the quest for innovative narrative avenues starring familiar yet refreshed favorites permeated every release.

Worlds of wonder

Recent and distant history was probed from the start. *Superman* detailed the hero's current adventures while *Action Comics* chronicled his first year in Metropolis. Ancient exploits offered traditional genre fare in *Demon Knights*, teaming Etrigan the Demon, Madame Xanadu, Shining Knight Sir Ystin, Vandal Savage, and others in the Dark Ages.

All-Star Western featured cowboys, Wild West pioneers, and other period antiheroes, all tightly woven into a grand continuity. Headlined by Jonah Hex, the title also informed Batman's

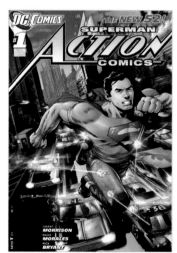

Survival of the fittest

The New 52 titles had close editorial scrutiny and were canceled quickly if they failed to find an audience. Branded as "waves," each major revision of the lineup replaced less popular titles with a selection of new concepts and characters, supplemented by specials, limited series, and one-shots. Between September 2011 and July 2016, *DC Comics: The New 52* experienced eight such regenerative waves.

Always aspiring to release 52 titles per month, the first cancellations—*Blackhawks, Hawk and Dove, Mister*

Terrific, OMAC, Static Shock, and *Men of War*—were soon balanced by a second wave consisting of *Dial H, Earth 2, World's Finest, G.I. Combat, Ravagers,* and *Batman Incorporated.*

As new titles began, the drive to address a broad range of genres and maintain contact with the company's illustrious past remained paramount. When *Men of War* was dropped with #8, *G.I. Combat* (#1, July 2012) replaced it, delivering iterations of revered military features *The War That Time Forgot, Unknown Soldier,* and *Haunted Tank,* honoring past successes while striving to satisfy modern sensibilities.

backstory revealing that Hex worked with asylum founder Amadeus Arkham in 1880s Gotham City. Modern combat was the arena in *Men of War*, which introduced the grandson of WWII legend Sgt. Rock, fresh looks for Gravedigger and GI Robot, and original features like Navy SEALS/ Human Shields.

Major crossover events were baked into the new line from the start. Creators crafted crucial first meetings, reinventing classic moments and

Speeding bullets
Writer Grant Morrison and artist Rags Morales told of Superman's first exploits with a fresh view of Clark Kent's early days in the big city.

setting surprises to catch readers off guard. As this reality dawned, Superman/Clark Kent would form a romantic relationship with Wonder Woman rather than Lois Lane, and Barry Allen was "just friends" with Iris West. Moreover, major crises were heralded—a Zero Year, war with Atlantis, Villains Month, and even a deadly invasion from a parallel Earth. ■

Key issues

All #1 issues (premiering November 2011)

Action Comics, All-Star Western, Animal Man, Aquaman, Batgirl, Batman, Batman and Robin, Batman: The Dark Knight, Batwing, Batwoman, Birds of Prey, Blackhawks, Blue Beetle, Captain Atom, Catwoman, DC Universe Presents, Deathstroke, Demon Knights, Detective Comics, The Flash, Frankenstein, Agent of S.H.A.D.E., Fury of Firestorm: The Nuclear Men, Green Arrow, Green Lantern, Green Lantern Corps, Green Lantern: New Guardians, Grifter, Hawk and Dove, I, Vampire, Justice League, Justice League Dark, Justice League International, Legion Lost, Legion of Super-Heroes, Men of War, Mister Terrific, Nightwing, OMAC, Red Hood and the Outlaws, Red Lanterns, Resurrection Man, Savage Hawkman, Static Shock, Stormwatch, Suicide Squad, Superboy, Supergirl, Superman, Swamp Thing, Teen Titans, Voodoo, Wonder Woman

"You just picked the **wrong** parallel universe."

Superman Calvin Ellis | *Action Comics #9*

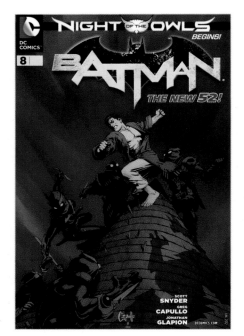

Homing instinct
Talons believed overwhelming force and surprise would be sufficient but miscalculated the ferocity of Bruce Wayne's defense of his ancestral lands.

Batman: Night of the Owls

April–May 2012

The new type of continuity unleashed by *DC Comics: The New 52* lent itself to different kinds of storytelling. **Batman: Night of the Owls** was an introduction to the new Gotham City. Growing from ongoing plot threads in *Batman* (writer **Scott Snyder** and artist **Greg Capullo**), *Nightwing* (writer **Kyle Higgins** and artist **Eddy Barrows**), an unconventional epic unfolded where secrets were exposed, alliances were forged, and the nature of family was tested to destruction.

Batman's goal is defending Gotham City, and when he discovered the truth of an old nursery rhyme about a secret society eternally observing everyone, he took drastic action. The fabled Court of Owls was actually a generational cabal of wealthy elite, seemingly formed in the 1600s, that manipulated events, ruthlessly removing obstacles for their own benefit.

Birds of ill omen

Secret chambers were constructed in countless buildings from which to observe potential allies and foes, and the Court's greatest weapons were money, influence, and secrecy. However, when direct action was called for, they deployed enhanced enforcers called Talons. For centuries, these fanatical, indoctrinated agents, augmented by

Ambush
Wayne learned first-hand how the Owls had haunted Gotham City for centuries, stealing secrets and delivering death from out of the city's very walls.

technology, operated as lethal ghosts in Gotham City. Talons are nearly impossible to kill but often become unstable. When this occurs, agents are frozen and stored in hibernation.

Young Bruce Wayne had become fascinated by the legend after his parents were gunned down but set aside such fantastic notions as he began preparing for his adult path as an avenger of wrongs. When Wayne first returned to Gotham City, proposing massive

rejuvenation for the city, he became the Talons's latest target.

The Court dispatched Talon William Cobb to kill him, but the assault failed, leading to Batman unearthing many of the Court's darkest secrets. The most disturbing was learning that Cobb was Dick Grayson's grandfather and that the Owls have for decades recruited Talons with extreme skill sets from street children and the circus where Grayson grew up. If fate had moved differently, the former Robin,

> "And when the bats came back... it was with a **vengeance**."
>
> **Alfred Pennyworth** | *Batman #9*

The Court is in session

Running primarily through (badged) Batman family titles over one month, *Night of the Owls* was the first major crossover of *DC Comics: The New 52*. Yet unlike most crossovers, it featured only in established titles, with no core series to act as its spine. That said, the sheer power and presence of the Court of Owls proved a highly effective addition to the Batman mythos.

The concept had been building from the very first Batman releases of the reboot. There had even been hints and foreshadowing in pre-*DC Comics: The New 52* limited series *Batman: The Gates of Gotham*. Written by Snyder, it advanced the notion of the city as a fully contributing character, detailing its history through its hereditary elites, the Cobblepot, Elliot, and Wayne families, whose latest generations spawned The Penguin, Hush, and Batman, respectively.

The influence of the Court was explored in all Batman titles and even period thriller *All-Star Western*, where Jonah Hex and

Amadeus Arkham challenged the Court in the 1880s. Even then, Gotham City toiled under its covert control, with the secret society busily anonymizing itself and creating a fairy-tale mythology around its existence and actions.

now operating as the hero Nightwing, would have been the next Talon.

With Wayne on their radar after he exposed his own grandfather Alan Wayne's links to the Court, and aware that their veil of secrecy has been pierced, the Owl's leaders mobilized all their forces in a huge retaliatory strike intended to eliminate Batman and remove Gotham City's official leadership. Abandoning anonymity and the shield of myth, they sought to steal the city, attacking Gotham to show that if they cannot rule in the shadows, they will command in person.

Grim fairy tale

It began in a mass attack on Wayne Manor and the Batcave, with an army of revived Talons attempting to kill Wayne, while solo agents sought to assassinate forty civic leaders and administrators, such as Police Commissioner James Gordon and Kane County Supreme Court Justice Jan Spitz. As the Dark Knight methodically and remorselessly cleaned house, devoted Alfred Pennyworth locked himself in and alerted every past partner and occasional ally that they were needed.

In 1880s Gotham, Jonah Hex and other western heroes battled a Talon, derailing and delaying an Owl scheme for decades. Their efforts proved that the Court could be defeated by exposure, but as part of the City's skeleton, they are not easy to excise. In present-day Gotham, Batgirl Barbara Gordon rescued her father, while Robin (Damian Wayne) saved the National Guard Commander, but Nightwing was only partially successful in saving Mayor Hady and the City Councillor. Also heeding Alfred's call, Catwoman, the Birds of Prey, Red Hood and the Outlaws, and others who had been touched by the shadow of the Bat strove to thwart the Owls, but their efforts met with limited success.

The Court was ultimately revealed to be part of a larger and more ancient conspiracy—a global Parliament of Owls stretching back into prehistory, complicit in a cosmic scheme to shatter the Multiverse. The goal was to make Batman a living gateway for invasion by bat-god Barbatos. However, even this

Suit up
The Talons soon learned that the Batcave was packed with imaginative combat systems in need of a thorough beta-testing workout.

was not the whole, unvarnished truth, as all Earth's Super Heroes would learn when Gotham City became the forge for *Dark Nights: Metal*. ▪

War in the air
In the final accounting, Batman's resolve and ingenuity proved superior to the Court's enslaved and augmented super-assassins.

Key issues

June–July 2012
Batman #8–9
Nightwing #8–9

Crossovers (July 2012)
All-Star Western #9, *Batgirl* #9, *Batman Annual #1*, *Batman and Robin* #9, *Batman: The Dark Knight* #9, *Batwing* #9, *Birds of Prey* #9, *Catwoman* #9, *Detective Comics* #9, *Red Hood and the Outlaws* #9

Rotworld

October 2012–May 2013

DC always understood the entertainment value of scary stories, pioneering supernatural heroes and anthology titles with great success. That experience was parlayed into groundbreaking titles from the 1980s onward, and, after some time away, the greatest of those characters rejoined DC's mainstream in *DC Comics: The New 52*. Celebrating the reunion, **Jeff Lemire**, **Scott Snyder**, **Steve Pugh**, and **Yanick Paquette** detailed a resurgence of terror in *Rotworld*.

Swamp savior
With conventional Super Heroes suborned to the Black, life on Earth needed to call on disturbingly different defenders.

Over decades, the nature of life on Earth and its precarious balance of existence was revealed in comic book sagas by many gifted, imaginative creators, generally in DC's horror and supernatural titles. By the time *DC Comics: The New 52* reunited far-ranging imprints into one grand continuity, accepted history revealed that as the new planet cooled, sentience sparked in all aspects and elements of the world. Magma, stone, water, winds, and even flame achieved a level of consciousness and formed Parliaments to steer their shared environment.

Living planet

When bacterial and cellular life developed, their combined sentience became linked and interactive: a primitive communal intellect. It was only superseded as flora and fauna evolved. These were shepherded by Parliaments of Tree and Bone—the Green and the Red. These hive minds worked slowly, reanimating dead creatures as physical avatars to execute their plans and manage their objectives.

Over millennia, Red and Green competed, reshaping environments to their needs and largely disregarding everything else. All Parliaments employed resurrected operatives, but eventually the Green gained the advantage, as Red Avatars were short-lived, impetuous, and easily distracted by primal urges.

As the factions jostled for dominance and instead achieved balance, they were challenged by another biologically determined grouping. Breaking away from the Grey, which represented fungal life, a rebel faction categorized itself as the Black—a Parliament of Decay intent on making death the true point of life. For billions of years, the Black pursued a slow, methodical approach, until their earthly agent, Anton Arcane, discarded their sluggish policies to pursue his own blighted agenda. His atrocities were countered by his own niece Abigail and her lover Alec Holland. As Swamp Thing, Holland was the most successful Green agent.

Secretly groomed from birth to be their champion, his bio-restorative formula should have ended world hunger. Instead, he was murdered by gangsters unwittingly working for Arcane. He attained his destiny after his personality merged with vegetable matter from the Louisiana swamps into which his burning body sank.

Darkness gathers
Anton Arcane's gambit to eliminate existence could only be countered by Life's greatest attributes—heroism, determination, hope, love, and, inevitably, sacrifice.

> "Abby. I can't have fought this hard just to **lose** you again. For **good**."
>
> **Swamp Thing** | *Swamp Thing* #18

Horror harvest
Turning Earth into a Rotworld unleashed every conceivable biologically debased horror, but Anton Arcane never anticipated that some monsters would fight for Life.

Kiss of death
After giving everything to restore Earth's natural order, the Black and Green avatars had to part forever or risk destroying each other through simple contact.

Far less successful was Red avatar Buddy Baker. A failed Super Hero dubbed Animal Man, his connection to the flesh and blood of Earth allowed him to channel any ability possessed by Earth's fauna. Despite wielding the powers of birds, beasts, bugs, and fish, his role was largely accidental and only temporary. The Parliament of Bones had actually chosen his preschool daughter Maxine as their true champion, with her father simply standing in until she matured.

Rotworld revealed how Arcane almost succeeded in destroying Earth. The death-obsessed fanatic knew better than his gods and masters, the Black, and his unsanctioned machinations unleashed transformative horror on all life. And, at first, no one seemed prepared to challenge him.

Initially resistant after enjoying recently renewed humanity, Alec Holland accepted the burden of battling the Rot as Swamp Thing only to save Abigail. She was Arcane's destined successor and realized she must sacrifice herself to defeat him. Animal Man fought the Red's war simply to save his children but was only partly successful.

Green politics

Arcane's assault transformed Earth. As Swamp Thing and Animal Man battled on separate fronts (assisted by other Red and Green agents Beast Boy, Poison Ivy, Black Orchid, Green Lantern Medphyll), conventional Super Heroes such as Superman and The Flash became ghastly Rot avatars. Even ghosts and reanimated corpses assisted the living—monster-hunter Frankenstein confronted the Rot while Boston Brand provided help as only a disembodied Deadman could.

Reversing the Rotworld's advance brought only misery to its victors. Abigail Arcane became a new, rational Rot avatar and, realizing he had lost Abigail forever, Swamp Thing comforted himself by joining Justice League Dark. For Buddy Baker, however, there was only torment and loss as he grieved the son he lost to the beasts that Animal Man failed to defeat. ◼

Survival of the fittest

An old-school crossover event, *Rotworld* was limited primarily to similarly themed and traditionally compatible series. Aimed at a more sophisticated audience, these specifically horror-tinged titles included core series—*Swamp Thing* and Animal Man—which had recently been readmitted to greater DC continuity after a period with the "mature-reader" imprint Vertigo.

The interwoven epic transformed reality and involved a wealth of other heroes, but only *Animal Man* and *Swamp Thing* were badged and numbered through their trade dress. As the epic unfolded, different stages reflected specific battles, namely "Rotworld: Prologue," "Green Kingdom," "Red Kingdom," "War of the Rot," and "Finale." An official tie-in, *Frankenstein, Agent of S.H.A.D.E.* #13–15 was badged with a substrand entitled "Rotworld: Secrets of the Dead."

Key issues

October 2012–May 2013

Animal Man #12–18
Swamp Thing #12–18
Frankenstein, Agent of S.H.A.D.E. #13–15
Animal Man #0
Swamp Thing #0
Swamp Thing Annual #1

Throne of Atlantis

November 2012–April 2013

When DC relaunched their entire line as *DC Comics: The New 52*, writer **Geoff Johns** was tasked with exploring the potential of veteran hero Aquaman. A tension-packed first year culminated in an epic crossover with key title *Justice League*, as pencillers **Ivan Reis**, **Pete Woods**, and **Paul Pelletier** charted a catastrophic clash that endangered America, and only ended with a bitter, reluctant hero reclaiming the *Throne of Atlantis*.

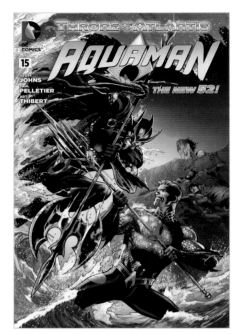

The sharp end
Ocean Master and Aquaman negotiated a deadly geopolitical crisis like savage beasts wielding magic weather-controlling tridents.

Aquaman was a major beneficiary of continuity-wide changes stemming from the *Flashpoint* event. In the reality of *DC Comics: The New 52*, he was a conflicted champion who rejected ruling Atlantis to pursue a hero's life. Adrift amid surface civilizations and an ancient empire, he sought to navigate a path of tolerance and cooperation between both.

Atlantis was founded on land 45,000 years ago and even its subsequent shattering submersion did not end it. Survivors adapted to undersea existence in seven sea realms: Atlantis, Kingdom of the Fishermen, Kingdom of the Trench, Kingdom of the Brine, Kingdom of the Deserters, the Lost Kingdom, and the Atlantean penal colony Xebel. Many of its people possessed hydrokinetic

Trident true
Vulko's plot sparked conflict between very different cultures and succeeded due to eons of mistrust between the "wet" and "dry" worlds.

powers, wielding water as a weapon. Aquaman's, wife, Mera was once its princess.

Family matters
Advanced in science and sorcery, Atlantis shunned all contact with surface humanity, brutally destroying any air-breather they encountered. This all changed when Queen Atlanna rebelled against her arranged marriage and fled to the surface. In Amnesty Bay, Maine, Atlanna fell in love with human lighthouse keeper Tom Curry, and they had a son.

However, their idyllic life ended when she was returned to Atlantis to wed King Orvax and provide an heir.

Raised by his father, Atlanna's first-born grew up to be truly extraordinary. Proudly embracing his human side, Arthur Curry developed incredible abilities and a profound appreciation of fairness and justice. Fully amphibian, with a body adapted to deep-sea conditions, he communicated with sea

> "He's not a **Super-Villain**. He's the leader of an underwater nation."
>
> **Aquaman** | *Aquaman* #15

life and from early on acted as a Super Hero, battling common criminals and bizarre super-foes like the Fisherman, Scavenger, and Black Manta.

When Tom Curry died, royal advisor Nuidis Vulko tracked down Atlanna's first son and helped install him as Atlantis's rightful ruler. An uneasy king, Arthur soon abdicated, leaving the position to his younger half brother. Dictatorial but honorable, Orm became Ocean Master but always felt Arthur should accept his regal responsibilities to their people.

This means war

Those wishes were cruelly granted in *Throne of Atlantis* when fanatical Vulko manipulated Aquaman and Orm into battling for the crown neither truly wanted. Tricked into believing America attacked the city-state, Orm employed ancient mystic tools to weaponize the waters, enacting war plans drafted by Arthur when he originally ruled. These were meant to ruthlessly punish human aggression while sending a signal to never mess with Atlantis.

Tactics involved a surprise assault on America's East Coast using massive tidal waves, before sinking the most damaged city forever as a warning of worse to come. Despite the rapid reaction of Justice Leaguers, an astounding upgrade to Cyborg, early activation of hopeful new recruits, and the best efforts of Aquaman and Mera, the deluge devastated

Perfect storm
Once Aquaman realized where his loyalties truly lay and what his responsibilities demanded, he let nothing stop him from ending the war.

Gotham City, Boston, Metropolis, and other conurbations. Atlantis had brought a brutal war to the surface world, a war that tested Arthur's loyalties to the limits.

The assault and casualty rate initially set Aquaman against his surface allies but had unintended consequences when the conflict unleashed the voracious Trench upon both sides. Bloodlust and honor were only satisfied when Arthur reclaimed the throne and surrendered his brother to the surface-worlders.

Throne of Atlantis repositioned Aquaman as a more dangerous and reluctant Super Hero trapped by unwanted responsibility and sacrificing happiness for the sake of fragile global peace. The consequences of the saga added layers of tension to the reality of *DC Comics: The New 52*, introducing characters who would play crucial roles in the forthcoming *Trinity War*. ■

Sunken treasures

Aquaman was created by Mort Weisinger and Paul Norris, for *More Fun Comics #73* (Nov. 1941). The Sea King was a genial second-stringer for most of his career yet swam on far beyond many "stronger" features. His adventures were illustrated by Norris, and many others—particularly Louis Cazeneuve, Charles Paris, and, latterly, Ramona Fradon, who drew almost every yarn between 1951–1961.

The Silver Age superhero renaissance saw DC update its costumed stars. After two decades of nautical service, Aquaman graduated from backup feature in *Adventure, Detective* and *World's Finest Comics*—via a run in *Showcase #30-33* (Feb.–Aug. 1961)—to his own title *Aquaman #1* (Feb. 1962). A Justice League of America

cofounder, he frequently returned to *Adventure Comics* (#441–478, Oct. 1976–Dec. 1980) whenever his own title briefly foundered, before inevitably relaunching as a solo star. *The New 52* was a place of constant crises, with many concurrent events building to a colossal universe-wide conclusion. *Throne of Atlantis* was a compact, self-contained crossover tale involving the regular monthly *Aquaman* and *Justice League* titles. The story took its starting place from another line-wide event, the "secret origin" story from *Aquaman #0* (Nov. 2012), itself part of a coordinated release of "zero issues." This disclosed the backstory of every title's stars one year after *DC Comics: The New 52* debuted.

Batman: Zero Year

June 2013–July 2014

As *The New 52* unfolded, its component characters blended contemporary exploits with glimpses of the past. With key title *Batman*, lead creators **Scott Snyder** and **Greg Capullo**, aided by writer **James Tynion IV**, and artists **Danny Miki**, and **Rafael Albuquerque**, made those untold stories the key to heroic futures. They explored players not yet Super Heroes who found their paths to duty and glory on Gotham City's ravaged streets in *Batman: Zero Year*.

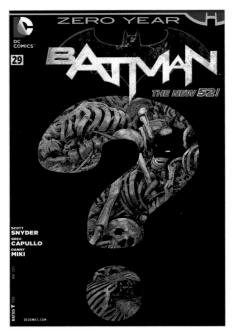

Marking time
Gotham City was a magnet for masterminds and maniacs, but it also created dedicated problem-solvers and miracle workers who could never allow evil to win.

Revitalizing an often retold origin story, *Batman: Zero Year* incorporated classic elements from seven decades of DC history into a new mythology. It detailed how Batman was a response to both Bruce Wayne's emotional needs and the rapid descent of Gotham City into chaos and terror—relating the hero's journey from traumatized crime victim to champion of the helpless for a new generation. The epic was divided into "Secret City," "Dark City," and "Savage City," detailing Batman's birth, first encounters with allies like James Gordon and Lucius Fox, as well as a terrifying trio of the uniquely baroque and bizarre villains Gotham City attracts.

Secrets and liars

After years away, Bruce Wayne quietly returned home. Having become sadly famous for witnessing his parents' murder, Bruce's hopes for anonymity were shredded by Wayne Enterprises CEO (and his uncle) Philip Kane and company strategist Edward Nygma. They "outed" the prodigal, making him an unwilling celebrity.

Wayne's return coincided with a Gotham City in meltdown, its corrupt government and police department helpless against constant attacks from seditious criminal gang the Red Hoods. Targeting business and influential citizens, the mystery men and their manic demagogue Red Hood One seemed to be ideologically motivated terrorists inflicting chaos and disruption for its own sake. Having trained himself to fight evil, Wayne retreated from the spotlight and stalked them in a variety of disguises. He failed and almost died.

Saved by distraught retainer Alfred Pennyworth, Wayne drew on early traumas, reinventing himself as Batman and allying with honest cop James Gordon to foil the Hoods' scheme to destroy Gotham with toxic weapons. However, his Uncle Philip— an unwilling member of the gang—died in the battle at Ace Chemicals before Red

Heroic influence
Batman's beginnings led him to become a unifying and inspirational beacon of hope to the fearful and weary of beleaguered Gotham City.

Hood One hurled himself into the toxic waste, declaring his war was not over.

Now making headlines as the new boss of Gotham City's biggest employer, Wayne invented Batman to channel his darker compulsions. However, while he hunted macabre serial killer Karl "Doctor

Death" Helfern, Nygma resurfaced. Depriving Gotham City of power and destroying its sea defenses just as Superstorm Rene hit, he ordered the panicked population to "get smarter or die" in *his* Dark City.

The catastrophe brought help from beyond the city. Clark Kent faced his physical limits battling Superstorm Rene while Oliver Queen (Green Arrow) rescued his mother from kidnappers. Special Forces soldier John Stewart (Green Lantern) extracted flood survivors from Seaside Coliseum while GCPD volunteer and rookie cop Barry Allen (The Flash) met Iris West.

Bright lights, dark city

James Gordon 's daughter Barbara (Batgirl/Oracle) discovered her strengths and limits while her dad started cleaning up the GCPD. Student Luke Fox (Batwing) realized he couldn't help everyone. Kate Kane (Batwoman)

Taking the fall
From the start, Batman knew his life may well end in the same way as that of his disturbingly similar opponents.

Group shot

Capitalizing on Batman's wealth of monthly titles, DC used the eponymous core title of the Batman Family franchise to establish his origin story over the course of a year, running the revelatory saga in parallel with ongoing modern-day storylines. However, in the context of the historical adventure, a number of other characters who would become Super Heroes were included in *Zero Year*, affording the opportunity for other creators to shine a light on the pasts of various DC stalwarts. Many January 2014 titles revealed untold tales of characters, who, for various reasons,

It's all connected
Men like The Riddler operated on a uniquely elevated level but always seemed able to find like-minded allies and enemies worthy of their undivided attention.

were drawn to Gotham City as Superstorm Rene struck.

Although set approximately six years in the past, *Zero Year* overlapped with the major company crossover event *Trinity War/Forever Evil*. As part of that mega-saga, all of *DC Comics: The New 52* issues for November 2013 generated stand-alone one-offs, spotlighting villains associated with the title. *Batman #23.1* to 23.4 (Nov. 2013) examined The Joker, The Riddler, The Penguin, and Bane.

reconnected with family at her uncle Philip's funeral, and Dinah Lance (Black Canary) lost a home and found purpose. Selina Kyle (Catwoman) simply learned better ways to steal. Crucially, juvenile offender Jason Todd (Robin/Red Hood) and headstrong circus acrobat Dick Grayson (Robin/Nightwing) both faced lethal foes on Gotham City's streets, inadvertently anticipating their future lives and destinies.

Over weeks, Nygma's Darwinian playground became a primitive jungle. His technology observed thousands dying by drowning, panic, violence, despair, hunger, and—in his eyes—stupidity, in the Savage City. Trapped survivors were reduced to beasts as Nygma, now calling himself the Riddler, awaited a worthy opponent to challenge his dominion. Meanwhile, child prodigy Duke Thomas rescued Batman from certain death, helped

him heal, and suggested a shrewd strategy to combat The Riddler.

Ultimately, Duke would become Batman Family member the Signal, but until then, Batman and his adult allies fought on until victorious. They defeated The Riddler, saving the city from annihilation by government bombing raids and giving its troubled inhabitants the hope that tomorrow would be better for all. ■

Key issues

August 2013–September 2014
Batman #21–27, 29–33

Tie-ins (January 2014)
Batman Annual #2
Action Comics #25
Batgirl #25
Batwing #25
Birds of Prey #25
Catwoman #25
Detective Comics #25
The Flash #25
Green Arrow #25
Green Lantern Corps #25
Nightwing #25
Red Hood and the Outlaws #25
Batman #23.2

> ## "You're not even going to **try** to answer me, are you?"
>
> **Edward Nygma, The Riddler** | *Batman #23.2*

Forever Evil

November 2013–July 2014

After two momentous and remarkable years, the darker, more precarious reality of *DC Comics: The New 52* faced its first multidimensional crisis, which saw evil triumphant and only overcome by a deeper, more insidious and unscrupulous morality. Touching many other series, the core limited series by writer **Geoff Johns** and illustrator **David Finch**, saw villains ascendant, with humanity's champions defeated and in retreat from a world *Forever Evil*.

Leader of the pack
After years battling Superman and his allies, Lex Luthor used his experience to lead Super-Villains against evil monsters and became a hero at last.

Since their formation five years previously, thwarting Darkseid's invasion, the Justice League had become a cornerstone of humanity's defense, but not a wholly trusted one. Deep-state operative Amanda Waller had repurposed A.R.G.U.S. to watch them and formed her own iteration— the Justice League of America—to counter their potential threat and monitor other superhuman forces like the Teen Titans, Doom Patrol, and the magical vigilantes unofficially operating as Justice League Dark.

No more heroes

Shrewd, meticulous, and ruthless, Waller already had a way to control Super-Villains. Those caught and convicted were set to work in her covert penal team Task Force X: the Suicide Squad.

Mirror monsters
Facing off against the Crime Syndicate convinced Luthor that his way to ultimate victory against the Justice League was to join them, not beat them.

That atmosphere of mistrust almost doomed the world when the various agencies and groups became entangled in the preliminary, quasi-mystical clash *Trinity War* (Aug.–Oct. 2013). This earlier conflict ended with Earth being invaded and overcome by a blitz attack from a dead planet in an alternate universe that had been devastated by an irresistible, collective alien presence.

With groundwork laid by sinister vanguard the Outsider, a merciless superpowered team—who were

> "The **Justice League** is **dead**. Superman is **gone**. **This** is a job for **Lex Luthor**."
>
> **Lex Luthor** | *Forever Evil #2*

Coming to America
Refugees from an expired alternate Earth, the Crime Syndicate planned to dominate, not assimilate.

Big reveal
The existential threat that forced the Crime Syndicate to flee their home universe was not Darkseid but a cosmic nemesis even he feared—the Anti-Monitor.

terrifying opposites of Earth's heroes—exploded onto Earth. Their first strike disabled all electronic infrastructure, infecting Victor Stone with sentient code Grid. It forced Cyborg's artificial parts to reject his organic remnants. As he lay dying, his comrades were absorbed and imprisoned inside Firestorm's nuclear matrix. Only Batman managed to avoid the trap.

After bringing Stone's dying remains to S.T.A.R. Labs' Red Room for emergency upgrades, Batman retrenched, seeking allies and finding Catwoman ready and willing to ignore the invaders' demands. The evil Justice League called themselves the Crime Syndicate—apex predators of a Darwinian society where might made right. When something even mightier drove them away from their own Earth, they invaded a new one, allowing Earth's Super-Villains to rule in return for eternal fealty and subservience.

The conquerors expected resistance from heroes but were unprepared for rebellion from Super-Villains like The Flash's Rogues. They cared nothing for

ruling the world but refused to knuckle under to the alien doppelgängers' reign of terror. Even more passionate in defiance was Lex Luthor, who formed his own army of evil to counter the Crime Syndicate. He even formed an uneasy alliance with Batman and devised the means by which the Justice League were restored to confront and overcome their evil alternates.

In truth, the Crime Syndicate brought with them the seeds of their own destruction. Green Lantern analogue Power Ring was consumed by terror generated by his ring, while Johnny Quick and Atomica's overconfidence and love for bloodshed made them fatally reckless. The Syndicate's Aquaman (Sea King) died on the journey across dimensions and their Firestorm was an actual zombie dubbed Deathstorm. But the true threat was pregnant Superwoman,

callously playing Ultraman against Owlman, deluding both into believing they were her romantic preference. Ultraman was already increasingly unstable, addicted to superpowered highs from ingesting every scrap of Kryptonite he could find.

Good works
Ultimately Earth's champions were restored, striking back beside criminal allies eager to reclaim their planet. With the Syndicate defeated, Superwoman revealed that she had planned to betray her comrades for the prisoner they had brought with them. Alexander Luthor was the smartest man on their Earth who carried its equivalent to the power of Shazam! (used by Billy Batson and Black Adam). Alexander was Superwoman's chosen mate and together they would rule whatever remained when the fighting was done, but he could not match wits with an outraged Lex Luthor and survive the experience.

An event that reshaped the DC Super Hero landscape, *Forever Evil* repositioned many villains as neither good nor bad but rather complex, compelling, and far more interesting.

Forever Evil grew out of the introductory crossover event *Trinity War* and was, in many ways, its second chapter. In that saga, a meticulous plot gathered Earth's Super-Villains into a single organization classified as the Secret Society of Super-Villains, while in the background, ancient mystical outcasts the Trinity of Sin renewed an age-old conflict.

"...Pandora's box can **open** a **gateway** to **another** universe. **Our** universe. **The birthplace of** *evil.*"

The Outsider | *Justice League* #23

Pandora's box

Trinity War saw Phantom Stranger and the Question trying to prevent the ancient and unjustly punished Pandora from finally opening the ominous artifact she was cursed to carry—a supposedly divine magical container in the shape of a gleaming golden skull.

Across the entire Earth, chaos reigned and people were terrified. The Justice League's satellite was destroyed, scattered across Happy Harbor, Rhode Island. Federal spymaster Amanda Waller sought to undermine and control Super Heroes through her own Justice League of America, while public opinion was turning against costumed champions. Even idealistic boy-hero Billy Batson

felt it was time to grow up and abandon his childish calling as Shazam!

Throughout the escalating chaos, Pandora challenged the greatest heroes and villains of the era to breach the accursed receptacle she had carried since the dawn of time. None could affect it, but its briefest touch turned Superman into a rampaging monster. A turning point in the web of deadly mystery came after the Man of Steel was revealed to have been poisoned by Kryptonite inserted directly into his brain.

Discovered far too late, the assassination attempt devolved into catastrophe when Superman's heat vision was hijacked and used to kill JLA member Doctor Light, triggering all-out war between the Justice League

The cursed gift
Pandora's box was a diabolical lure planted in prehistory to generate conflict and open dimensional doors.

and Waller's JLA. With hidden super-foes and traitors inside the Justice League, the climactic battle between assorted well-intentioned champions suddenly ceased when Pandora's burden was ultimately unsealed by mystery player the Outsider. His abrupt actions allowed the Crime Syndicate of an alternate Earth to cross to Earth and signaled the end of the heroic ideal.

With evil victorious and Earth now colonized by the survivors of Earth-Three, sidebar series traced how the world coped without its greatest

Playthings of the gods
The *Trinity War* found damned immortals battling Super Heroes, all unaware their fate was orchestrated by extradimensional exiles seeking fresh worlds to conquer.

Cold comfort
The Rogues always took whatever they wanted—but never a tyrant's orders or disrespect from wannabes and copycats.

Evil intentions

Shining a spotlight on the darkest corners of the DCU, mass crossover *Forever Evil* was vast and sprawling—the first major event of the *DC Comics: The New 52* era. It comprised a core limited series plus tie-ins, with supplemental fixed-length titles like *Forever Evil: A.R.G.U.S.*, *Forever Evil: Arkham War*, and *Forever Evil: Rogues Rebellion* fleshing out repercussions of the invasion for specific sectors of reality. The first issue of the core limited series was the bestselling comic book for September 2014.

Another overlapping story arc—*Forever Evil: Blight*—ran through regular series

Justice League Dark, *Trinity of Sin: Pandora*, *Trinity of Sin: Phantom Stranger*, and *Constantine*, with most (but not all) carrying the requisite banner above the title logo declaring it as part of the main event.

A subsequent event-within-the-event, "Villains Month" took place between issue #23 and #24 of a third of DC's titles, highlighting past and present deeds of Earth's greatest evildoers. Numbered #23.1 to 23.4, many featured 3-D/ lenticular motion covers. Four of the titles starring Batman foes—The Joker, Riddler, Bane, and Penguin—placed in September 2014's top-ten bestsellers list.

---

defenders. Crafted by writer Sterling Gates, and artists Philip Tan, Neil Edwards, Javier Piña, and others, *Forever Evil: A.R.G.U.S.* the valiant efforts of Justice League liaison and intelligence operative Steve Trevor to liberate Earth's Super Heroes. He led the remnants of the Advanced Research Group Uniting Super-Humans and a cadre of metahumans like Killer Frost, who were increasingly unhappy with Secret Society interference and Crime Syndicate rule.

Wicked kingdom

With Gotham City overrun by its Super-Villains, a battle for supremacy between the Penguin and Bane erupted in *Forever Evil: Arkham War* by writer Peter Tomasi and artists Scot Eaton and Jaime Mendoza, with the victor having to face

a returned, resurgent, and enraged Dark Knight in the epilogue episode *Forever Evil Aftermath: Batman vs. Bane* #1 by Tomasi, Eaton, Mendoza, and artist Scott Hana.

Perhaps the most significant tale was *Forever Evil: Rogues Rebellion*, written by Brian Buccellato and illustrated by Patrick Zircher and Scott Hepburn, which tracked the members of The Flash's Rogues Gallery as they were ruthlessly hunted by the Secret Society and Crime Syndicate super-stooges for refusing to surrender their independence and join the New World

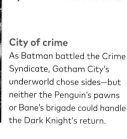

City of crime
As Batman battled the Crime Syndicate, Gotham City's underworld chose sides—but neither the Penguin's pawns or Bane's brigade could handle the Dark Knight's return.

Order. Eventually, some rebels joined the fightback, finding new avenues for their innate antisocial tendencies.

The invasion and spiritual triumph of the villains deeply affected Earth's magical aura, manifesting a presence of pure evil throughout the planet. Supernatural champions led by John Constantine, Zatanna, Phantom Stranger, Swamp Thing, Night Nurse, and many more united in an epic war fought on many fronts to cleanse the planet and repel the horrific avatar of despair, the Blight. ■

Key issues

November 2013–July 2014
Forever Evil #1–7, Justice League #24–30, Justice League of America #8–14, Suicide Squad #24–30

December 2013–May 2014
Forever Evil: A.R.G.U.S. #1–6, Forever Evil: Arkham War #1–6, Forever Evil: Rogues Rebellion #1–6

December 2013–May 2014
Forever Evil: Blight, Justice League Dark #24–29; Trinity of Sin: Phantom Stranger #14–17; Constantine #9–12; Trinity of Sin: Pandora #6–9

June 2014
Forever Evil Aftermath: Batman vs. Bane #1

The Multiversity

October 2014–June 2015

The Multiverse holds worlds beyond number and the concept of 52 linked universes had long been a critical DC universe component. Cataloging some of the least explored and expanding the notion of Super Heroes, writer **Grant Morrison** and many top artists exposed a treasure trove of untapped potential and promoted future creations while telling a primal tale of good overcoming malevolent evil in *The Multiversity*.

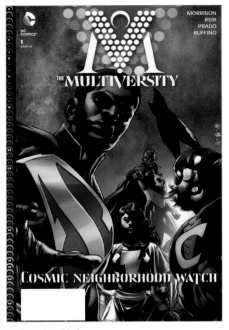

Hail to the chief
President Superman and cartoonist Captain Carrot championed vastly different worlds but united to save all life from ultimate evil.

The DC Multiverse is a concept of infinite scope conceived in part to allow creators abundant range to tell stories. Within its limitless confines, time and space are simply directions, and an infinity of potential alternate realms have been devised. In 1999's *The Kingdom*, Mark Waid and Grant Morrison introduced super-dimensional Hypertime—a "vast, interconnected web of parallel time-lines that comprise all reality"—as another means of describing and defining how DC's increasingly complex and labyrinthine fictional expanse functioned.

The notion of a multiverse even enabled "destroyed" worlds and deceased characters, such as pre-*Zero Hour* heroes, to enter a form of deep storage, where they could be called upon if new story ideas

demanded their return. Incorporated into Morrison's universe-warping, fourth-wall busting sagas, *The Multiversity* delivered epic adventure as parallel existences were attacked by astonishing predatory beings from even further "out there."

Infinite inspiration

Morrison's stated aim was to open up possibilities for DC creators by making its many past worlds viable in modern continuity. By reinventing characters/ scenarios, such as a world populated by former Charlton Comics heroes (who inspired *Watchmen*) or another populated by the original Fawcett Comics pantheon derived from *Shazam!*, Morrison hoped to provide a playing field bursting with variety and potential.

Delayed, deferred, and reworked for years, the event became a blend of classic try-out titles such as *Showcase* or the *Brave and the Bold,* and 2005's *Seven Soldiers* experiment. *The Multiversity* utilized minor characters from parallel Earths— previously seen in multi-reality events such as *52, Countdown, Infinite Crisis,* and *Final Crisis*—united

These island Earths
No matter how strangely varied or bizarrely shaped by their environments, all denizens of every Earth were born to resist the Gentry.

in a pan-dimensional coalition to save last surviving Monitor Nix Uotan, the Superjudge, and all the worlds that he oversees.

Starting and concluding in *The Multiversity* #1–2 (illustrated by Ivan Reis, Joe Prado, and Eber Ferreira), the far-reaching tale unfolded across seven one-shots. Each one-shot carried the underlying war against enemies from outside existence in stand-alone segments that were, in truth, test bed tales for wildly differing superhero concepts, ranging from pulp nostalgia to ironic deconstruction.

When not being a comic book obsessed young human, the Superjudge occupies cosmic citadel the House of Heroes, but after the parasitical, extra-existential invaders The Gentry destroy Earth-7 of the 52-Earth Orrery

Multiversal guide

Masterminded and scripted by Morrison, *The Multiversity* metaseries employed a broad range of artistic and typographic styles to match the variety and range of the content. It also eschewed standard trade dress, using a subtle and simple spine icon of ring binding to alert readers to individual issues.

The event generated a large and imaginative number of variant covers exploring tantalizing alternate realities in faux and nostalgia-based covers. Many referenced classic and esteemed earlier experiments in alternate continuity, like DC's decades-long "Imaginary Stories" strand and "Elseworlds" imprint.

Produced as a celebration of DC's beloved 80-Page Giants, the pivotal *The Multiversity Guidebook* #1 (the first issue Morrison wrote) also advanced the greater story in brief yet telling installments, but its true purpose was to definitively catalogue the current 52 Earths comprising the Local Multiverse, via a vast who's who of artists and an indispensable Multiversal map by Morrison and acclaimed designer Rian Hughes.

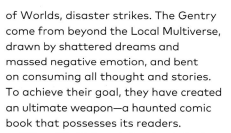

Wonderful worlds
Thanks to the infinite capacity of Hypertime, ideal moments of inspiration and triumph can never be lost.

of Worlds, disaster strikes. The Gentry come from beyond the Local Multiverse, drawn by shattered dreams and massed negative emotion, and bent on consuming all thought and stories. To achieve their goal, they have created an ultimate weapon—a haunted comic book that possesses its readers.

When Nix Uotan strikes back, he is captured and corrupted, forcing House of Heroes' A.I. Harbinger to conscript champions (many fancifully familiar analogues of each other) to save the Superjudge and repel the invasion. As they gather, Calvin Ellis, Superman of Earth-23 and President, reluctantly becomes their Commander-in-Chief.

Beyond Multiversity

All prefixed and designated "The Multiversity," the one-shots were released on a monthly schedule. The saga began with *The Society of Super-Heroes* #1 (illustrated by Chris Sprouse, Karl Story, and Walden Wong), which starred Earth-20's gritty, 1940s iteration of the classic Justice Society of America, while *The Just* #1, drawn by Ben Oliver, visited Earth-16, populated by the celebrity children of Super Heroes. Frank Quitely illustrated *Pax Americana* #1 where bleak modern iterations of Charlton's heroes battled terrorists on Earth-4.

In *Thunderworld Adventures* #1, drawn by Cameron Stewart, the Golden Age Shazam! applied charm and horror to overcome catastrophe on Earth-5, while Jim Lee and Scott Williams depicted the Nazi triumph of Earth-10 in *Mastermen* #1. Doug Mahnke and Christian Alamy rendered readers helpless as Earth-33 took delivery of the parasites' haunted secret weapon—*Ultra Comics* #1, before the united army of Super Heroes finally rescued Uotan, and repelled—for now—The Gentry. ◾

Key issues

October 2014–June 2015

The Multiversity #1–2, The Multiversity: The Society of Super-Heroes #1, The Multiversity: The Just #1, The Multiversity: Pax Americana #1, The Multiversity: Thunderworld Adventures #1, The Multiversity Guidebook #1, The Multiversity: Mastermen #1, The Multiversity: Ultra Comics #1

Convergence

June–July 2015

When cataclysm and Armageddon are daily occurrences, any mass reset of reality calls for something special—an end to top all previous endings. The result was multiple series revisiting beloved eras and iterations, steered by a core miniseries from writers **Jeff King**, **Scott Lobdell**, and **Dan Jurgens**, and artists **Stephen Segovia**, **Aaron Lopresti**, **Ed Benes**, **Eduardo Pansica**, **Andy Kubert**, and **Carlos Pagulayan**, who brought about a calamitous *Convergence*.

Sense of wonder
Having survived Darkseid and the destruction of Earth-2, the wandering Wonders' greatest remaining problem was each other.

After four years of experimentation and innovation, DC was ready to re-embrace past aspects of its momentous history. Always meticulous planners, the company's creative staff carefully guided its shared-continuity titles toward a single point, setting up game-changing crossover events to conclude in a mighty, nostalgia-fueled *Convergence*.

In a comparatively short time, Prime Earth's Super Heroes had seen their share of cosmic events. As part of a Multiverse of 52 realities, the world designated Earth-2 had failed to fight off Darkseid and had been ultimately destroyed, with its survivors cast adrift in space arks searching for a new home. The epic tale concluded in *Earth-2: World's End*, running in parallel with *The New 52: Futures End*,

All together now
Telos delivered the message "fight or die," utterly unaware that the true prize would be his own freedom from Brainiac.

which revealed the probable fate of Prime Earth's heroic stars five years into the future.

Collector of worlds

In the concluding chapter *Futures End: Booster Gold*, the guardian of time was captured by the pitiless marauder

Brainiac and tortured for the secrets of Vanishing Point. The result was Brainiac learning to move beyond his own reality and travel across and beyond the Multiverse. He could now access and attack through Hypertime and target previous existences.

Brainiac was the most feared being in space—a ruthless intelligence taking segments of planetary cultures as specimens for idle study. He preserved

> ## "I am always intrigued by those who triumph over death."
>
> **Brainiac** | *Convergence #0*

those stolen fragments and pruned them into discrete units of data before destroying the worlds from which his specimens originated.

Convergence revealed that, like Super Heroes and Super-Villains, Brainiac was constantly reinvented across countless realities. However, one version escaped the bounds of mere universes and evolved into a hyper-dimensional plunderer. Where universal iterations scoured galaxies for civilizations to reduce in size and secure in bottles, the Over-Brainiac gathered cities from divergent timelines and expired realities and sought to destroy his parallel selves.

In an indefinable moment, the remaining Super Heroes of *DC Comics: The New 52*'s Earth-2—called "Wonders"—and variants of the original Justice Society of America arrived on a vast desolate world. They had been seeking a new planet for the survivors of

Reality check
The chaos of seeing all his treasured specimens struggling together to save existence gave the Collector of Worlds a life-altering fresh perspective.

Darkseid's attacks but learned that this prospective refuge was sentient and hostile. Living planet Telos was the slave of the Over-Brainiac, overseeing innumerable, impenetrable domed cities. Most contained variations of Earth's costumed champions, taken at critical turning points of previous realities and preserved with their lives precariously on hold.

Telos then delivered a chilling proclamation. The enclaves had to battle against each other to determine which of them were worthy of continued survival and restoration to full existence. However, as Telos arranged the bouts, notions of rebellion and autonomy blossomed and he began working against his master and for freedom.

Points of origin
As a myriad of cities complied, with various degrees of willingness or reluctance the Wonders had to survive a devious power-grab by wizard Deimos of Skartaris, who escaped his enclosure and tricked the Wonders into summoning the ultimate Brainiac.

Homeward bound
Experiencing the novel emotion of regret, the repentant Over-Brainiac surveyed his ruined relics one last time before restoring everyone to their points of origin.

Attempting to steal the cosmic collector's power, Deimos destabilized the entirety of creation, before being eliminated by Hal Jordan in his past worst self as Parallax.

Defeated and demoralized, the Over-Brainiac was revealed as the pre-*Flashpoint* New Earth iteration, who had survived but was mutated by successive reality shifts. His attempt to make amends by undoing the effects of the original *Crisis on Infinite Earths* were a genuine but ultimately doomed failure. As he returned all survivors to their points of origin, his most crucial decision was to place one Superman—with his wife, Lois, and their infant son, Jon—on Prime Earth in its recent past.

Now liberated, Telos began a search for his own true history and identity, and offered himself as the new world the survivors of Earth-2 could colonize.

While *Convergence* detailed how and why portions of the past still existed, the event's true allure was glimpsing key moments of DC history through the lens of modern sensibilities. By pitting these heroes and villains in gladiatorial contests for their very survival, new readers could experience, and veteran fans relive, the power and compelling charisma of DC's vast character canon.

Testing times

Like *Flashpoint*, the supplemental series took place alongside the main narrative arc and led toward its conclusion. All captive cities were told they must appoint champions to battle those of other cities, with obliteration for losers and continued life for victors, until only one—the most worthy—remained.

Individual releases were subdivided into themed categories. These included tales relating to *Crisis on Infinite Earths*, *Flashpoint,* and *Zero Hour*, or to specific A-List heroes like Batman and Superman during memorable moments in their long careers. In effect, this meant stories prior to those major events: tales set on the remnants of previous realities, plus other extraordinary encounters like

Justice League Detroit battling the Earth-9 heroes of the Tangent Universe (aka The Secret Six), or the adult Robin and Huntress of 1970s Earth-2 dueling the Soviet Superman of Earth 30.

Drama was paramount but room was also made for humor and whimsy. Set on Earth-S, *Convergence: Shazam!*, by writer Jeff Parker and artist Evan Shaner, saw the lighthearted Captain Marvel Family and Bulletman pause their fight against the Monster Society of Evil to duel Victorian-era denizens of Earth-19's Gotham (by Gaslight) City.

In *Convergence: Harley Quinn*, by writer Steve Pugh and artists Phil Winslade and John Dell, Harleen Quinzel was appalled to discover—in the middle of much-needed therapy and dosed up on mood stabilizers—that she had been chosen as sole champion of Gotham City. To compound the real-world craziness,

her opponent was a cartoon character with the powers of Superman. Protector of Follywood, Califurnia, Captain Carrot was generally easygoing, but that changed when his Justa Lotta Animals comrade Pig-Iron was apparently murdered by Harley. Fortunately, the frame-up by Telos's agents was uncovered and both factions joined a growing army of heroes freed from captivity to unite against Deimos, Telos, and ultimately, Brainiac.

Many tales doubled down when revisiting classic characters, and orchestrated outrageous situations. These included nuclear war survivors the Atomic Knights (from a very different 1986) clashing with the 30th century Legion of Super-Heroes (*Convergence: Superboy and the Legion of Super-Heroes,* by writer Stuart Moore and artists Peter Gross and

Men of action
The nostalgia-drenched 1960s-era "Action-Heroes" confirmed that style, swagger, and unbridled "cool" never went out of fashion.

Future proof
Brainiac's storehouse of miracles proved that pasts and presents were not fixed and that Earth's future was also infinitely mutable.

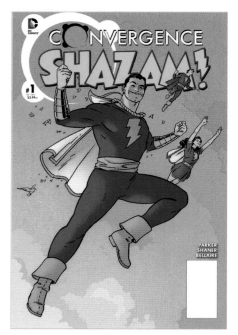

Good old days
The trials of Billy Batson and the Shazam family harked back to simpler, happier times when it was far easier to tell good guys from bad guys.

Mental agility
Harley and her BFFs could survive only if their chosen champion was, quite literally, out of her mind.

Variety, the spice of life

Cover-dated June and July, weekly event *Convergence* ran from April to May 2015. Starting with #0, the nine-part core limited series was supported by 40 separate two-issue "micro-series."

Narratively, the tale continued plot threads from *Earth-2: World's End* and crossover event *The New 52: Futures End*, combined with a selection of historical, pre-*Flashpoint* scenarios like *Crisis on Infinite Earths* and *Zero Hour*. Also included were many beloved time periods and series, such as the Silver Age Atomic Knights stories from the pages of *Strange Adventures*, as well as previous DC experiments like the Tangent Comics universe.

Editorially, the event saw the end of the *DC Comics: The New 52* branding. After *Convergence*, new and resuming titles simply carried DC's then imprint symbol the "DC Peel."

All in-continuity titles were suspended, and during the hiatus, each micro-series (subdivided into character-themed blocs) featured cherished, long-vanished iterations of characters on one final adventure. It was a wave of nostalgia deployed to prepare readers for another all-encompassing reboot/reality correction a year later. Each of these—even faux title *Convergence: Crime Syndicate*—carried event graphics and banner, positioned above classic original versions of individual title logos.

Mark Farmer), or the original 1939 Superman of Earth-2 (from the 1950s), battling beside his cousin Power Girl against Soviet (*Red Son*) Superman and Earth-30's Wonder Woman. In the end, they united in the cause of peace to oust Russian dictator Josef Stalin (*Convergence: Action Comics*, by writer Justin Gray and artist Claude St. Aubin) before turning to deal with Brainiac.

Closure

The project provided many powerful moments such as writer Dan Abnett and artists Tom Derenick and Trevor Scott's *Convergence: Justice Society of America*. In this epic and moving tale, DC's first Super Hero team came out of retirement to save their Metropolis from the marauding Weaponers of Qward, while writer Paul Levitz and artists Jim Fern, Shannon Wheeler, and Joe Rubinstein exulted in old-fashioned costumed capers as the original Seven Soldiers of Liberty also battled Qwardians. Writer Brian Buccellato and artist Phil Winslade broke new ground with *Convergence: Crime Syndicate* as the classic evil-twin

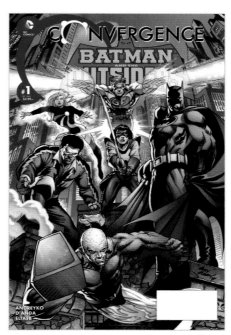

Outside interests
Batman's covert ops team was fine fighting Super-Villains like Kobra, but were unprepared for "The World That's Coming" when OMAC attacked.

analogues of the Justice League of America clashed with Justice Legion Alpha from the 853rd century, as never seen in *DC 1,000,000*.

All sidebar sagas were perfect introductory and celebratory fare—a collection of heartfelt tributes to the heroes and villains of DC's long history. They also served a subtler purpose, as a buildup for the final clash and ultimate redemption of the Over-Brainiac. ■

Key issues

Prelude (November 2014)
Future's End: Booster Gold #1–2

All issues June–July 2015
Convergence #0–8

Convergence (two-issue micro-series)
Batgirl, Batman and Robin, Harley Quinn, Justice League, Nightwing/Oracle, Speed Force, Superman, The Atom, Titans, The Question, Aquaman, Batman: Shadow of the Bat, Catwoman, Green Arrow, Green Lantern/Parallax, Justice League International, Suicide Squad, Superboy, Superman: The Man of Steel, Adventures of Superman, Supergirl: Matrix, Batman and the Outsiders, Green Lantern Corps, Hawkman, Justice League of America, New Teen Titans, The Flash, Wonder Woman, Superboy and the Legion of Super-Heroes, Action Comics, Detective Comics, Infinity Inc., Justice Society of America, World's Finest Comics, Crime Syndicate, Blue Beetle, Shazam!, Plastic Man and the Freedom Fighters, Booster Gold

DC Rebirth

July 2016–November 2017

Constant renewal and imaginative innovation are critical aspects of comic book publishing. However, when your raw material consists of some of the greatest and most popular characters in fiction, looking back is also something with instant appeal and proven benefits. Spearheaded by writer and co-publisher **Geoff Johns**, a company-wide relaunch was focused around a merging of old and new universes that would generate a **DC Rebirth**.

Reach for the sky
History realigned, forgotten heroes returned, and diverging realities rejoined, but behind it all was an unknown and probably hostile force manipulating heroes and villains like toys.

The era of *DC Comics: The New 52* ended with the death of its Superman, before fantasy and reality collided as DC used the tragedy to trigger a complete overhaul of their mainstream continuity. While adjusting their publishing output to a changing market, DC found a way to restore its potent and vast legacy of characters.

The signature 52 regular titles were canceled prior to relaunch, beginning with an oversize one-shot cover-dated July 2016. Based on the 80-Page Giants of DC's Silver Age, *DC Universe: Rebirth Special* #1 hit stores on May 25, 2016.

Alternate agendas
Unlike 2011's *The New 52*, these comic books came in waves rather than as a unilateral release. The *Rebirth Special* preceded 32 debuting regular titles (plus limited series and specials). The previously top-selling 17 titles increased to twice-monthly release, while the rest stayed monthly. Prices were reduced and later regraded, with top titles costing least. Commitment to digital publishing was confirmed with December 2016's second wave of releases, as physical copies included product codes to redeem digital copies.

Restoring DC's long legacy and rich history, key titles *Action Comics* and *Detective Comics* reverted to their original numbering by adding the 52 *New 52* issues to the overall count. *Action Comics* #957 and *Detective Comics* #934 (both Aug. 2016) joined other titles that restarted with new volumes and first issues, while 23 titles were also awarded additional prologue one-shots.

Narratively, *Rebirth* marked a bold return to a familiar tapestry that was

Leading the charge
The new-old reality overflowed with daring champions and mighty defender, but faced even greater and more terrifying threats no one could anticipate.

dramatically acknowledged by the shock return of a major character. The Prime Earth of *The New 52* resulted from The Flash (Barry Allen's) creation of *Flashpoint* and subsequent attempt to undo the damage that caused. The event had erased a number of heroes and villains, including his own protégé and successor Wally West, who explosively reappeared in *Rebirth* at the vanguard of several baffling happenings.

> ## "I can feel it, even now, Barry... we're being watched."
>
> **The Flash (Wally West)** | *DC Universe: Rebirth Special* #1

Watch this space
Aware that something was amiss with reality,
the World's Greatest Detective's first solid clue
was an impossible object in the most unlikely place.

Meticulously crafted by writer Geoff Johns, and illustrated by Gary Frank and other artists, *DC Universe: Rebirth Special* paved the way ahead for years to come, planting clues and laying groundwork for a number of continuity-related events. Wally's return was contingent on him finding an emotional anchor, or else suffering ultimate dissolution because no one remembered him.

Memento

After Batman, his former Teen Titan allies, and even Linda Park—who had been his wife before *Flashpoint*—failed to recognize him, Wally's salvation came when his mentor Barry Allen literally pulled him back into existence. It was a moving moment but merely a prelude to disaster. From his vantage point beyond this restored reality, Wally West had witnessed how it was being systematically altered and edited by a powerful outside force that was changing timelines and the ages of everybody he knew.

The clandestine actions of this external agency, however, had not been entirely seamless. Batman noticed there might be three different Jokers in existence. Elderly hero Johnny Thunder hunted for a Justice Society that never existed, and a girl from the future remembered a Legion of Super-Heroes that would never exist.

Superman was dead and yet another—complete with wife, Lois, and son, Jon—remained ready for action, despite the warnings of hooded stalker Mister Oz. Portents were everywhere. When a survivor of the *The New 52* reality, Pandora, was eliminated by a blue hand and the Dark Knight found a bloodstained "smiley" button ominously embedded in the wall of the Batcave, the only conclusion to be drawn was that catastrophe was coming.

Rebirth carefully curated and ordered a merging of elements from previous continuities, using a gripping cosmic mystery to foreshadow storylines like *The Button* and *Doomsday Clock*. It fully merged past and present in *Superman Reborn*, and many other soon-to-unfold storylines, all gradually building to huge revelations in *Dark Nights: Metal*, *Dark Nights: Death Metal,* and the *Future State* of the *Infinite Frontier* beyond. ■

Key issues

July 2016

DC Universe: Rebirth Special #1

August 2016–May 2017

Action Comics #957, All-Star Batman #1, Aquaman: Rebirth #1, Aquaman #1, Batgirl and the Birds of Prey: Rebirth #1, Batgirl and the Birds of Prey #1, Batgirl #1, Batman: Rebirth #1, Batman #1, Batman Beyond: Rebirth #1, Batman Beyond #1, Batwoman: Rebirth #1, Batwoman #1, Blue Beetle: Rebirth #1, Blue Beetle #1, Cyborg: Rebirth #1, Cyborg #1, Deathstroke: Rebirth #1, Deathstroke #1, Detective Comics #934, The Flash: Rebirth #1, The Flash #1, Green Arrow: Rebirth #1, Green Arrow #1, Green Lanterns: Rebirth #1, Green Lanterns #1, Hal Jordan and the Green Lantern Corps: Rebirth #1, Hal Jordan and the Green Lantern Corps #1, Harley Quinn #1, The Hellblazer: Rebirth #1, The Hellblazer #1, Justice League: Rebirth #1, Justice League #1, JLA #1, JLA: Rebirth #1, JLA: The Atom Rebirth #1, JLA: Killer Frost Rebirth #1, JLA: The Ray Rebirth #1, JLA: Vixen Rebirth #1, New Super-Man #1, Nightwing: Rebirth #1, Nightwing #1, Red Hood and the Outlaws: Rebirth #1, Red Hood and the Outlaws #1, Suicide Squad: Rebirth #1, Suicide Squad #1, Suicide Squad War Crimes Special: Rebirth #1, Supergirl: Rebirth #1, Supergirl #1, Superman: Rebirth #1, Superman #1, Super Sons #1, Superwoman #1, Teen Titans: Rebirth #1, Teen Titans #1, Titans: Rebirth #1, Titans #1, Trinity #1, Wonder Woman: Rebirth #1, Wonder Woman #1

Face time

Expert in supporting its major events, DC teased and advertised the big change well in advance in all sectors of the media and were ready with in-world events and ubiquitous trade dress on all participating titles—a bold blue curtain being drawn back.

The company announced that they would cut back on variant and specialty covers to concentrate on the stories inside. Many first issues and one-shots carried extreme close-ups of the lead character as a way of reminding readers that the way forward was beloved characters in compelling tales. *DC Universe: Rebirth Special #1* eventually went through five printings and a hardback deluxe edition and one-shots *Superman: Rebirth*, *Batman: Rebirth*, *Green Lanterns: Rebirth*, and *Green Arrow: Rebirth* had second printings, with the trade dress in different colors.

The *DC Rebirth* branding continued on covers until the end of 2017, when the event officially ended with the trade dress replaced by a simple "DC Universe" corner colophon.

Superman Reborn

May–June 2017

With Superman dead again, writers **Peter Tomasi**, **Dan Jurgens**, and **Paul Dini**, and pencillers **Doug Mahnke**, **Patrick Gleason**, and **Ian Churchill** clarified how Jon Kent's debut during *Convergence* affected continuity and revealed how Pre-*Flashpoint* Superman and Lois Lane—and their son—fitted into a reconstructed DC Universe. *Superman Reborn* heralded a return to greatness for the Man of Steel and his family.

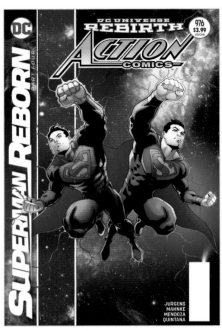

Split decision
Although reality reeled at the reunion of Superman Red and Superman Blue, the result was a more resilient universe and a hero better able to safeguard it.

Since *Crisis on Infinite Earths*, reality had become inherently unstable. Successive shifts and cosmic events that further damaged the fabric of creation would ultimately prove to be the work of a guiding intelligence.

Family ties
Now fully part of the world, the Superman family was ready for any adventure and as much fun as they could find.

The Superman family

Reality and history often changed for Earth and its population, and after *Flashpoint* created Earth-0 in the Multiverse of *DC Comics: The New 52*, cracks began to show. As a new, more aggressive Superman lived and died, followed by his close friend but never wife, Lois Lane, it was revealed that survivors from a previous existence had been hiding on Earth for years.

They were Superman and Lois Lane-Kent of New Earth (the singular cosmos created after *Crisis on Infinite Earths* merged five alternate realities into one). Long married and raising their son, Jonathan, in secrecy and isolation, "Mr. and Mrs. Smith" had chosen to live apart from this world's Super Heroic demands.

Everything changed with the deaths of their counterparts. Strange crimson energies had inundated the New Earth refugees and Prime Earth's Lana Lang (resulting in her brief costumed hero career as Superwoman), and after much discussion, Lois and Clark decided that, as Earth would always need a Superman, they would secretly adopt and continue the lives of their deceased mirror selves.

It was not a seamless transition. As they lived quietly on a farm in Hamilton County, 300 miles away in Metropolis, Lex Luthor was attempting to rebrand himself as the city's true Superman, while in China, well-meaning hero Kong Kenan was making headlines as the New Super-Man. Most worryingly, at *The Daily Planet*, an utterly human Clark Kent already existed. When challenged, he claimed to be the real deal and Superman was the imposter.

Events came to a head on Mr. and Mrs. Smith's wedding anniversary, when "Kent" delivered a photo album of their lives on New Earth and an eerie blue flame began absorbing Jon. With memories of their previous lives being

> ## "We didn't lose Jon. That **Clark Kent** took him..."
>
> **Clark Kent (Superman)** | *Superman* #18

overwritten and replaced by those of Prime Earth's Lois and Clark, the doppelgänger revealed himself as Fifth-Dimensional entity Mr. Mxyzptlk.

Together forever

The powerful sprite explained he had been held captive by a scheming being called Mister Oz (ultimately revealed as a corrupted, time-lost Jor-El, stalking the survivors of his own family). After an impossible length of time waiting to be rescued by his old sparring partner Superman, Mr. Mxyzptlk felt rejected and lost his temper. Escaping to Earth, the imp discovered Superman was dead and hid from Mister Oz by becoming Clark Kent, complete with altered memories so that even he believed in the subterfuge.

When he discovered another Superman existed, Mxyzptlk targeted young Jon Kent because his "old pal" preferred the kid to him. Mxyzptlk erased their son from the transplanted Kents' new life, hoping the boy would be

Kent vs Kent
Clark Kent's impossible imposter was initially a convenient secret-identity aid, but he was soon revealed as too dangerous to live.

his new playmate. The mischief-making imp then invited New Earth Superman and Lois to play a game to get Jon back, sweetening the deal by explaining the truth of their existence. Some unknown force (later revealed as atomic god Doctor Manhattan) had tampered with the fabric of the universe, splitting cosmically inseparable Superman and Lois into separate—and lesser— couples, characterized by blue energy for New Earth and red energy for the less connected Prime Earth pair.

When the latter couple died, their spiritual force and

Myx-ed blessings
Before answering all Superman's questions, the 5-D imp could not resist testing his favorite straight man to near destruction.

Cosmic consequence

Although a short and relatively low-key story arc that appeared as part of a far-larger tapestry of tales, *Superman Reborn* was arguably the most significant tale of 2017, resulting in a major change to continuity during the vast and ongoing *DC Rebirth* mega-event.

The core *Superman* and *Action Comics* issues carried a spine banner announcing the tale, but not every contributing tie-in added a badge declaring participation in the event.

memories were released and began dissipating. However, as Jon Kent struggled in Mxyzptlk's pocket dimension, the Prime Earth couple began to reform, nurturing Jon, and becoming more substantial. Meanwhile, their New Earth counterparts started to fade as their memories of their son abated.

When Mxyzptlk reneged on his deal, the red couple sacrificed themselves, surrendering their lives and individuality, merging with the blue family to sustain them. This reunited universal strands and divergent timelines into one cohesive whole. This selfless demonstration of love reshaped reality once more, resulting in stronger, more balanced and complete existence. ■

Key issues

Convergence: Superman #2 (July 2015)

May–June 2017

Superman #18–19, Action Comics #975–976, Superwoman #8–9, New Super-Man #10, Trinity #8

Dark Nights: Metal

August 2017–May 2018

The DC universe is a place of constant revelation, always with a new secret about its major heroes and villains to be exposed. In 2017, Batman-team writer **Scott Snyder** and artist **Greg Capullo** shared the greatest mystery of all, as Bruce Wayne reviewed his own life and discovered the true nature of reality and his critical role in its continued survival during a transformative crisis—*Dark Nights: Metal*.

Full metal justice
Before repelling the invasion of Barbatos, the Justice League first had to convince teammate Batman to let them help him.

A chain of linked events that would dominate and reshape continuity began when Scott Snyder and Greg Capullo completed a long association with Batman by revising his history, while creating a legion of dark doppelgängers and a major new villain—The Batman Who Laughs.

When the Justice League returned from a space mission, they found a mountain had materialized in Gotham City. It was the HQ of legendary adventurers the Challengers of the Unknown, and its reappearance presaged catastrophe. More information came from Hawkgirl Kendra Saunders, then leader of the Blackhawks, who revealed the secret history of Earth and the true nature of existence. As chaos spread throughout Gotham City and champions responded, Kendra explained that Multiversal existence—both positive matter and Antimatter—had a hidden underside, a region of dark matter known as the Dark Multiverse. Here the brother of Monitor and Anti-Monitor made new universes. The World Forger's efforts were constant, and his standards high, and he rejected countless universes for being malformed or unstable.

Food for thought

Those discarded were consumed by The World Forger's "Bat-God" dragon Barbatos, who grew mighty on rejected realities. Barbatos constantly craved unsuitable universes, and turned on his creator, extending his influence by allowing corrupted realities to fester and grow. Aware of the Multiverse above, Barbatos warped

Bat to the bone
By plundering the sickest realities of the Dark Multiverse, Barbatos assembled the deadliest killers in existence—and they were all Batman.

time, influenced human history, created cults to worship him, and founded the Court/Parliament of Owls.

His focus was Batman. Bruce Wayne's life was subtly altered to forge him into a portal allowing Barbatos entry to the Multiverse. He even claimed to be the bat Wayne saw the night he resolved to fight crime. Barbatos systematically

> **"All roads lead to Barbatos...** and now the world will sink... into darkness...**"
>
> **Batman** | *Dark Nights: Metal #3*

tempered his unwitting human tool via a progression of extra-Multiversal "divine" metals—Electrum, Dionesium, Promethium, Nth Metal, and more—in a process called "mantling."

After reading Hawkman Carter Hall's diary and receiving a prophetic warning from abstract entity Dream of the Endless, Batman abandoned his well-meaning Justice League comrades and their efforts to combat the incursion. The Dark Knight sought to travel back in time and undo the mantling, unaware this was also part of Barbatos's plan. After inadvertent exposure to "Batmanium," Wayne became the doorway and the Bat-god entered, inflicting monstrous mutation and terror while forcing the Dark Multiverse to absorb established realities above it.

Into the abyss

Weaving his plan over eons, Barbatos had removed reincarnating warrior Carter Hall from existence after Hawkman deduced the secrets of Nth Metal, transforming him into a ghastly puppet guarding the World Forge. Free at last, Barbatos sought to subsume Earth's positive matter Multiverse with deviant realities deemed unworthy of existence and

Tables turned
The upside of an infinite number of Batman iterations was that the majority of them fought for justice and the light.

Batman deviations drawn from the most twisted universes. Meanwhile, heroes invaded his abandoned domain, rescuing his former slaves and puppets.

As Batman struggled on, Barbatos unleashed variant Dark Knights in a full-scale assault on creation. A repulsive amalgamation of Batman and the Joker, the "Batman Who Laughs" was in command, a cosmic wildcard who would ultimately grow beyond his origins and seize control of creation.

At this time, however, the Batman Who Laughs was defeated by Batman and the true Joker working together, even as an army of resurgent Super Heroes acting in unison and employing Nth and Tenth Metal weapons and armor counterattacked. Using exotic elements inimical to Dark Multiversal beings, they battled valiantly and were eventually victorious. Reality was restored and the natural order returned, but dangerously altered and only at tremendous cost.

The battle created a crack in the infinite Source Wall at the end of space. As well as triggering primordial and catastrophic cosmic repair systems, it also allowed the oldest menace to creation fresh access to the Multiverse. In the end, Perpetua would be the most incredible disaster humanity and reality would ever face. ■

Key issues

Prelude (August–September 2017)
Dark Days: The Forge #1, Dark Days: The Casting #1

October 2017–May 2018
Dark Nights: Metal #1–6

One-shots (November 2017–January 2018)
Batman: The Red Death #1, Batman: The Red Death #1, Batman: The Dawnbreaker #1, Batman: The Drowned #1, Batman: The Merciless #1, Batman: The Devastator #1, The Batman Who Laughs #1

Tie-ins (January–April 2018)
Batman: Lost #1, Hawkman: Found #1, Dark Knights Rising: The Wild Hunt #1

Gotham Resistance crossovers (November– December 2017)
Teen Titans #12, Nightwing #29, Suicide Squad #26, Green Arrow #32

Bats out of Hell (December 2017– January 2018)
The Flash #33, Justice League #32–33, Hal Jordan and the Green Lantern Corps #32

Spin-off series (March–August 2018)
Damage #1, The Silencer #1, Sideways #1, The Terrifics #1, The Curse of Brimstone #1, The Immortal Men #1, New Challengers #1, The Unexpected #1

Striking gold

Dark Nights: Metal reunited Snyder and Capullo (with inker Jonathan Glapion) following their stellar, groundbreaking run on *Batman*. Their previous triumphs began in 2011 and included *The Court of Owls*, *Death of the Family*, *Zero Year*, and *Endgame*, with this final crossover saga linking and unifying them all.

Editorially, a range of trade dress was employed, with banners for tie-ins specifically tailored to the sub-storyline—like *Bats Out of Hell* or *Gotham Resistance*—while the main story arc and one-shots carried the key graphic.

As well as setting the scene for the redefining sequel *Dark Nights: Death Metal*, the saga was equally significant for reviving many past triumphs.

Reintroducing Neil Gaiman's Sandman to mainstream continuity, it also reinvigorated classic properties such as Challengers of the Unknown and Hawkman. Dark Multiverse contamination was the spark used to ignite a wave of new titles, like weird science super-team the Terrifics (uniting Plastic Man, Phantom Girl, Metamorpho, and Mister Terrific) and entirely original characters like Derek James, who gained the power to teleport and became hapless teen hero Sideways after falling into a portal.

Doomsday Clock

January 2018–February 2020

In 2017, after years of pressure for an official sequel to the groundbreaking *Watchmen*, DC announced that fans' wishes had come true. Written by **Geoff Johns** and illustrated by **Gary Frank**, a saga that fully integrated the landmark story into DC continuity was launched. It revisited an alternate past, only to introduce all of DC's superstars to the all-too present and imminent peril of the ***Doomsday Clock***.

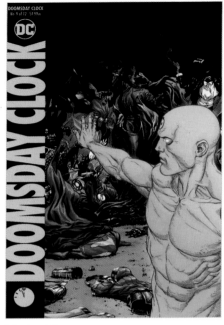

It's about time
Doctor Manhattan preferred to make minor alterations to realities that had profound consequences but was not afraid to also trade blows with the mightiest heroes in existence.

Narratively, *Doomsday Clock* began seven years after *Watchmen* ended. Adrian (Ozymandias) Veidt's scheme to save humanity from itself had been exposed and he was now a fugitive. The geopolitical situation was still dire, with the US and the Soviets both readying their nukes to fly.

Convinced that Doctor Manhattan could still save the planet, Veidt tricked new Rorschach Reggie Long (son of the original's prison psychiatrist), into springing convict lovers Mime (Marcos Maez) and Marionette (Erika Manson) to help him retrieve the atomic god from an alternate reality.

Armageddon

Promised cash and the restoration of their baby—confiscated from Marionette upon her arrest—the voyagers boarded Nite Owl's converted craft, just as nuclear missiles struck their world. Although it managed to cross universes to Doctor Manhattan's last detectable location,

the severely damaged Owlship crashed into the worst part of Gotham City.

As the lethal lovers met this Earth's most dangerous costumed criminals, Rorschach encountered Batman. After a brief stint in Arkham, Reggie convinced the Dark Knight his incredible story was true, but by then Veidt's real plan was underway and Ozymandias approached this world's intellectual equivalent of himself. The meeting with Lex Luthor ended when they were all ambushed by a man he murdered years ago. Some unknown force had plucked

the Comedian from his death plunge and sent him after Ozymandias.

This Earth was also the verge of Armageddon. Overflowing with super-beings, a recent exposé indicated that America had been deliberately creating them—triggering latent "metagenes" by arranging accidents or just trying to kill volunteers to trigger the creation of superpowered soldiers.

Branded as misinformation, false-flag tactics, or simply lies, the "Supermen Theory" scandal made Earth an unstable armed camp, with formerly independent Super Heroes and Villains aligning along

Tide turned
Doctor Manhattan unmade his time tapestry and sparked an explosion of Super Heroes encompassing past, present, and future generations.

Power of perspective
The ferocious blow Manhattan had seen heading towards him ever since he had arrived in this reality finally landed... on a threat he had never perceived.

national lines and demanding that the US stand down its overwhelming metahuman forces.

Previously considered neutral and impartial, Superman became a global pariah after hundreds died when he tried to prevent Firestorm's meltdown in Red Square. Sidelined by the faked crisis, Superman had no idea his existence had been continually altered.

Adrift in time, Doctor Manhattan had first arrived on Earth in 1938, befriended an actor named Carlton Carver, and watched the very first manifestation of Superman. Aware of all time simultaneously, Manhattan embraced a spirit of impartial inquiry, but, after literally seeing no future for himself, began making changes.

Instinctively aware of Super Heroes' potential threat, he tailored reality, preventing the 1940s proliferation and the existence of the Justice Society. However, every effort to delete Superman had simply pushed the infant's arrival on Earth forward a number of years. Doctor Manhattan could not shake the belief—glimpsed as a partial vision from the future—that one day Superman would end him.

Cover story

Doomsday Clock exceeded most fans' expectations and was a sales hit despite taking almost a year longer than anticipated to complete. The reality warping series became an integral component of the overarching continuity from the moment it concluded.

Major timeline changes were deliberately ambiguous, neither confirming or denying whether it occupied mainstream continuity or a parallel one closely resembling it. Plot threads like America's secret project to create metahumans have been largely ignored, but Doctor Manhattan's presence and actions have impacted mainstream events as seen in *DC Rebirth*, *The Button*, *Dark Nights: Death Metal*,

Flash Forward, *Generations*, and the 2021 *Infinite Frontiers* relaunch.

Like its progenitor, *Doomsday Clock* provided supplementary in-world materials—excerpts from police files, letters, records and dossiers, faux film articles on murdered actor Carlton Carver and his private eye screen (and comic book) alter ego Nathaniel Dusk, as well as other features that fleshed out the tale. *Watchmen*'s design style and cover logo was retained, including modifying the back covers' flowing blood motif to signify the centrality of Superman to the drama. One new bonus was a range of variant and special-effects covers and the many reprintings made possible by rapid improvements in print technology.

Ultimately, he reasoned this reality was, in fact, a sentient Metaverse, the prime reality where Kal-El's landing and the inevitable advent of Superman could not be excised. Attempts to negate his influence only delayed the arrival of the Man of Steel to serve another generation equally in need of his powers and inspiration.

Promised land

As both Manhattan and Ozymandias manipulated events, Batman and Luthor each deduced some incredible extra-universal force had been editing time and independently acted to preserve Superman. With the war of words between nations boasting their own metahumans becoming bloody deeds on Earth, an army of Super Heroes voyaged to Mars to confront the now-exposed Doctor Manhattan.

His ultimate showdown with Superman did—in a way—eliminate him. The pointless murder of Carver long ago sparked a flash of clarity, restoring Doctor Manhattan's connection to humanity. Once again he amended time—recreating moments that created the Justice Society, Legion of Super-Heroes, and all other inspirational figures. He did not stop there; he returned to his home world to punish Ozymandias and repair the planet's wounds to fashion a paradise for all. ◾

> ## "I am a being of inaction, on a crash course with a man of **action**."
>
> **Doctor Manhattan** | *Doomsday Clock* #10

Key issues

September 1986—October 1987
Watchmen #1–12

July 2016
DC Universe: Rebirth Special #1

June—July 2017
Batman #21–22; *The Flash* #21–22 (The Button)

January 2018—February 2020
Doomsday Clock #1–12

November 2019—April 2020
Flash Forward #1–6

November 2020
Dark Nights: Death Metal Speed Metal #1

Partners in peril
To save his people, Colu's computer overlord Brainiac compiled a collection of alien and human heroes and villains. He had no expectation of surviving his mission.

Justice League: No Justice

July–August 2018

Although Earth's heroes had successfully turned back a horrific Multiversal incursion in *Dark Nights: Metal*, the cost of their victory was that creation began unraveling almost immediately. With ancient mechanisms awakening, writers **Scott Snyder**, **James Tynion IV**, and **Joshua Williamson** joined artists **Francis Manapul**, **Marcus To**, and **Riley Rossmo** in laying groundwork for the next all-encompassing crisis as reality was pushed to the brink in *Justice League: No Justice*.

After *DC Rebirth* realigned diverging timelines, ever-escalating crises and reality-warping incidents plagued the Multiverse. With tension, destruction, and casualties mounting everywhere, constant rapid change inevitably led to another threat—this time from the beginnings of existence.

Short and sharp, *Justice League: No Justice* presaged a monumental epic set to shake up everything. In its wake, interlinked story arcs *Year of the Villain, Heroes in Crisis, Event Leviathan*, and more, culminated in *Dark Nights: Death Metal, Future State,* and *Infinite Frontiers,* forging an utterly altered DC Multiverse.

In *Dark Nights: Metal,* Earth's defenders damaged the Source Wall to save humanity from the Dark Multiverse. The incomprehensible barrier dividing Multiverses was as old as existence, and legend stated that behind it lay a benevolent cosmic force. Now, an army of Green Lanterns worked tirelessly to repair the crack, forgetting that not all myths and legends are true.

Alien alliance
On Earth, Collector of Worlds Brainiac incapacitated many of its heroes—the Justice League, Teen Titans, Titans, and Suicide Squad—before abducting a selection to assist with what he claimed was a rescue mission. His home world Colu—home to the universe's most intelligent race—was besieged by primordial Omega Titans, and he needed specific sentient weapons to defeat them. His armory also included villains Lobo, Sinestro, Deathstroke, Starro, Etrigan the Demon, and Lex Luthor—a true Legion of Doom.

Think again
Despite finally defeating the Super Heroes who had so often frustrated his plans, Brainiac could not destroy them until his greater agenda had been completed.

The Omega Titans embodied the primal concepts of Entropy, Mystery, Wonder, and Wisdom. When planets neared their end by tipping too far toward one concept—such as Wisdom on Colu—that world perished. These towering, inscrutable cosmic gods were drawn to trees that represented their concept, which somehow spontaneously germinated and destroyed unbalanced worlds. This allowed the Omega Twins

> ## "You and your friends on the Justice League **broke** the damn universe."
>
> **Guy Gardner** | *Justice League: No Justice #1*

Titanic
Omega Titans fed on planets, using the power to sustain the Source. By saving Earth, its heroes had imperiled all life.

THE OMEGA TITANS, PLANET EARTH.

to feast on the energy that was released after the death of the planet.

Equipping the heroes with new uniforms to augment the movement of the trees' collected energy stores, and splitting the heroes into teams representing the primal concepts,

Brainiac led them into rebalancing the equation on Colu. This was done by enhancing Mystery, Wonder, and Entropy to counter the deadly overabundance of Wisdom. Brainiac stressed that they must follow his instructions exactly… but disaster struck.

From Earth, a psychic assault by Amanda Waller's Taskforce XI hacked, data-mined, and destroyed Brainiac, transferring all his knowledge back to her. However, to ensure his captive army's compliance, the computer tyrant had planted a cosmic seed

on Earth, which would germinate and summon the Omega Titans if Colu was destroyed. Now humanity was doomed.

Out of space

As Waller and Green Arrow desperately hunted for Earth's seed, Colu's fate was sealed when it became clear that the heroes couldn't balance the trees' damage. In response, the planet's inhabitants proved their legendary intelligence by fleeing into space. However, Colu's obliteration also inadvertently liberated thousands of worlds that had previously been shrunk and bottled by Brainiac to be studied.

In an instant, the region of space was filled with squabbling civilizations, forming a "Ghost Sector" of worlds desperately in need of peacekeepers. Also freed was Brainiac's "son" Vril Dox, aka Brainiac 2.0, who testily explained how everyone had been deceived and Earth had always been earmarked for annihilation. There, the cosmic seed had already spawned four energy trees, gradually preparing the planet for consumption by the Omega Titans, who now loomed over every horizon.

The Omega Titans' true purpose was lost to history. No one knew that at the dawn of creation they were built as self-sustaining tools to maintain the integrity of the Source Wall and ensure that the powerful being imprisoned behind it stayed there forever. As that entity watched on, heroes and villains rushed to Earth to avert catastrophe. Here, a last-ditch attempt involving Amanda Waller's data-mined download, Brainiac 2.0's revelation of his "father's" duplicity, and Cyborg's inbuilt Apokoliptian technology resulted in the Omega Titans turning on each other at the final moment. ▨

Justice variations

Justice League: No Justice was a visually spectacular, blockbuster intended to set the scene for bigger things. The self-contained tale launched with a teaser prelude in promotional title *DC Nation #0*, with official ties-ins *Titans Special #1* and *Green Arrow Annual #2* being suitably badged. However, the event's repercussions spread far further and wider.

The energy leaking from the cracked Source Wall was referenced in many titles as it affected emotional states and mutated beings across infinity. With fan favorite Beast Boy ferociously changed, the Justice League appointed the Titans to seek out and counter situations caused by the contamination. This left Robin (Damian Wayne) free to form his own

Teen Titans team to execute his own extreme agenda. Luthor regained his status as DC's primary villain, with his actions here directly leading to his becoming the prophet of Doom in a world dedicated to evil.

The biggest shake-up was to the entire Justice League franchise. The current volumes of *Justice League of America* and *Justice League* wrapped up (#29 and #43 respectively, both June 2018) and were replaced by *new Justice League #1* and *Justice League Dark #1* incarnations.

Springing directly out of *Justice League: No Justice*, the cosmically dystopian new series *Justice League Odyssey* was set in the recently liberated Ghost Sector, where Cyborg and a constantly shifting team of space-based characters confronted Darkseid.

Key issues

July–August 2018

Justice League: No Justice: #1–4, *DC Nation #0, Green Arrow Annual #2, Titans Special #1*

Spin-off series (August–November 2018)

Justice League #1, Justice League Dark #1, Justice League Odyssey #1

Heroes in Crisis

November 2018–July 2019

Comic creators have always strove to blend the unbelievable with the conceivable and the astonishing with the authentic. Realism remains something to which many aspire, and this endeavor reached new heights in a harrowing drama from writer **Tom King** and illustrators **Clay Mann**, **Travis Moore**, **Lee Weeks**, **Mitch Gerads**, and **Jorge Fornés**, who took a long, hard look at costumed crusaders in modern society and discovered *Heroes in Crisis*.

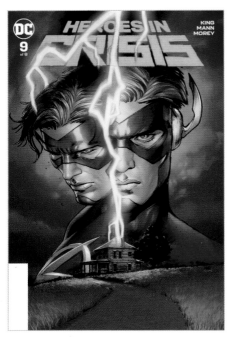

Death by misadventure
The horror of a senseless mass murder was made infinitely worse when one hero became both victim and perpetrator.

Speedsters hold a unique position in the DC universe, their connection to the enigmatic Speed Force granting them a dangerous potential for creating unwelcome, reality-rending change. Despite this, they also seem unable to outrace personal tragedy.

Super Heroes are no strangers to trauma and grief, and in the aftermath of countless incidents of personal crisis, Superman, Batman, and Wonder Woman created a top-secret refuge and rehabilitation project where metahumans received counseling for mental-health problems afflicting the more (or less) than human. Some even underwent psychiatric treatment for post-traumatic stress disorders.

Sidekicks and strangers

Sanctuary—as the refuge was called— was located in the rural Midwest: an isolated, fully automated facility where heroes, reforming villains, and superpowered teens could unload and share the pressures only they and people like them endured.

Everything changed when the majority of patients at the facility were murdered in a single attack. Alerted by alarms, Super Heroes converged on the site to find multiple bodies and four potential culprits missing. Among the many casualties were Arsenal, Poison Ivy, Wally West, Blue Jay, Red Devil, Protector, Tattooed Man, Gunfire, Lagoon Boy, Gnarrk, Commander Steel, and Hot Spot. Meanwhile, prime suspects Booster Gold and Harley Quinn were violently attacking one another—each convinced the other was the killer.

Speed kills
Drowning in depression and mired in survivor's guilt, the third Flash's toxic emotional state was ejected from him as lethal Speed Force energy.

Batman's investigation confirmed sabotage of Sanctury's systems and indicated an inside job. This was seemingly corroborated by enigmatic whistleblower "the Puddler," who fed confidential recordings made by patients to *Daily Planet* journalist Lois Lane.

> "Our hope for... **Redemption**... is now just another **hunt** for vengeance."
>
> **Batman** | *Heroes in Crisis* #1

Now knowing it was the scene of multiple murders, Lois could no longer suppress Sanctuary's existence, no matter what her husband, Superman, wanted. The news grew into public scandal, with citizens justifiably terrified that their heroic "walking super-weapon" idols could be as crazy as any abused schoolkid, burned-out cop, or troubled war veteran. Tensions mounted, and Superman, Batman, and Wonder Woman's hasty press conference only further alienated the public and their own costumed allies.

On the run and both suffering memory loss, Booster and Harley found allies to help clear their name. Former Blue Beetle Ted Lord happily helped his erstwhile JLA buddy, but Quinn had a far tougher time convincing Batgirl Barbara Gordon of her innocence. Their individual investigations pointed to baffling anomalies, confirmed when Wallace West—a distant cousin also connected to the Speed Force—stated that assumed victim and frequent time traveler Wally West was still alive.

Reexamination of West's body revealed it was from five days in the future, and confirmation of Wally's

Reconciliation
The hardest task Wally West ever accomplished was forgiving himself and finding the strength to go on.

Personal issues

Playing out as a murder mystery, *Heroes in Crisis* used DC's compelling and expansive continuity to explore real-world issues. Feeling comics had always reflected major issues of their time, author Tom King wanted to highlight the effects of violence; adapting the phenomenon of mass killings to the superhero idiom to promote wider debate on how modern culture seemingly accepted death by massacre as normal. It was a comic book response to the societal issue of living with violence in the same way drug issues were first explored in the 1970s *Green Lantern/Green Arrow* series.

In the aftermath, Wally West became a Multiversal wanderer, gaining the powers of fellow nomad Doctor

Manhattan in limited series *Fast Forward* and becoming a key component of massive reality shifts in *Dark Nights: Death Metal*. This culminated in the DC Universe entering a Future State of Infinite Frontiers.

In keeping with its sombre themes, *Heroes in Crisis* carried no trade dress on the core miniseries or tie-in crossovers dealing with superhero survivors coping with the loss of partners. However, among many variant covers augmenting the main series was a sequence of "dossier images" depicting shocking moments from DC history— the deaths of Superman, Barry Allen, and Jason Todd, Aquaman losing his hand, Bane breaking Batman's back, Wonder Woman's execution of Maxwell Lord, and more.

guilt came after he resurrected Poison Ivy and, as the Puddler, sent a video confession to Lois. When *Flashpoint* created the *DC Comics: The New 52* universe, Wally's wife, Linda, and children, Irey and Jai, were erased from reality but never restored in subsequent reality realignments.

Dead and alive

Wally's tragic spiral hit bottom in Sanctuary, which he believed was created out of pity solely for him. In a delusional state, he lost control, and a burst of raw Speed Force energy ended the lives of everyone in range. Still lost, Wally killed a willing future self and left evidence framing sole survivors Harley and Booster.

Resolved to avoid accidentally creating another *Flashpoint*, Wally needed to murder himself, but

seasoned time traveler Booster Gold offered another solution to close the time loop caused by The Flash's simultaneously dead and living bodies. If they clone Wally's body in the far future, that could be used for the crime scene rather than his real body. Accepting his guilt in multiple counts of manslaughter, Wally surrendered himself to Justice League custody. ■

Key issues

November 2018–July 2019
Heroes in Crisis #1–9

Tie-ins (December 2018, March–May 2019)
Green Arrow #45, 48–50, The Flash Annual #2, Batman #64–65, The Flash #64–65

Spin-off series (November 2019–April 2020)
Harley Quinn and Poison Ivy #–6, Flash Forward #1–6

Dark Nights: Death Metal

August 2020–March 2021

For all of eternity, conflict and catastrophe had beleaguered living beings across every universe, and inevitably champions and defenders had risen to resist darkness and doom. A core limited series written by **Scott Snyder** and illustrated by **Greg Capullo** inspired a host of creators in supplementary titles to at last reveal the meaning of life and the nature of existence in *Dark Nights: Death Metal*.

Metal storm
Reality might be completely overwritten by evil, but the noble spirits of its champions shone through any malign metamorphosis.

The world had become a perilous place with destruction and discontent everywhere. Its defenders reeled from one crisis to the next in a constant holding action against cosmic calamity. Eventually, an amalgamation of Super-Villains known as the Legion of Doom, led by Lex Luthor (in a hybrid superpowered form dubbed "Apex Lex"), resulted in the death of the Justice League and the birth of a nightmare reality. Only then did answers come, as hopes of a better world were rekindled by a Multiversal nomad—Wally West.

Spiritual component

When dragon Barbatos first attacked from the Dark Multiverse, he devised monstrous alternate-Earth versions of Batman as his army, accidentally unleashing a universal threat in The Batman Who Laughs, a deadly melding of Bruce Wayne and the Joker. This crazed, unpredictable schemer grew far beyond his creator. His duel with Batman left Barbatos defeated by Earth's Super Heroes, but also caused the Source Wall that encapsulated the universe to rupture.

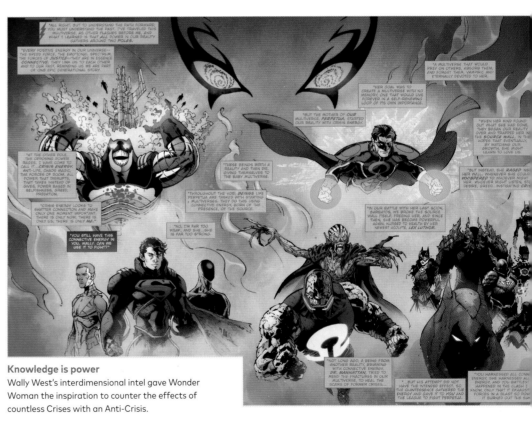

Knowledge is power
Wally West's interdimensional intel gave Wonder Woman the inspiration to counter the effects of countless Crises with an Anti-Crisis.

Transformative energies escaped and primordial mechanisms activated to seal the breach. The actions of the "Omega Titans" were, unfortunately, misinterpreted by the Justice League, who defeated the giants, inadvertently sealing the fate of the Multiverse.

The truth became known only after an escalating war across creation revealed existence's true origins, the competing forces fueling it, and how crucial spiritual components drove it. By then, however, life had become the plaything of a pitiless foe.

Robin
Earth's ravaged remnants were policed by the most malicious, malevolent, and maladjusted Doom doppelgängers of Batman and Robin.

All existence stems from an ineffable fountainhead known as The Presence, which itself exists beyond the Source. It ordered Perpetua, the personification of creation, to fashion a Multiverse of life and sentience. She was required to surrender her own energies to sustain it, but instead built fiercely competitive worlds, encouraging savage, undiluted competition, and selfish goals. Her species violently clashed, devoid of any positive sentiments or influences intended by The Presence to provide balance and equilibrium for evolving sentients. Instead, Perpetua's system of forces in opposition came to underpin reality—good against evil, order vs. chaos, positivity and negativity, generosity or selfishness, Connectivity and Crisis, Justice and Doom.

Her cosmos was designed to preserve Perpetua, who lived for billions of years developing warrior predators to battle her superiors when they eventually discovered her dereliction of duty. Ultimately, her firstborn creations—Alpheus the World Forger, Mar Novu the Over-Monitor, and Mobius the Anti-Monitor—became aware of her deceit and notified The Presence's Sixth Dimensional intermediaries.

The Presence's Cosmic Raptor captured Perpetua, reversing time to restart a Multiverse divided into self-contained autonomous universes, separated by a transdimensional wall. Segregating space-time yet connecting everything to the Source, the eternal barrier became her prison. Over eons, Perpetua watched and schemed. Realizing living beings' actions, choices, and emotions generated energies that empowered her, Perpetua began influencing worlds beyond the Wall to maximize "Crisis Energies."

Infinite universes filled with beings embraced her philosophy of Doom, but life generally tilted toward benevolent advancement—Justice. Greed, cruelty, and evil were everywhere resisted by ordinary mortals and more extraordinary creatures—defenders, champions, and heroes. In recent times Super Heroes emerged, but their well-intentioned actions seemed to attract the chaos and negativity Perpetua needed.

Doom vs. Justice

Cosmic close-calls and disasters averted by Super Heroes strengthened Perpetua, allowing her to formulate existence-threatening, time-altering events—Crises. As these mounted and intensified, cracks appeared in the Source Wall restraining Perpetua. Following time-tampering by Doctor Manhattan, subsequent reality fractures granted Perpetua even greater influence. She imposed her solipsistic beliefs on the arrogant, avaricious Lex Luthor via hallucinations, eventually recreating him as her disciple.

He fostered further evil deeds through his Legion of Doom, while spreading her "me-first" doctrine, which slowly poisoned humanity's collective-consciousness, tipping the planet's ethical balance away from fairness and justice toward self-serving Doom.

Run for your lives
Infused with the knowledge of New God Metron and touched by the power of Doctor Manhattan, Wally West led speedsters in the race to restore the Multiverse.

Titans together
Costumed champions from across time and space were called to a final battle for the life and soul of all that ever was.

Own worst enemies
Life's most implacable and terrifying foes were its greatest champions twisted into monsters.

After a prolonged campaign or terror and constant clashes across Earth's timeline, the events of the *Year of the Villain* changed Earth. Presented with a choice of sacrifice or self-preservation, humanity sided with the dark side. With evil ascendant everywhere, Apex Lex finally liberated Perpetua from the Source Wall and she began remodeling existence to suit her needs and desires.

For life and Justice

Seeking sustenance and inspiration, she began consuming and reshaping alternate Earths, still attempting to build the ultimate warrior species to defend her from the consequences of her sins. Covertly impacting creation from the start, by triggering Crises to weaken the fabric of existence and her prison, she had duped and indoctrinated Luthor with her creed of Doom, making him a human-Martian hybrid and high priest for gathering recruits, an Apex Predator.

The Justice League was still alive, saved by mystic cabal The Quintessence. As the heroes regrouped, Apex Lex was stripped of his powers and ejected in favor of superior predator The Batman Who Laughs. Luthor would make Perpetua regret her choice. He hired Lobo to scour realities for a retaliatory weapon and in the nightmare of New Apokolips the infallible bounty hunter finally secured enough exotic "Death Metal" to meet his client's needs. Life would soon turn the tables.

The counterattack began after Multiversal wanderer Wally West returned, bearing the truth about Perpetua. Rallying the scattered disciples of Justice for one last strike, he used Earth-0's fluid nature and his own new powers to summon multiple incarnations of Super Heroes from every past, possible present, or future Earth that could ever be.

Perpetua was distracted, consuming worlds and universes until little more than Earth-0 remained. It was a chaotic, vile arena where—whether mutated, debased, or dead—Life's last champions struggled against her deputy The

Outcompeted
By stealing the Crisis Energy fueling Perpetua, her former flunky became the greatest terror in reality.

> "See it for what it has become. See what **my** actions have made it."
>
> **Lex Luthor** | *Dark Nights: Death Metal Guidebook #1*

Who's laughing now?
Wonder Woman and The Darkest Knight warred across time, with the turning point coming in the frozen moment before creation began.

Knight confirmed the validity of her egocentric, twisted beliefs by his very existence. He gained power by stealth and force, outcompeting her on her own celestial level. However, his triumph was short-lived as he defeated Perpetua, only to ultimately succumb to amassed Anti-Crisis energies and the resolute ethics of the Multiverse's greatest champion and defender, Wonder Woman, clad in the mystic armor of Death Metal.

Golden tomorrows

After the Darkest Knight destroyed Perpetua, he battled the golden Amazon across all time and space before being beaten and destroyed in the heart of the last sun in existence. He fell to the pure might of Justice as wielded by ascended Wonder Woman, who had fulfilled the multibillion-year expectations so long ago set in motion by the will of The Presence.

As confirmation of this outcome, the Multiverse was restored as an Omniverse—expanded and unlocked in anticipation of intriguing Futures State and horizons where an Infinite Frontier beckoned. ▨

Darkest Knight (formerly the Batman Who Laughs). After ousting Lex Luthor, he became Perpetua's new lieutenant, carrying out her wishes in return for stewardship of the last enclave of humanity in a reality remade and harvested by Perpetua. This reality was policed by variant versions of Batman and other champions reimagined as templates of terror.

The Darkest Knight presided over Earth-0, not caring that even after their transformation, true heroes remained dedicated to Justice and would strive to save who and what they could. Gradually, the Life's last survivors united to end the nightmare. Valiant resistance proved the enduring, unyielding nature of Justice and, thanks to Wally West, a winning ploy was enacted. The resisters struck back by triggering an "Anti-Crisis" fueled by the positivity of Connective energy. The Darkest Knight, meanwhile, concentrated on his own plans.

Despite her own long-gestating manipulations, Perpetua was defeated by a usurper. The Darkest

Mine of information

Dark Nights: Death Metal officially drew a line under the *Flashpoint*, *The New 52*, and *DC Rebirth* chapters and signified DC was now looking forward, not back, and exploring the broadest potential and interpretations of its legendary characters.

The core limited series was seven issues, with 12 interconnected giant-sized one-shots specials released during the run. It followed an epic string of linked stories beginning in *Justice League* #1 (Aug. 2018), which culminated in the team's defeat and demise in *Justice League* #29–39 (Oct. 2019–Mar. 2020). Other elements of the Multiversal makeover were explored in *Flash Forward* #1–6 (Nov. 2019–Apr. 2020), and *Year of the Villain: Hell Arisen* #1–4 (Feb.–May 2020) before *Death Metal* brought the old DC era to an end.

Trade dress consisted of the electrifying logos and titles on the front covers of tie-ins. A large number of variant covers were produced, many using metallic inks to emphasize the elemental themes.

Future State Infinite Frontier

March–August 2021

Creative revolution came in a parade of innovation. DC's legendary pantheon was reimagined, producing fresh prospects and incarnations waiting at an *Infinite Frontier*. Supervised by writer **Joshua Williamson** and delivered by a host of top creators, that path was preceded by a preliminary event offering a taste of things to come as tradition-draped stars underwent fantastic new permutations in a wave of limited series from a *Future State*.

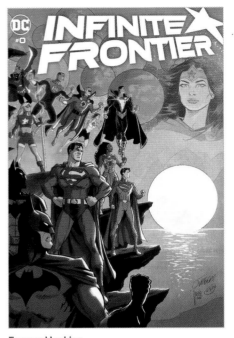

Forward looking
Whatever the future might bring them, DC's indomitable and versatile pantheon would meet it head on and always triumph.

The conclusion of *Dark Nights: Death Metal* saw Wonder Woman elevated to practical godhood. She was then offered—but rejected—a role with supernatural supervisors The Quintessence. Her guide throughout this ascendant excursion was a representative of The Presence (one of "The Hands" so frequently reoccurring throughout DC's creation stories) taking the form of her own 1940s incarnation from pre-*Crisis on Infinite Earths*.

The divine visitation explained that Diana's noble actions had prompted the Higher Powers responsible for all realties to rethink their methodology, and henceforth, all past

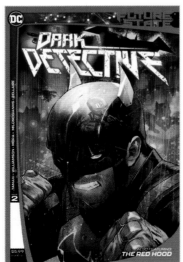

State your name
The latest permutations and innovations confirmed the measureless versatility and infinite potential of archetypal characters like Batman.

Multiverses and variant realties would be restored and coexist. In practical terms, continuity would resume from the point where it was interrupted by Perpetua's attack, but every individual universe's substructure had changed.

Prime Earth was no longer the center of its Local Multiverse. Reality now lay between opposing planetary "poles" that dictated the spiritual balance of Life—one a wildly variable "Elseworld" of limitless potential, and the other an evil oppressive Omega Earth, controlled by the ultimate merger of all Darkseids.

Latest projections

The ignominious defeat of Perpetua and her unexpected wild card nemesis The Darkest Knight changed reality for in-world characters. It also opened up the creative environment to accommodate nearly any permutation and iteration of past stars and tomorrow's sensations.

To celebrate the evolution and emphasize the end of the three-year-long epic, which had begun with the invasion of Barbatos in *Dark Nights: Metal*, DC demonstrated just how versatile and intriguing the days ahead would be through a range of speculative limited series with a shared theme. *Future State* ran in January and February 2021 and offered new and dangerous visions of how the new reality might evolve.

When *Dark Nights: Death Metal* ended, DC placed all its mainstream titles on hiatus. For the first two months of 2021 (cover dates March and April), publishing event *Future*

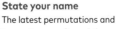

> **"I don't think we're on Earth anymore... well, at least not our Earth."**
>
> **Aquaman (Jackson Hyde)** | *Future State: Aquaman #1*

Inheritance
The relentless drive for change would soon see Kal-El surrender his position as Superman to his anxious but dutiful son, Jon.

State saw them replaced with new titles set ahead of current continuity. Divided into three "families"—Batman, Superman, and Justice League, and supplemented by a catch-all "Aftermath" group—the 33 limited series and one-shots explored possible paths to be taken by those who might follow today's established stars.

With the changes of *Death Metal*'s conclusion now an active and vital component of continuity, DC officially relaunched in March with The *Infinite Frontier*. Beginning with May cover-dated titles, all past iterations of DC character continuity were simultaneously "true," "real," and viable, housed in one vast shared comic book continuity.

Anything goes

This Omniverse was forward-looking and, rather than the old system where a new continuity reset would exclusively replace and render obsolete the previous one, the new status quo maintained that readers and creators concentrate on great storytelling, not bookkeeping, score-card checking,

Interesting times

Each new event featured unique and instantly identifiable trade dress, *Future State* titles were identified by a framing device down the spine and a series information bar above the logo simulating a computer tablet. When The *Infinite Frontier* launched, new series and debuting titles all carried a stylish but restrained corner symbol reminiscent

of the classic DC bullet colophon, to differentiate issues from other imprints such as the mature-reader DC Black Label titles.

Many of the impending changes were trailed and detailed in promotional magazine *DC Nation Presents New Frontiers*, which offered artwork, short promotional features, and interviews with the many writers and artists involved in the ambitious endeavor.

or admin. Everyone now remembered infinite alternate existences.

The transition from Multiverse to Omniverse was further explored between September 2020 and February 2021 in time-bending event *Generations* (*Generations Shattered*, *Generations Forged*, *Flash Forward*) and crossovers in *Wonder Woman* #750 (Mar. 2020), *The Flash* #750 (May 2020), and *Detective Comics* #1027 (Nov. 2020) before the never-ending battle resumed in a wave of new and resumed titles.

Among the new releases was the eponymous core title *Infinite Frontier*—a Multiversal romp starring a super-team recruited from various Earths, plus a new version of the Crime Syndicate of Earth-3, a new career for Superman's son, Jon Kent, a fresh and fierce Suicide Squad led by the Peacemaker, and a controversial and challenging series tracing the ongoing duel between former GCPD Commissioner James Gordon and The Joker. ∎

Key issues

Future State (March–May 2021)

All issues prefixed with Future State.

Aquaman #1–2, Batman/Superman #1–2, Catwoman #1–2, Dark Detective #1–4, Green Lantern #1–2, Harley Quinn #1–2, Immortal Wonder Woman #1–2, Justice League #1–2, Kara Zor-El: Superwoman #1–2, Legion of Super-Heroes #1–2, Nightwing #1–2, Robin Eternal #1–2, Shazam! #1–2, Suicide Squad #1, Superman House of El Lex #1–3, Superman of Metropolis #1–2, Superman vs. Imperious Lex #1–3, Superman/Wonder Woman #1–2, Superman: Worlds of War #1–2, Swamp Thing #1–2, Teen Titans #1–2, The Flash #1–2, The Next Batman #1–4, Wonder Woman #1–2

Infinite Frontiers—finite series and specials (February 2021–June 2022)

Infinite Frontiers #0–6, Man-Bat #1–5, Batman/Superman #16–22, Crime Syndicate #1–6, Justice League #59–75, Superman #29–32, Superman: Red & Blue #1–6, Sensational Wonder Woman #1–14, Batman: The Detective #1–6, The Next Batman: Second Son #1–4, DC Festival of Heroes: The Asian Super-Hero Celebration, Future State: Gotham #1, Legends of the Dark Knight, Justice League: Last Ride #1–7, Mister Miracle: The Source of Freedom #1–6, Stargirl Spring Break Special #1,

Wonder Girl #1–7, Checkmate #1–6, Crush & Lobo #1–8, DC Pride #1, Green Arrow 80th Anniversary 100–Page Spectacular #1, Infinite Frontiers Secret Files #1, Supergirl: Woman of Tomorrow #1–8, Blue & Gold #1–8, Shazam! #1–4, Superman and The Authority #1–4, Aquaman 80th Anniversary 100–Page Spectacular #1, Batman: Fear State Alpha, I Am Batman #0, Aquaman: The Becoming #1–6, Black Manta #1–6, Suicide Squad: King Shark #1–6, Titans United #1 –7, Aquaman/Green Arrow: Deep Target #1–7, Arkham City: The Order of the World #1–6, Task Force Z #1 –12, Wonder Woman 80th Anniversary 100–Page Spectacular #1, Dark Knights of Steel #1–12, DC vs. Vampires #1–12, Justice League Incarnate #1–5, Robin & Batman #1–3, Robins #1–6, Wonder Woman: Evolution #1–8, World of Krypton #1–6, Batman: The Knight #1–10, Justice League vs. the Legion of Super-Heroes #1–6, Dark Crisis #1–7

Ongoing *Infinite Frontier* series—start issues (March 2021 and beyond)

Action Comics #1029, Batman #106, Batman: Urban Legends #1, Catwoman #29, Detective Comics #1034, Harley Quinn #1, Nightwing #78, Suicide Squad #1, Teen Titans Academy #1, The Flash #768, The Joker #1, The Swamp Thing #1, Green Lantern #1, Robin #1, Superman: Son of Kal-El #1, Deathstroke Inc. #1, I Am Batman #1, Nubia and the Amazons #1, Batgirls #1, One Star Squadron #1, Aquamen #1

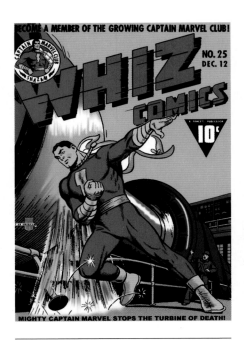

The Origin of Captain Marvel. Jr.

December 1941

Superman, Matinee Idol

December 1942

The Planet That Came to a Standstill!

May 1962

Before DC acquired them, Fawcett Comics' top titles were released every two weeks. The company pioneered multi-issue crossover events while creating classic Super-Villains to challenge their heroes. Months before America officially entered WWII, *Master Comics'* lead feature Bulletman took up the cause with "The Coming of Captain Nazi" (#21, Dec. 1941) by writer William Woolfolk and artist Mac Raboy, with Captain Marvel helping the hero fight the Nazi menace.

The story continued in *Whiz Comics #25* (Dec. 1941) as Captain Marvel battled the Aryan invader in "The Origin of Captain Marvel Jr.," by writer Ed Herron, art by C.C. Beck, and Raboy. It saw the defeated Nazi flee, callously attacking teenager Freddy Freeman and his grandfather. The elder died and Freddy was crippled, but with the help of the wizard Shazam, Captain Marvel saved the injured boy by bestowing him with some of his powers. Thus Freddy became Captain Marvel Jr., joining the fight and assuming the lead spot in *Master Comics* with #22 (Jan. 1942). A new manner of storytelling, a major villain debut, and creation of new hero all make this a true comics landmark.

Imaginary stories explored scenarios outside continuity while using established in-world tenets. Such significant deviations comprised a major strand of DC output from the late 1950s all the way up to and culminating in "Whatever Happened to the Man of Tomorrow?" (*Action Comics #583* and *Superman #423*, Sep. 1986)—the last Superman story prior to *Crisis on Infinite Earths* (Apr. 1985–Mar. 1986).

In the 1960s, DC regularly offered book-length thrillers like "The Death of Superman!" (*Superman #149*, Nov. 1961) or occasional series like "Mr. and Mrs. Clark (Superman) Kent!" The concepts became so popular that imaginary stories gained an imprint— *Elseworlds*—in 1990.

The first foray into imaginary stories was "Superman, Matinee Idol," by writers Jerry Siegel and Joe Shuster, and artist John Sikela in *Superman #19* (Dec. 1942). The story delightfully broke the fourth wall as reporters Lois Lane and Clark Kent watched a Superman cartoon depicting the hero changing into Kent—a shameless yet exceedingly inventive "infomercial" plug for the Fleischer Brothers animated shorts.

Long before the superhero renaissance of the Silver Age, DC published serial stars in other popular genres like westerns, war, and science fiction. One of the most compelling was an ordinary Earthman having spectacular adventures on other worlds. Armed with ray-gun, jetpack, and sharp wits, Adam Strange was the brainchild of editor Julius Schwartz and his team of creative stalwarts. As lead feature in the anthology title *Mystery in Space*—and courtesy of scripter Gardner F. Fox and illustrator Carmine Infantino—Adam and alien hero Alanna battled threats to her far-distant world of Rann as it rebuilt from atomic Armageddon a millennium in the past.

Soon after the Justice League of America debuted, Fox, Infantino, and artist Murphy Anderson crafted a legendary team-up in *Mystery in Space #75* (May 1962), with Adam and the JLA battling the despicable extraterrestrial tyrant Kanjar Ro in "The Planet That Came to a Standstill." This is a key moment in the development of cross-series continuity as DC's Super Hero and science-fiction universes were confirmed as one and the same.

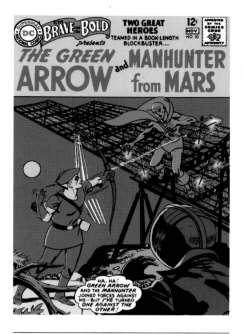

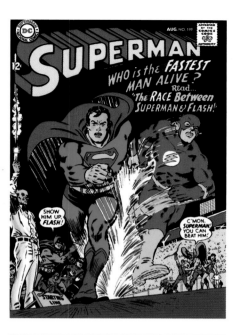

Wanted—the Capsule Master!

November 1963

Twilight of the Challengers!

March 1966

Superman's Race with The Flash!

August 1967

The Brave and the Bold premiered in 1955, an adventure anthology addressing the era's fascination with sword and sandals films. As tastes changed, it became a try-out vehicle and the superhero revival saw it launch Task Force X: the Suicide Squad, Hawkman, and the Justice League of America before sparking a new subgenre—the team-up.

From 1954, DC enjoyed great success pairing Superman with Batman and Robin in a single story in *World's Finest Comics* and in 1963 sought another top-selling duo from their growing Super Heroes stable. At this time, few superhero stories acknowledged the jurisdiction or even existence of other masked champions. When *The Brave and the Bold* offered successive team-ups, it paved the way for the development of future close-knit continuity.

The Brave and the Bold #50's "Wanted—the Capsule Master!" by writer Bob Haney and artist George Roussos, saw Green Arrow and the Manhunter from Mars in a fast-paced, book-length battle against the marauding alien Vulkor. Other heroic unions followed, culminating in a regular Batman plus guest format.

One of *DC Showcase*'s earliest triumphs was the Challengers of the Unknown. Their uncanny exploits played a major part in reviving the fortunes of costumed adventurers, and by 1963, their innovation had become a trend, with the "freakish" Doom Patrol debuting as part of a wave of new champions.

Both teams were considered edgy outsiders at a time when superheroes were reestablishing themselves and latterly participated in a milestone experiment in cross-selling. Scripted by Arnold Drake and illustrated by Bob Brown, *The Challengers of the Unknown #48* (Mar. 1966) declared a "Twilight of the Challengers" with the death-cheaters found dead and the Doom Patrol vengefully stepping in to hunt down their murderers.

The cliffhanger asked readers to buy a different title—specifically *Doom Patrol #102* (Mar. 1966), by Drake and artist Bruno Premiani—where super-genius The Chief resurrected the Challengers and formed a coalition with his squad to crush a cabal of bizarre Super-Villains in the explosive conclusion "8 Against Eternity."

Comic books have never been "just for kids," but whatever a reader's age, some questions cannot be ignored or rationally justified. They're just thought to be crucial and cool.

Who hasn't asked "who'd win if..." or "who's strongest/smartest/fastest...?" Comics editors generally avoided such questions, wary of upsetting sections of the tenuous and supposedly transitory fan base. However, teenaged scripter Jim Shooter knew better—writing a tale that's resonated down the years and been constantly revisited. As the superhero boom slowed, a definitive race between the Man of Steel and the Fastest Man Alive became an increasingly enticing, sales-worthy proposition.

Illustrated by Curt Swan and George Klein "Superman's Race with The Flash" in *Superman #199* (Aug. 1967) has the United Nations ask the heroes to raise funds to fight World Hunger via an exhibition race. Naturally they agreed, but the clever global handicap, circling the planet three times, is subverted by rival criminal syndicates staging the greatest gambling coup in history...

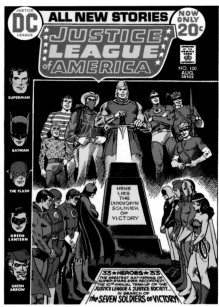

Hard traveling heroes

April 1970–April 1972

The Unknown Soldier of Victory

August–October 1972

Apokolips Now

October–December 1980

As America reeled from cultural unrest in the late 1960s/early 1970s, *Green Lantern* suffered a sales downturn that similarly affected superhero comic books. Editor Julie Schwartz took a chance on an audacious experiment that became a movement—augmenting traditional action fare with socially relevant, mature themes.

Writer Denny O'Neil and artist Neal Adams delivered dissent-driven stories for the retitled *Green Lantern/Green Arrow.* Former millionaire Oliver Queen became a passionate, liberal voice for a generation-in-crisis, crossing the nation to open the eyes of conservative, space cop Hal Jordan—representing the well-meaning but oblivious establishment—to other, subtler kinds of evil.

Alongside Black Canary and a Guardian of the Universe, their travels (spanning *GL/GA #76–89*, Apr. 1970–Apr. 1972) confronted racism, rampant capitalism, poverty, crooked politicians, Native American rights, and other hot-button topics. Their journey garnered awards and critical acclaim, introducing DC's first black Super Hero John Stewart, and addressing drug abuse in groundbreaking tales that revolutionized the industry.

Like many titles in the early 1970s, *Justice League of America* explored more socially aware avenues of adventure before moving away from relevancy and returning to epic, action-oriented Super Hero dramas. The revival began in anniversary issue *JLA #100* with the annual *Justice League of America/Justice Society of America* summer blockbuster extended to three chapters (#100–102, Aug.–Oct. 1972) and featuring almost every hero in DC's current pantheon.

Written by Len Wein and illustrated by Dick Dillin, Joe Giella, and Dick Giordano, "The Hand that Shook the World!" depicted the champions of two Earths undertaking a quest through time to retrieve forgotten heroes—the Seven Soldiers of Victory. The lost team's greatest enemy had returned and the "Law's Legionnaires" held the answer to defeating a criminal mastermind literally holding the world (of Earth-2) to ransom.

The rescue mission spanned seven eras before demanding the ultimate sacrifice from one Justice Society of America stalwart in the thrilling concluding chapter "And One of Us Must Die!"

The eagerly awaited annual alliance of the Justice League and its inspirational predecessor Justice Society of America delivered many classic tales, especially when paired with other groups such as the Legion of Super-Heroes or Shazam-aligned Earth-S champions. *Justice League of America #183–185* (Oct.–Dec. 1980) co-starred Jack Kirby's New Gods in a stirring tale by writer Gerry Conway and artists Dick Dillin, George Pérez, and Frank McLaughlin.

Transported to New Genesis, the heroes joined Orion, Mister Miracle, Big Barda, Oberon, and Metron in rescuing their captive fellow gods from Apokolips. Darkseid had been killed by Orion, but his restless spirit recruited Earth-2 villains the Shade, Icicle, and Fiddler to resurrect him and insert Apokolips into normal space currently occupied by Earth-2. Rendered by rising star Pérez, "Crisis Between Two Earths or, Apokolips Now!" and "Crisis on Apokolips or, Darkseid Rising!" saw the champions spectacularly triumph, but without a true resolution. Such is the nature of undying evil.

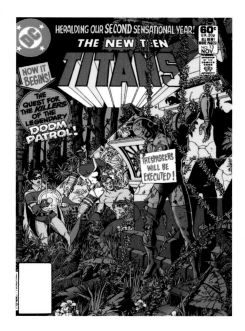

Hunt for the Doom Patrol

November 1981–January 1982

The Judas Contract

May–July 1984

Cosmic Odyssey

December 1988–March 1989

In 1980, Marv Wolfman and George Pérez, with inker Romeo Tanghal, reimagined a fan favorite as *The New Teen Titans.* A huge hit thanks to sophisticated character interaction, sizzling action, and playful storytelling that cleverly mined DC history, it blended modern sensibilities with potent nostalgia.

The story saw Robin (Dick Grayson), Kid Flash (Wally West), Wonder Girl, and Beast Boy/Changeling join new creations Raven, Cyborg, and Starfire. An extended plot-strand followed Changeling and his stepfather Steve "Mento" Dayton's hunt for Madame Rouge and General Zahl—who had killed the original Doom Patrol—culminated in *The New Teen Titans* #13–15 (Nov. 1981–Jan. 1982). The ensuing clash freed captive sole-survivor Robotman and also uncovered a plot to conquer rogue nation Zandia. With Changeling injured, the Titans united to handle his family business, coincidentally foiling the secret revival of the Doom Patrol's greatest enemies in "The Brotherhood of Evil Lives Again!" before defeating Rouge and Zahl in a saga setting up decades more drama and skullduggery.

The New Teen Titans was DC's foremost 1980s Super Hero series, and its creative peak was "The Judas Contract," by Wolfman and Pérez and inkers Dick Giordano and Mike DeCarlo, in *Tales of the New Teen Titans* #42–44 (May–Jul. 1984) and *Tales of the New Teen Titans Annual* #3 (Jul. 1984).

The New Teen Titans #39–41 (Feb–Apr. 1984) of the retitled series had revealed big changes. Dick Grayson surrendered his Robin identity and Wally West retired, unaware that Slade Wilson, aka Deathstroke the Terminator, was exploiting metahuman teen Tara Markov. She infiltrated the team as Terra, and Wilson learned her teammates' secret identities and weaknesses before his final strike. Betrayed and awaiting death, the team was saved by Grayson in his new heroic identity as Nightwing, assisted by Wilson's estranged wife, Adeline Wilson, and their psychic son, Joseph, who joined the Titans as Jericho.

Controversially, Terra was revealed—to readers at least—as Deathstroke's lover and pawn. She was a psychotically murderous, self-destructive wild card whose plan almost succeeded before she tragically lost control and died trying to kill everyone.

Experimenting with new production materials and book styles, DC struck gold with "Prestige Format" limited series *Cosmic Odyssey.* Written by Jim Starlin, illustrated by Mike Mignola and Carlos Carzon, colored by Steve Oliff, and lettered by John Workman, the four-issue series revealed how Darkseid and Highfather discovered that the Anti-Life Equation was sentient and aggressively malevolent.

Dispatching four aspects of itself to destroy Rann, Thanagar, Xanshi, and Earth and trigger the collapse of the Milky Way galaxy, it forced a New Gods alliance and the recruitment of Superman, Batman, Green Lantern John Stewart, Martian Manhunter, Starfire, Doctor Fate, and the Demon Etrigan, to save existence. By turns darkly brooding and spectacularly cathartic, the scheme was ultimately thwarted, but betrayal and disaster were never far away. One particularly shocking moment saw arrogantly complacent Stewart miscalculate, triggering the utter destruction of planet Xanshi. The tragedy would haunt him and shape his personality and the DC universe for decades to come.

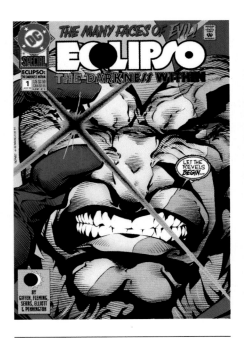

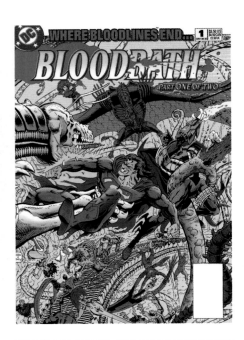

The Darkness Within

July–October 1992

Panic in the Sky!

February–April 1992

Bloodlines

August–December 1993

With crossover events now an indispensable part of comic book storytelling, DC began treating them as blockbuster chapter plays running through each year's annuals and usually supported by a limited series.

In 1992, Eclipso was reinvented by writers Robert Loren Fleming and Keith Giffen and artist Bart Sears as an ancient demon of vengeance and scourge of humanity. From his lunar citadel, Eclipso duped wandering Daxamite Lar Gand (Valor) into unleashing hell on Earth, successively possessing heroes and their loved ones when they succumbed to hatred or rage. The critical weapon was shards of black diamond that magnified dark emotions. The event's first issue came with a free plastic replica embedded in the cover.

Bookended by *Eclipso: The Darkness Within* #1 and 2, the epic war for humanity's souls ran through 18 double-length annuals and *Starman* #42–45 (Jan.–Apr. 1992, featuring the Will Payton Starman) before Eclipso was finally foiled by his human nemesis Dr. Bruce Gordon. The tale led to a solo series for *Eclipso* (#1–18, Nov. 1992–Apr. 1994) and *Valor* (#1–23, Nov. 1992–Sep. 1994).

Alien invasions are a timeless staple of comics, and Superman group editor Mike Carlin, writers Dan Jurgens, Jerry Ordway, Louise Simonson, Roger Stern, and artists Dan Jurgens, Jon Bogdanove, Tom Grummett, Bob McLeod, Brett Breeding, Doug Hazlewood, Dennis Janke, and Denis Rodier delivered a perfect example in *Action Comics* #674–675, *Superman: The Man of Steel* #9–10, *Superman* #65–66, and *Adventures of Superman* #488–489 (all titles Feb.–Apr. 1992).

Roaming intergalactic shape-shifter Matrix encountered battle-planet Warworld, before, in her Supergirl form, succumbing to Brainiac's mind control. She joins fellow super-slaves Maxima and Draaga as Warworld heads to Earth. In response, Superman rallies Super Heroes into two teams, one defending Earth from aliens and another to directly attack Brainiac. Recruits included the New Gods, Metal Men, Justice League International, Aquaman, Deathstroke, Nightwing, Wonder Woman, and numerous Green Lanterns in last-ditch defense and attack modes, delivering all-out action, suspenseful drama, and tripwire tension.

Otherworldly invaders were used to create a whole stable of new DC characters in twinned events "Bloodlines" and culminating in two-issue micro-series "Bloodbath." As so often in the 1990s, the crossovers ran through that year's annuals, 23 in all, subdivided into movie-style acts "Outbreak," "Earthplague," and finally "Deathstorm," the climactic closing two-parter.

The tale saw seven shape-shifting extradimensional horrors feeding on humans by draining their spinal fluid, unaware that for a large proportion of their victims, what looked like death was actually the coma of metagene activation and that resurrection would leave the victims amnesiac, angry, and superpowered. Known as "New Bloods," 28 super-beings were initially created. Some won their own titles, most notably Hitman, Loose Cannon, Anima, and Blood Pack.

The closing series was written by Dan Raspler with art by Chick Wojtkiewicz, Bill Willingham, Sal Velluto, and Val Semeiks, with the invaders' true purpose and ultimate aim thwarted as a legion of Super Heroes and New Bloods battled their vile creator the Taker.

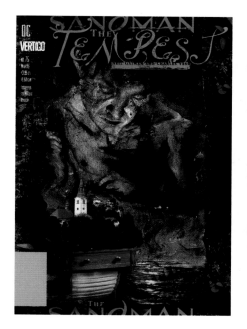

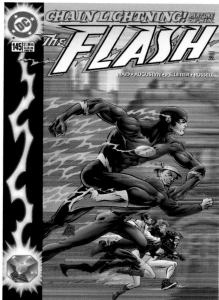

The Wake!

August 1995—March 1996

Chain Lightning

February—July 1999

The Joker's Last Laugh

December 2001—January 2002

Only notionally based on mainstream DC characters, writer Neil Gaiman's award-winning *Sandman*, published by the company's Vertigo imprint, was generally "continuity adjacent." It explored the nature of stories with poetic style, terror, and disquiet. When the saga was done, the signature star passed away on his own terms.

The founding concept was that in the early 20th century, evil occultists imprisoned Morpheus, aka Dream of the Endless. This abstract being oversaw the universal ability to dream and in its absence, Wesley Dodds, Garrett Sanford, Dr. Destiny, and Hector Hall each responded to the ensuing metaphysical perturbations in the dream realms in Super Hero terms.

Morpheus's death was marked by a six-part commemoration "The Wake," illustrated by Michael Zulli, Charles Vess, Bryan Talbot, John Ridgway, and Jon J. Muth (*The Sandman #70–75*, Aug. 1995–Mar. 1996). Here, all the powers of creation and even the dream-selves of Justice Leaguers and other icons paid tribute to his passing in advance of successor Daniel of Dream becoming the new, mainstream continuity Sandman.

In all incarnations, The Flash is rich in history and potential. Writers Mark Waid and Brian Augustyn,and artists Paul Pelletier and Vince Russell took that idea to the limit in the six-part story arc "Chain Lightning" (*The Flash #145–150*, Feb.–Jul. 1999) as third scarlet speedster Wally West embarked on a 1000-year odyssey through time to save his descendants.

Minor villain Cobalt Blue is defeated and found to be Barry Allen's lost twin. Also an ancestor of Reverse-Flash, Cobalt Blue's hatred of Allen and the Speed Force spans centuries. He controls a mystic blue flame, and through his children and his own later return to power, he confidently boasts his intention to destroy all future speedsters. Marshaling his current fast friends, Wally West races into the future to save the unborn speedsters, encountering untrustworthy friends and unlikely foes throughout future history, unaware that he is the prime target of a millennial plot and should not trust anyone.

This complex, clever, and compelling yarn breaks all boundaries in time-travel tales and offers fresh perspective on classic events you only thought you knew.

When a medical examination at super-max prison "the Slab" revealed an inoperable brain tumor leaving him only weeks to live, The Joker decided to take everyone with him. Using Joker-toxin mixed with super-steroid Venom, he turned fellow Super-Villain inmates into Joker-duplicates, and let them run riot. The "Jokerized" terrors triggered a global killing spree and humanity seemed doubly doomed when the Harlequin of Hate seeded clouds to ensure everyone alive died laughing!

The Joker eagerly anticipated Earth as his cackling funeral pyre while President Lex Luthor scoured Earth for the transformed escapees, who had spread far and wide—even into the Super Hero community.

The core limited series was written by Chuck Dixon and Scott Beatty and illustrated by Pete Woods, Marcos Martin, Walter McDaniel, Andy Kuhn, Ron Randall, and Rich Burchett. It encapsulated 25 additional sardonic, zany, and action-packed crossovers from DC's best creators, before the clown was caught, a medical mistake was admitted, and the world was left to pick up the pieces.

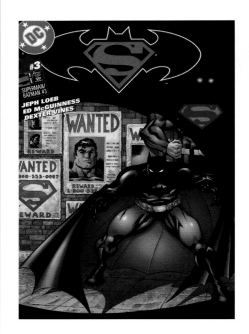

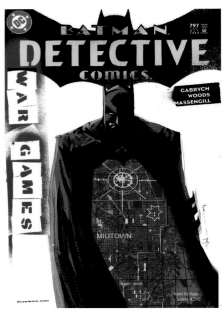

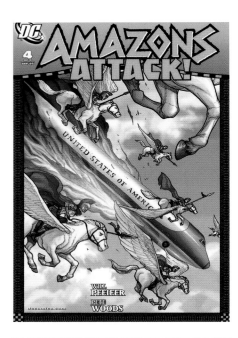

Public Enemies

October 2003–March 2004

Batman: War Drums

August 2004–January 2005

Amazons Attack!

June–October 2007

Originating in *Superman/Batman #1–6* and *Superman/Batman Secret Files* 2003 (Oct. 2003–Mar. 2004), by writer Jeph Loeb and artists Ed McGuiness, Dexter Vines, and Tim Sale, *Public Enemies* detailed how President Lex Luthor learned an Australia-sized Kryptonite asteroid would strike Earth. Accusing Superman of summoning it and Batman of complicity, Luthor issued arrest warrants, convened a metahuman task force, and used TV to denounce Superman and offer a billion dollar bounty.

Adding to their woes, the heroes were visited by an older version of Superman, warning against making a mistake that would end life on Earth. With Super Heroes and villains polarized into hunting or helping, Batman and Superman acted to save Earth and topple Luthor, who was now addicted to Kryptonite-enhanced super-steroid Venom and spiraling into madness. With extinction imminent, Superman prepared an 11th-hour suicidal salvation machine (built by Toyman) but was ambushed by Captain Atom who took his place, riding a missile into the K-asteroid. Believed dead, the hero actually crossed realties into the WildStorm universe.

In *War Drums*, *War Games*, and *War Crimes*, Batman titles *Detective Comics #790–799, 810*, *Batman #631–633, 644*, *Batman: The 12-Cent Adventure #1*, *Batman: Legends of the Dark Knight #182–184*, *Batman: Gotham Knights #56–57*, *Nightwing #96–98*, *Robin #126–131*, *Catwoman #34–36*, *Batgirl #55–57*, and *Gotham Central #25* (all Aug. 2004–Jan. 2005) revealed the causes and effects of criminal rivalries in Gotham City.

It began when Batman fired fourth Robin Stephanie Brown, who then tried proving her worth by activating a Batman training scenario—an underworld takeover by Matches Malone. Brown had no idea that Batman was Malone and as the scheme unfolded without his oversight, it triggered a bloodbath as enraged factions hunted each other and the nonexistent mastermind.

As casualties mounted, martial law was declared, forcing Batman to actually attempt taking over Gotham City. After Stephanie's apparent death, the Dark Knight and his Batman Family allies had to face restoring the status quo with both the police and the underworld against them.

Comprising a six-issue limited series plus crossovers *Catwoman #69–70*, *Supergirl #20*, *Teen Titans #48–49* and *Wonder Woman #6–13* (all titles Jun.–Oct. 2007), *Amazons Attack!* detailed savage war on American soil. When the Department of Metahuman Affairs arrested Wonder Woman (on the orders of shape-shifter Everyman impersonating Director Sarge Steel), it was at sorceress Circe's instigation. Resurrecting Queen Hippolyta, the witch compelled her to attack America, ignoring the fact that American agent Nemesis had already helped Diana escape.

Washington, DC, Kansas, Gotham City, and more reeled from assault by Amazons, and the President declared anyone with Amazon connections a potential terrorist. Batman deduced the deeper game in play, Superman proved the power of true nobility, and Wonder Woman confronted ugly truths before the scheme was foiled.

Writer Will Pfeiffer and artist Pete Woods made telling points about real-world wars in Iraq and Afghanistan while the conflict was ultimately revealed as a covert chapter of *Countdown to Infinite Crisis*.

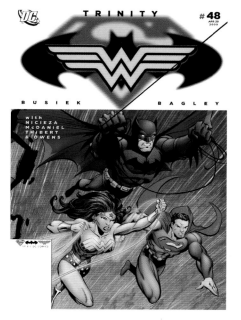

Trinity

June 2008–May 2009

Rise of the Third Army

October 2012–March 2013

Justice League vs. Suicide Squad

February–March 2017

Superman, Batman, and Wonder Woman are "The Trinity," which acknowledges their exalted status and longevity. The term inspired writers Kurt Busiek and Fabian Nicieza, and artists, including Mark Bagley, Scott McDaniel, and Jerry Ordway, to use DC's third yearlong weekly series *Trinity* (Jun. 2008–May 2009) to explore the three heroes' metaphysical importance. Featuring lead chapters with connected backup tales, the fable revealed a faith-powered, reality-warping web covering the Multiverse as hidden forces usurped the cosmic significance of the trio.

At the heart of existence, an ancient, immensely powerful being struggled to smash its prison. The effort resonated on Earth as Clark Kent, Bruce Wayne, and Diana Prince shared the same dream of a monster escaping. Eventually every aspect of reality shifted as belief in the Trinity was manipulated, with alien Despero, sorceress Morgaine Le Fey, and mystery mastermind Enigma groomed to replace Superman, Wonder Woman, and Batman as cornerstones of universal existence. Ultimately, undying friendships and the power of legend ensured the restoration of true reality.

When 30th century time-traveler Volthoom arrived in reality's earliest era, the Guardians of the Universe confiscated his "Travel Lantern" to master the Emotional Spectrum. The Oans imprisoned him for billions of years while using his tech to make power rings. Seeking to neutralize emotion and chaos they recruited strong-willed sentients, but their Green Lantern Corps proved as unreliable as their first army—the robotic Manhunters who abandoned their programming to butcher an entire Space Sector.

As Green Lanterns questioned the Guardians' actions, the immortals imposed cold rationality via a bio-manufactured Third Army. In response, Lanterns of all hues—including new GL Simon Baz—joined a cosmic war that killed most Guardians and freed vengeful Volthoom to unleash hell.

Written by Geoff Johns, Peter Tomasi, Tony Bedard, and Peter Milligan, the interlocking sagas spanned *Green Lantern Annual #1*, *Green Lantern #0, 13–16*, *Green Lantern: New Guardians #0, 13–16*, *Green Lantern Corps #13–16*, *Green Lantern Corps Annual #1*, and *Red Lanterns #13–16* (Oct. 2012–Mar. 2013).

With DC celebrating a *Rebirth*, writer Joshua Williamson and artists Jason Fabok, Robson Rocha, Fernando Pasarin, Jesus Merino, Tony S. Daniel, and Howard Porter crafted a no-nonsense blockbuster romp *Justice League vs. Suicide Squad* (Feb.–Mar. 2017) in six weekly installments. Designed to delight fans and celebrate the reboot, it starred the company's top teams who were duped into tackling each other by resurrected spy-master Maxwell Lord.

He set the Super Heroes against rival spook Amanda Waller and her felonious Super-Villain Suicide Squad as a distraction while he acquired Eclipso's gem The Heart of Darkness. His scheme included reactivating the merciless first Suicide Squad—Doctor Polaris, Emerald Empress, Lobo, Rustam, and Johnny Sorrow—suborning the Justice League, and spreading chaos and carnage. The game of bluff and multi-bluff spiraled out of control as the liberated spirit of darkness, Eclipso, endangered all life. That was until Batman and reformed felon Killer Frost outwitted him, Lord, and Waller, leading to a new life, freedom, and friends for the former ice queen in the JLA.

Index

Acknowledgments

The Publisher would like to thank:

Neal Adams
Rafael Albuquerque
Marlo Alquiza
Murphy Anrderson
Jim Aparo
Bernard Baily
Michael Bair
Eduardo Barreto
Eddy Barrows
Cary Bates
C.C. Beck
Tony Bedard
Adam Beechen
Jon Belfi
Ed Benes
Otto Binder
Jerry Bingham
Steve Bissette
Bret Blevins
Jon Bogdanove
Brian Bolland
Brett Booth
Russell Braun
Mark Bright
John Broome
Bob Brown
Jack Burnley
John Byrne
Greg Capullo
Nick Cardy
Mike Carlin
Mauro Cascioli
Joe Casey
Bobbie Chase
Ian Churchill
Andy Clarke
Vince Colletta
Max Allen Collins
Gerry Conway
Denys Cowan
Alan Davis
Mike DeCarlo
J.M. DeMatteis
Paul Dini
Chuck Dixon
Scot Eaton
Steve Englehart
Jason Fabok
Wayne Faucher
David Finch
Bill Finger
Ben Flinton
Jorge Fornes
Gardner Fox

Gary Frank
Kerry Gammill
Ron Garney
Pat Garrahy
Stirling Gates
Mitch Gerads
Vince Giarrano
Dave Gibbons
Ian Gibson
Joe Giella
Keith Giffen
Dick Giordano
Jonathan Glapion
Patrick Gleason
Adrian Gonzales
Al Gordon
Alan Grant
Justin Gray
Dan Green
Sid Greene
Chad Grothkopf
Tom Grummett
Renato Guedes
Pia Guerra
Edmond Hamilton
Bob Haney
Scott Hanna
Ed Hannigan
Tony Harris
Irwin Hasen
Don Heck
Phil Hester
Everett E. Hibbard
John Higgins
Kyle Higgins
Adam Hughes
Rian Hughes
Dave Hunt
Jamal Igle
Stuart Immomen
Carmine Infantino
Mikel Janin
Dennis Janke
Klaus Janson
Phil Jimenez
Oscar Jiminez
Jock
Geoff Johns
J.G. Jones
Dan Jurgens
Viktor Kalvachev
Bob Kane
Gil Kane
Robert Kanigher

Kano
Stan Kaye
Joe Kelly
Karl Kerschl
Karl Kesel
Jeff King
Tom King
Jack Kirby
Leonard Kirk
Scott Kolins
Andy Kubert
Joe Kubert
Paul Kupperberg
Robert L. Washington
Jose Ladronn
Andy Lanning
Jae Lee
Jim Lee
Jeff Lemire
Paul Levitz
Steve Lightle
Scott Lobdell
Jeph Loeb
Aaron Lopresti
Tula Lotay
Emanuela Lupacchino
Dev Madan
Kevin Maguire
Larry Mahlstedt
Doug Mahnke
Alex Maleev
Francis Manapul
Clay Mann
Bill Mantlo
Guillem March
Pablo Marcos
William Moulton Marston
Cynthia Martin
Alvaro Martinez
Jose Marzan Jr.
Sheldon Mayer
Dave Mazzucchelli
Trevor McCarthy
Scott McDaniel
Luke McDonnell
Dwayne McDuffie
Todd McFarlane
Ed McGuinness
David McKean
Sean McKeever
Mike McKone
Brad Meltzer
Jamie Mendoza
Mike Mignola

Danny Miki
Steve Mitchell
Doug Moench
Sheldon Moldoff
Alan Moore
Travis Moore
Dan Mora
Mark Morales
Rags Morales
Grant Morrison
Win Mortimer
Charles Moulton
Todd Nauck
Martin Nodell
Graham Nolan
Oliver Nome
Dennis O'Neill
Glen Orbik
Jerry Ordway
John Ostrander
Carlos Pacheco
Carlos Pagulayan
Jimmy Palmiotti
Eduardo Pansica
Yanick Paquette
Fernando Pasarin
Bruce D. Patterson
Paul Pelletier
George Pérez
Harry G Peter
Al Plastino
Alberto Ponticelli
Howard Porter
Joe Prado
Bruno Premiani
Steve Pugh
Yasmine Putri
Mac Raboy
Stefano Raffaele
Humberto Ramos
Norm Rapmund
Fred Ray
Ivan Reis
James Robinson
Denis Rodier
Marshall Rogers
Prentis Rollins
Alex Ross
Riley Rossmo
George Roussos
Stephane Roux
Mike Royer
Joe Rubinstein
Greg Rucka

Steve Rude
Marco Rudy
Bernard Sachs
Jesus Saiz
Lew Sayre
Mark Schultz
Julius Schwartz
Bart Sears
Stephen Segovia
Mike Sekowsky
Val Semeiks
Declan Shalvey
Evan Shaner
Liam Sharp
Howard Sherman
Joe Shuster
Jerry Siegel
John Sikela
Louise Simonson
Walt Simonson
Cam Smith
Matthew Smith
John K Snyder III
Scott Snyder
Ryan Sook
Jim Starlin
Joe Staton
Brian Stelfreeze
Karl Story
Curt Swan
Romeo Tanghal
Art Thibert
Roy Thomas
Jill Thompson
Marcus To
Anthony Tollin
Peter Tomasi
Alex Toth
Sal Trapani
Michael Turner
James Tynion IV
Ivan Velez Jr.
Ron Wagner
Mark Waid
Lee Weeks
Len Wein
Mort Weisinger
Greg Weisman
Mike Wieringo
James Williamson
Judd Winick
Marv Wolfman
Pete Woods
Kim Yale

The Publishers have made every effort to identify and acknowledge the artists whose work appears in this book.